Acing

The Bar Exam

A Checklist Approach to
Taking the Bar Exam

Suzanne Darrow-Kleinhaus

Assistant Professor of Legal Process
and Director of Academic Development

Touro College
Jacob D. Fuchsberg Law Center

Series Editor
A. Benjamin Spencer

THOMSON
™
WEST

Mat #40550840

Thomson/West have created this publication to provide you with accurate and authoritative information concerning the subject matter covered. However, this publication was not necessarily prepared by persons licensed to practice law in a particular jurisdiction. Thomson/West are not engaged in rendering legal or other professional advice, and this publication is not a substitute for the advice of an attorney. If you require legal or other expert advice, you should seek the services of a competent attorney or other professional.

© 2008 Thomson/West
    610 Opperman Drive
    P.O. Box 64526
    St. Paul, MN 55164–0526
    800–328–9352

Printed in the United States of America

ISBN: 978–0–314–17706–3

 TEXT IS PRINTED ON 10% POST CONSUMER RECYCLED PAPER

To Murray, for his love and constancy

*

PREFACE AND ACKNOWLEDGMENTS

I was reminded that *Acing the Bar Exam* might be a curious title for this book since it is not necessary to "ace" the bar exam but only to pass it to be successful. Still, the image is an appropriate one because "acing the bar exam" means that you're the one in control of the exam and not the other way around. It's the attitude you need when preparing for the bar exam.

But attitude will take you only so far. You need to prepare thoroughly and properly. This means understanding the bar review process, using your strengths and weaknesses to define a workable study plan, and learning the black letter law as tested in your jurisdiction. Here is where this book can help: it provides a complete guide to the bar exam—from pre-planning considerations through the bar review course and sitting for the exam. Every aspect of the process is explained in detail and by example. The bar exam is de-constructed, section by section, with suggested approaches for learning the black letter law, setting study schedules, and answering essay and multiple-choice questions. Each task is summarized in checklist format to help you chart and monitor your progress.

The bar exam is not an easy exam, but it is a doable one. As you get caught up in your bar review course, it may help to realize this and to know you are not alone—thousands of students take their state's bar exams every year and pass. They are not any smarter than you. You must believe that you can pass the bar exam and put in the effort. Then it will happen.

Thanks to my husband, Murray, for his love and encouragement, and especially for reminding me not to take everything so seriously. Thanks to Meredith, who demonstrates daily what it means to be a thoughtful and loving wife, mother, and daughter. Thanks to Benjamin, for possessing the most delightfully engaging young mind and sharing it so readily with me. Thanks, too, to my parents, for showing me first the joy of learning.

I would like to thank Myra Berman, my dearest friend and colleague. She is one of the most amazingly talented women I have ever known and an extraordinary teacher. I am incredibly lucky that I get to work with her and learn from her.

Also, I would like to thank my students, for whom this book is intended and without whom it would not have been written. I am fortunate to be a part of their education and have learned as much from them as they have learned from me.

My deepest appreciation to Touro College, Jacob D. Fuchsberg Law Center. I am proud to be an alumna and prouder still to be a member of its faculty. I am grateful to Dean Lawrence Raful and Vice Dean Gary Shaw for their continued support and encouragement.

I am especially thankful to Heidi M. Hellekson, Associate Publisher for the West Law School imprint at Thomson-West Publishing Company. I greatly value her judgment and admire her thoughtfulness, diligence, and insight. Her commitment to her authors is without parallel and is returned in kind. Thank you, Heidi.

I've endeavored to make clear throughout the book that the candidate's best friends during this time are the bar examiners. Both the National Conference of Bar Examiners ("NCBE") and the state boards make numerous materials available to bar candidates.

The Multistate Essay Examination ("MEE") has been "Reprinted by Permission" from the July 1998 MEE. Copyright © 1999 National Conference of Bar Examiners. All rights reserved. The Multistate Bar Examination ("MBE") questions have been "Reprinted by Permission" from the following NCBE publications: Sample MBE February, 1991 (© 1991 by the National Conference of Bar Examiners), Sample MBE 1996 (© 1996 by the National Conference of Bar Examiners), Sample MBE III July,1998 (© 1998 by the National Conference of Bar Examiners) and the 2006 Information Booklet (© 2005 by the National Conference of Bar Examiners). The Multistate Performance Test ("MPT") has been "Reprinted by Permission" from Test 2 of the July 1997, MPT, State v. Devine (© 1997 by the National Conference of Bar Examiners).

Like the NCBE, individual state bar examiners make vital information available to its bar candidates. Most of this information is readily available on the internet and I made extensive use of this vital resource. I urge all candidates to do the same. The reprinted essay selections and sample answers have all been downloaded from the states' websites, in large part to illustrate the accessibility of these materials.

In New York, the Board of Law Examiners release answers which received scores superior to the average scaled score awarded for the relevant essay. However, the Board is careful to make no representation as to the accuracy of the answers; they are simply considered above average responses. Like New York, the bar examiners in New Jersey, Florida and California publish essay questions and answers after each bar examination administration. The Florida Board of Bar Examiners Study Guide is copyrighted and the selections reproduced here are under the express written permission of the Florida Board of Bar Examiners.

SUZANNE DARROW-KLEINHAUS

Bellmore, New York
September, 2007

*

Table of Contents

*

CHAPTER 1

Preliminary Matters

Passing the bar exam is only one of a number of jurisdictionally-set criteria candidates must meet before gaining admittance to the practice of law. Each state sets its own requirements for admission to the practice of law within its jurisdiction, which includes the precise composition of its bar exam, the score required for passage, and the computation of that score. In addition to bar passage, states typically impose age, education, and moral character requirements.

Still, it is the bar exam that comes first to mind when we think about getting licensed to practice law. For most law students, concern about passing the bar exam is second only to succeeding in law school. This is not surprising since the bar exam is what might well be the most important test of your life: a two or three day marathon event designed to see whether you have mastered the legal skills and general knowledge that a first year practicing attorney should possess.

In truth, the bar exam is a tough exam, but not an impossible one. Quite the contrary: it is meant to be passed and the vast majority of candidates do pass their bar exam.

What Is Required of You

The goal of the bar examiners is to test your competency for the practice of law. To pass the bar exam, therefore, you must demonstrate a firm grasp of the "black letter law" and a solid grounding in basic analytical, reading, and writing skills.

As a subsequent chapter details in great length, your bar exam will most likely consist of the National Conference of Bar Examiners ("NCBE") Multistate Bar Exam ("MBE") and a state-based essay component. Some jurisdictions also include objective-style questions on state law and many include a performance test that requires you to complete a typical lawyering task such as drafting a client letter or writing a persuasive memo. Through the combination of these types of questions, the bar exam tests your abilities in the following areas:

- problem solving

- identifying and formulating legal issues

- organizing information

- separating relevant from irrelevant facts

- communicating effectively in writing

- managing time efficiently to complete an assignment

Why the Bar Exam Is Challenging

Much of the talk about the bar exam is understandable: it is taken by almost every law student and is often the final hurdle for admission to law practice. It is also a very public event and, unfortunately, failures are visible. What you must remember, however, is that while the bar exam is a challenging exam, it is also a doable exam. Countless others before you have done it and you'll do it too.

One perspective

Let's consider some of the reasons why the bar exam seems so daunting to test-takers:

1. It tests so many subjects at one time.

2. There is not enough time, either to prepare for the bar exam or to take it.

3. The pressure to pass is overwhelming.

So many subjects . . .

Depending on your jurisdiction, you might be responsible for the substantive law in anywhere from six to over twenty different subject areas. This is a lot of material to be responsible for at one time.

In law school, on the other hand, exams were spread out over a two-week period and the maximum number of exams you had to take was usually three or four and never more than five. Further, you were tested on only one subject at a time, you knew which subject it was going to be, and then you had at least one day (usually more) before you were tested on another subject.

Finally, the material covered on the exam was limited to what the professor covered during the semester. Most professors probably gave you some idea of the topics to be tested. Some even gave a review class before the final. If you were lucky, your professor kept some old exams on file, and if you were really lucky, there were some sample answers available too. The result was that you had a pretty good idea of what to expect when you walked into the exam.

In contrast, when you walk into the bar exam, you're facing what seems like the entire legal universe. You are responsible for all the subjects tested in your jurisdiction. Further, they are tested in a completely random manner so that both the subject matter and the level of difficulty may vary as you proceed from question to question. And to make matters that much worse, you're tested on everything in a two or three day period.

. . . so little time

Most candidates feel the time crunch immediately because bar review classes can begin before you've attended your law school graduation ceremony. But that's the least of it: by the end of the first week of bar review, you are overwhelmed by the sheer volume of the material and the pace by which you are moving forward. When combined with the time pressures of the exam itself, it's not unusual to feel more than just a little bit anxious.

These feelings are entirely normal. There would be something wrong with you if you didn't have them. There is a real basis to your anxiety—which leads to the next concern—the stress factor.

The pressure to pass

When you study for the bar exam, you are facing one of the most stressful periods of your life. You may be consumed with thoughts of "what if"—*what if I fail; what if I have to do this again; what if I don't get the job that I want; what if I disappoint my family, my friends, my teachers, myself.*

These are very normal fears; we all have them. In fact, a certain level of anxiety is a good thing but too much prevents you from doing your job. And you must be able to do your job of studying the law. You can't afford to lose control because of the pressure.

Another perspective

What if we consider these issues from an entirely different perspective? Here is what we might see instead:

1.   The bar exam has definite boundaries even though it tests multiple topics.

2.   There is enough time to prepare for the bar exam *if you plan for it.*

3.   A certain level of stress can be productive.

The bar exam has "boundaries"

As you'll learn in a subsequent chapter, the national and state bar examiners define the universe of what is tested on your jurisdiction's bar exam. I will show you how to use what they provide, what you learn from your bar review course, and what you know of your own strengths and weaknesses to tailor a study program that puts you in control.

Consider the following:

☐   The number of subjects tested on the bar exam is finite.

For the Multistate Bar Examination, the National Bar Examiners provide a subject matter outline that indicates the scope of coverage for each subject with a breakdown by percentage of questions from each category.

Similarly, most jurisdictions provide candidates with a list of the topics covered on their bar exam. This allows you to define the scope of your exam and put yourself on the same footing as you did for law school exams. Also, you'll study from released bar exam questions just as you worked with your professors' old exams in preparing for finals.

☐ There is breadth to the bar exam but not necessarily the same depth as on law school exams.

Perhaps to compensate for the wide range of subjects tested on the bar exam, the questions typically do not require the same depth of analysis as on a law school exam. Of course you will have to make this determination after a careful review of released exam questions in your jurisdiction, but it is likely you will find this to be true.

There's enough time if you plan properly

The bar exam requires a major commitment of time and effort to succeed. Bar review courses are structured to lead you through the material, but you must make the effort to learn it. It takes time to memorize black letter law and to practice problems. This part is neither fun nor easy. Still, it is possible to prepare adequately during the usual bar review period of six to eight weeks—*if you devote your time exclusively to bar preparation.* Unfortunately, this is not always a possibility for everyone. If it isn't for you, then you need to consider alternatives.

Whether it is a question of time to prepare or if you have one or more of the recognized "risk factors" associated with bar passage—one of which is "time"—you might want to consider beginning your bar preparation earlier than the traditional bar review period. Here a word or two about "risk factors" is in order before we proceed: such factors are based on statistics of groups of past bar takers and you are an individual. Statistics do not decide whether you'll pass the bar exam—only you will do that. Nonetheless, if you find you have one or more of the traditional risk factors, there are steps you can take to compensate by beginning your bar preparation before graduation.

The good news is that you have options. For example, since the ABA's approval of bar courses for credit, law schools are beginning to make such courses available to its students. This would give you the option of beginning your bar preparation during your last year of law school and jump start the bar review process. You have other choices as well and they are outlined in the Checklist, "*Would You Benefit From a "Head Start" on Bar Preparation?*"

Still, it is important to realize that even if you had all the time in the world, there are limits to how much information you can retain and how long you can maintain the level of intensity required during the preparation period. In many respects, it might well be a good thing that the bar prep period is finite. You just couldn't keep it up much longer!

The time pressure of the exam itself is a whole other issue, but one that you address through careful preparation. By the time you sit to take the actual bar exam, you will have practiced so many questions that your timing should be well under control.

Some stress is unavoidable

A little anxiety can be a good thing before an exam. Some anxiety is absolutely normal and very necessary. It's useful because the adrenaline ensures that you'll operate at peak performance. It helps to keep you focused. The problem occurs when it interferes with your performance.

Preparation is the recommended antidote to test anxiety. It is the best way to provide the confidence necessary to ward off the usual exam jitters. You must go into the bar exam knowing that you've done everything possible to prepare. In fact, you've over-prepared. In this case, you'll be in position to find the "exam zone." Whether you call it "auto-pilot" or "muscle memory," what happens is that your preparation takes over and you'll respond to the questions as you've trained yourself to do.

The Need for Preparation

By now it should be clear that studying for the bar exam will be an experience unlike any other. Taking the bar exam is a lot like running a marathon. And you need to prepare the same way—you must be in top physical and mental form to compete successfully. It won't be easy, enjoyable, or anything less than the tremendous pain that it is. But it is doable and countless others before you have done it and you'll do it too. And you should plan on doing it only once. If you put in the time and effort required for the period involved, then it will be behind you forever—unless you choose to take the bar exam in another jurisdiction. But then it will be your choice, not the bar examiners.

Admittedly, this is a challenge. But so was law school and you made it through or you wouldn't be here now. The good news is that law school prepared you for this exam. Now it's up to you to complete the job.

WOULD YOU BENEFIT FROM A "HEAD START" ON BAR PREPARATION?

The traditional bar review course begins around the time of your law school graduation and continues for the next six or eight weeks, ending a week or so before the bar exam. It provides all the law you need to know in a structured, cohesive package. This insures that you will cover all the law necessary to succeed on the exam. This is the route followed by most bar candidates—and it is usually sufficient to do the job. However, it is not the only way to go, nor is it suited to all candidates. In a number of instances, there is much to recommend a "head start."

As you'll learn in a subsequent chapter, a bar review course is just that—a review of the law. While it covers all the basic black letter law you need to know, a bar review course assumes a great deal about you. For example, it "assumes" that:

- you have a basic knowledge of most of the substantive law and the review course is just review

- you know how to study and juggle the competing demands on your time

- you know how to combine memorization with application

- you know how to take multiple-choice exams

- you know how to write essays in the format and structure of legal analysis

A. Would you benefit from early preparation? If you answer "yes" to any of the following questions, then you should strongly consider beginning your bar preparation before graduation by following one of the options outlined below in B.

    ☐ 1. Do you have serious gaps in your substantive knowledge in some of the subjects tested in your jurisdiction?

Since you cannot retain all the black letter law you need to know for the bar exam *too* many months beforehand, you must focus on only those subjects that will be the most efficient use of your time.

How do you know which subjects to target for an early intervention?

    a. What are the specific topics tested on your bar exam?

You need to know exactly what will be covered on your jurisdiction's bar exam. Refer to Chapter 5 and complete the *Checklist For State–Based Components*. This will lead you through the steps to identify the specific subjects tested on your bar exam.

    b. Are you weaker in some areas of the law than others?

Everyone has strengths and weaknesses, but now is when you must be completely honest with yourself—only you know what you know and what you don't know, which courses you did well in and those where, let's just say, your performance was less than stellar (anything with a grade in the "C" range or below). Make of list of these subjects.

_____

_____

_____

_____

_____

_____

c. Compare the list of bar-tested subjects (which should include the six multistate subjects) with your personal subject list and highlight the subjects that appear on both lists.

d. Select four or five subjects from this list and write them here. By narrowing your focus to only a few subjects, retention of the material until the bar exam is more likely.

_____

_____

_____

_____

Although you've already identified the subjects that warrant your attention, some subjects are "worthier" than others. In choosing from this pared down list, ask:

(i) Is it an area that is heavily tested on the bar exam?

Not all topics are accorded equal treatment on the exam. Some are tested more heavily than others. For example, there are 33 or 34 multiple choice questions on each of the six MBE subjects and, in some jurisdictions, these subjects are tested on the essay questions as well. Concentrating your study time in any of these areas would be highly productive.

(ii) Is it a subject that I will be learning for the first time during bar review?

Although it is not possible to eliminate all the new material you may encounter, it is best to minimize what you need to "learn for the bar" and focus instead on "reviewing for the bar."

After using these criteria to further narrow your list, two or three subjects should remain:

_____

_____

_____

☐ 2. Do some *types* of exam questions pose more difficulty for you than others? In considering this question, ask:

a. Did you score lower on objective, multiple-choice exams than essay exams in law school? If so, then you are going to want to devote more practice time to working with MBE questions.

b. Alternatively, did your professors make the comments "conclusory," "lacking analysis," or "sketchy on the law" in your exam books? If so, then you are going to spend more time working on your essay writing skills.

☐ 3. Do you have something less than "ideal" study habits?

a. Did you have major difficulties juggling your workload of balancing four or five subjects during the course of the semester?

b. Did you find yourself struggling at the end of each semester to finish your outlines and without sufficient time to write out essay questions or practice multiple choice questions?

c. Did you have trouble setting study goals and maintaining a realistic work schedule?

☐ 4. Do you have any of the traditional "risk factors" associated with low bar passage?

Admittedly, the bar exam is challenging and candidates do fail. This is not a secret: jurisdictions publish their pass rates so these numbers are readily available. What is not so readily available, however, are the reasons candidates fail the bar exam. While the explanations tend to be as varied as the candidates themselves, some factors are identifiable and thus useful for our purposes.

If you find yourself answering "yes" to any of the following criteria, you should strongly consider incorporating one or more of the suggested options for beginning your bar preparation during your last year of law school.

a. Academic standing: Do you have a low law school GPA? Do you rank in the bottom 20—25% of your graduating class? Did you have a low LSAT? [1]

Research shows that the strongest predictor of bar passage is law school GPA: the higher the law school grade point average, the greater the likelihood of passing the bar exam. Still, you are not doomed to failure if your law school grades are less than spectacular. Grades are not destiny. But they should tell you something: you need to take your preparation efforts seriously—*very* seriously.

b. Did you not take many of the bar-tested courses in law school, or if you did, were your grades in the "C" range?

c. Will you have to work or have primary care of your family (or both) during the bar review period?

d. Are you a non-traditional student? That is, are you an older student, a part-time student, or have more economic and familial responsibilities than the typical full-time law student? [2]

e. Are you not planning to take a bar-review course?

---

1. See, e.g., Denise Riebe, *A Bar Review for Law Schools: Getting Students on Board to Pass Their Bar Exams*, 45 Brandeis L.J. 269, 284 (2007).

2. See, e.g., Linda Jellum & Emmeline Pau-lette Reeves, *Cool Data on a Hot Issue: Empirical Evidence That a Law School Bar Support Program Enhances Bar Performance*, 5 Nev.L.J. 646, (2005).

Almost all students take a bar review course and I strongly recommend that you find the time and the money to do so. Some law schools offer bridge loans to get you through this period. After all the time and money you have spent on your education, this is not the time to economize. The longer it takes you to pass the bar exam and get your law license, the longer it will take you to start earning a salary.

f.   Do you perform poorly on essay exams? Multiple-choice exams?

Recognizing specific test-taking weaknesses early enough in the preparation process allows you to devote extra time to practice in areas you need to improve.

g.   Are you or a close family member facing a health or personal crisis?

It's pretty easy to see that the bar review period takes all of your emotional and physical energy. Illness or any significant life crisis—either personal or that of a loved one—can seriously detract from your ability to focus and study. If this is the case, you have several options, depending on your circumstances. You might seek professional help, emotional support, or consider whether this is the best time for you to take the bar exam.

h.   Do you have excessive fear or anxiety about test taking?

As we discussed, there is a real basis for anxiety about the bar exam and it is natural to be anxious. But it cannot be the kind of anxiety that prevents you from focusing on your studies. This kind of fear can sabotage your efforts and stand in your way of succeeding. If you find the suggestions in this book insufficient to overcome your fears, then you might want to consider getting professional help.

B.   How should you proceed if you want to begin your bar preparation early?

☐ 1.   Does your law school offer an early bar preparation program?

If your law school provides this opportunity, take it. Look for the following possibilities at your school:

a.   Is there a course identified as bar preparation, whether for-credit or not? Increasingly, law schools are providing students with bar preparation courses during the third year. Since the name of the course may not tell you what to expect, be sure to consult with the Registrar or Academic Dean at your school.

b.   Is there a course in state law or state procedural law you can take? Many schools offer classes that teach state-specific law such as New York Practice, Florida Law, Texas Oil and Gas Law. Typically, such courses provide a solid foundation in the substantive and procedural law tested on the state-based portion of your bar exam.

c.   Are there workshops about the bar exam? Even if formal classes are not offered, many schools provide information about the bar exam. Look for the following:

☐   Advisement sessions about the bar application process.

☐   Lectures previewing the components of the bar exam, sometimes offered by professional bar preparation experts at a small or no-fee. They may just require your attendance, but to be of any real value, count on giving it your full and active participation.

☐   Informational visits from members of your jurisdiction's bar examining committee.

☐   2.   If your law school does not offer a formal bar preparation course, consider creating your own "informal" bar review program by using other resources available to you:

a.   Does your school offer a course in Remedies?

If so, this course is an excellent vehicle for reviewing the substantive law in several areas—Torts, Contracts, and Civil Procedure. Typically, these were first year courses and looking at them again from the vantage point of your third year will let you see things you did not see earlier while reviewing the substantive material at a time much closer to the bar exam.

b.   If you have not already done so, do you still have time to take courses in such heavily tested bar subjects as

☐ Evidence?

☐ Trusts and Estates?

☐ Business Organizations?

☐ Family Law?

☐ Sales?

☐ Negotiable Instruments?

☐ Criminal Procedure?

These are just some of the possibilities. Many schools do not require these courses for graduation, but if you can take courses in the areas tested on your state's bar exam, it makes sense to do so. You do not need to sacrifice the electives you want to take—just try to balance them with the courses that will help you prepare for the bar exam as well. Besides, these "so-called" bar prep courses are usually basic law courses and should be part of every law student's legal education.

c. Does your school have an academic support department?

If so, you can meet with the academic support professional and work together on setting up an independent study program—one that is tailored to your individual strengths and weaknesses.

☐ 3. Do you plan to pursue an early bar preparation program on your own? This requires a bit more effort on your part, but it is possible.

Begin by identifying and working with the two or three subject areas most worthy of your attention based on the considerations outlined in section A. You will strengthen your substantive knowledge in these areas and transfer the skills gained from reading, analyzing, and answering questions in one subject area to others when you begin your formal bar review.

Use the study guidelines outlined in Chapter 7 for learning the substantive law in these areas. You can work with the subject matter outlines from your bar review course—these are usually given to you as soon as you sign up to take the course and are probably sitting somewhere in your room. If you don't have access to these materials, then use commercial outlines. After reviewing the black letter law, you are ready to move on to practice questions.

Follow the approaches in the chapters on the essays, the MBE, and the Multistate Performance Test to do the following:

a. Work with released essay exams from your jurisdiction to develop your essay writing skills.

b. Practice answering MPTs if your jurisdiction includes this component on its bar exam.

c. Develop your multiple-choice test-taking skills by:

☐ Using the Subject Matter Outlines from the Bar Examiners to target study areas.

☐ Studying the black letter law and then practicing the questions in that area by working with released MBE questions.

☐ 4. Does your bar review course allow you to attend its lectures twice—where the first time is **before** your graduation from law school (i.e., before your first taking of the bar exam)? For example, if you are planning to graduate in May and sit for the July bar exam, then you would take the bar review course offered the previous December—which is the course typically taken by candidates sitting for the February bar exam.

Since some bar review courses offer candidates a repeater course if their first attempt at the bar exam is unsuccessful, it can't hurt to ask if you can sit through the course prior to your actual bar course period. This can be very helpful:

a. Attending the bar review classes in advance would let you devote the entire bar review period to studying your notes and practicing problems instead of sitting in lectures.

b. It would be enormously beneficial to hear the material twice if you are an auditory learner.

*

CHAPTER 2

The Bar Planner

Calendar Countdown

Taking the bar exam is a major event in your life. And like any other event, it takes careful planning. Planning ensures that you won't forget things you need to do and puts you in a position of control over the preparation process.

Since preparing for the bar exam involves a number of tasks over a period of time, the most practical approach is to calendar the activities. This allows you to keep track of what you have done and what you may still need to do—and to do so at a glance.

The following pages provide checklists to guide you through the phases of the bar preparation process. The time frames are not definitive and tasks may overlap so use them as a general guide. If you are getting a bit of a late start, don't despair. Most of the early tasks can be made up along the way. Of course there are some you can't make up—such as the "jump start" program outlined in the previous chapter—but for the most part, you will be in fine shape if you follow the suggested guidelines. Extremely time-sensitive tasks are marked with a clock so can't miss them. There is really only one critical deadline you can't afford to miss: registering for your bar exam. You will want to verify and comply with this date as soon as possible.

The following Bar Planner Checklists take you through the entire bar preparation period, from the initial planning phases to the actual days of your bar exam. ***The "countdown" is to the start of your bar review class.*** As you work your way through each stage, you will most likely find your own points to add to the list.

Bar Planner Checklists

9–12 Months Ahead

4–6 Months Ahead

3 Months Ahead

3–4 Weeks Ahead

During Your Bar Review Class

    First 4 Weeks of Bar Review

    Next 2 Weeks of Bar Review

    Final 2 Weeks of Bar Review

The Days of the Bar Exam

After the Bar Exam

9–12 MONTHS AHEAD

☐ Are you familiar with the bar exam and the bar review process so you know exactly what to expect? (Chapters 1, 3, 4, 5)

    ☐ Procedurally? (the application and licensing process, bar review courses, and the bar review period?)

    ☐ Substantively? (the content and subjects tested on your bar exam?)

☒ Would you benefit from a "head start" on bar prep? (Chapter 1)

☐ Now that you are close to completing your law school education, are you sure you want to practice law?

- [ ] If not, and you are considering another path, is it necessary to take the bar exam?

- [ ] Even if you are planning a career where your law license is not essential, would it be beneficial to have it nonetheless? If so, then continue.

- [ ] Assuming you plan to take the bar exam, is now the best time for you to do so?

  - [ ] Are there family or health issues that require your full attention?

  - [ ] Are their financial issues you cannot overcome at this time?

  - [ ] Would the July or February bar exam be a better "fit" for you? (Chapter 6)

- [ ] Have you decided where you will be practicing law?

- [ ] Are you planning to take a bar examination in more than one jurisdiction? If so, it is your responsibility to determine the requirements for each jurisdiction and whether or not it is feasible for you to take a concurrent examination.

- [ ] Have you located the contact information for your chosen licensing jurisdiction(s)? (Chapter 4)

- [ ] Have you contacted your licensing entity to learn the following?

  - [ ] Your state's admission information with respect to:

    - [ ] Requirements for Admission?

    - Character and Fitness?

      Resolve any "character and fitness" matters well before you seek admission.

  - [ ] Your state's registration requirements for the bar exam with respect to:

    - [ ] Application packet and forms?

    - [ ] Application fees?

    - [ ] Filing deadlines?

    - [ ] Dates of the bar examination?

    - [ ] Test center locations?

⚰ Test accommodations?

Since each jurisdiction has its own policy and procedures with respect to test accommodations, you must verify that policy well in advance of your test date to allow sufficient time to comply with any requested documentation.

☐ Does your jurisdiction require the Multistate Professional Responsibility Exam ("MPRE")? If so,

    ☐ What is the required passing score?

    ☐ When must you pass it in relation to the bar exam?

    ☐ If you have not already taken the MPRE, when do you plan to take it?

        ☐ March   ☐ August   ☐ November

    ☐ What is the application deadline for the MPRE administration you will take?

        Date: _____

☐ Have you selected a bar review course? (Chapter 6)

☐ Have you considered your finances to ensure that you have enough to cover your living expenses during the bar review period?

    ⚰ If finances are an issue, can you borrow the money you need?

☐ If you are a working student,

    ☐ Can you take time off during the bar review period by using accumulated sick and vacation time?

    ☐ Can you take time off without pay?

    ☐ If finances are an issue, can you borrow the money you need?

☐ Have you set up your bar calendar to record all information about your bar application, bar review, and bar licensing activities? Have you noted:

    ☐ Filing dates?

    ☐ Exam dates?

☐ Bar review schedule?

Notes:

_____

_____

_____

4–6 MONTHS AHEAD

☐ Have you selected and registered with a bar review course? (Chapter 6)

    ☐ If you are pursuing an early bar preparation program, are you:

    ☐ Working with released essay exams from your jurisdiction to develop your essay writing skills?

    ☐ Practicing MPTs if your jurisdiction includes this component on its bar exam?

    ☐ Developing your multiple-choice test-taking skills by:

        ☐ Using the Subject Matter Outlines from the Bar Examiners to target study areas?

        ☐ Studying the black letter law and practicing questions in that area by working through released MBE questions?

☐ Have you started to fill out your bar exam application?

    ☐ Have you considered whether you need to request a change in the Test Center Location?

    ☐ Do you have the option to type your bar exam?

    ☺ Have you completed and filed your request for test accommodations if you require them?

Notes:

_____

_____

_____

_____

_____

_____

_____

3 MONTHS AHEAD

☐ Have you completed and submitted your bar application?

    ☐ If you are a re-applicant, have you verified the filing deadline since it may differ from first-time applicants?

     Have you requested test accommodations if you require them?

☐ Have you made hotel reservations near the Test Center?

☐ Have you scheduled any necessary medical exams?

    ☐ Doctor?

    ☐ Dentist?

    ☐ Vision exam?

Notes:

_____

_____

_____

_____

_____

_____

3–4 WEEKS AHEAD

☐ Have you finalized your bar review preparations with respect to:

    ☐ Financial arrangements?

    ☐ Living arrangements?

    ☐ Childcare?

☐ If you are planning to study in your home (as opposed to the library), have you readied your study area? (Chapter 3)

☐ Have you decided whether to take the morning or evening session of your bar review course?

☐ Even if you are not working and can attend day sessions, would you benefit from evening sessions? (Chapters 6, 7)

☐ Have you spoken with family and friends to let them know what you will be doing during the bar review period, how long it will last, and what it may require from them? (Chapter 3)

☐ Have you made travel arrangements for the days of the bar exam?

⊘ Have you made hotel reservations near the Test Center?

☐ Have you visited the drug store, supermarket, office supply store, etc. to purchase basic supplies and personal necessities?

☐ Have you planned a day (or weekend if you have the time and resources) to do something you really enjoy *before* your bar review class begins?

☐ Have you made plans for *after* the bar exam so you have something to look forward to when the exam is over?

Notes:

_____

_____

_____

DURING THE BAR REVIEW PERIOD

First 4 Weeks of Bar Review

Goal: To define a workable routine and maintain it

☐ Have you set a realistic work schedule that allows for

    ☐ Lecture time?

    ☐ Review time?

    ☐ Practice time?

    ☐ Relaxation time?

☐ Have you defined realistic study goals based on your strengths and weaknesses?

☐ Are you varying your study activities sufficiently throughout the day to maintain your concentration level?

☐ Have you set up a daily work schedule to include time for

    ☐ Attending your bar review class?

    ☐ Reviewing the material covered in each class?

    ☐ Consolidating your notes?

    ☐ Working through practice questions? (Chapter 7)

        ☐ Approximately 15 to 20 MBE questions?

        ☐ One or two essay questions?

        ☐ One MPT per week?

    ☐ Taking mini-study breaks and exercising?

☐ Have you set up a weekly schedule that includes one afternoon or evening away from your studies?

The following are suggested study schedules:

Assuming you take a morning bar prep course:

7:30—9:00 a.m.	Shower, breakfast, dress, and travel to bar review class.
9:00—12:30/1:00	Bar review course.

1:00—2:00	Lunch break.
2:00—4:00/4:30	Thorough review of notes from morning's session; make flashcards for black letter law; consolidate notes.
4:30—5:00	Break—go for a walk with your dog, exercise, call a friend.
5:00—6:30	Work through 15 to 20 MBE questions in the subject you have just studied.
6:30—7:30	Dinner break.
7:30—9:30	Work through another group of 15 to 20 MBE questions, one to two essays from a released bar exam, or an MPT, depending on your study needs.
9:30—11:00	Review materials for next day's bar review session; review notes from one subject covered earlier in the bar review period.
11:00/12:00	Relax. Watch *Law and Order.* Pass out.

Assuming you take an evening bar prep course:

7:30—8:30 a.m.	Shower, breakfast, and dress.
8:30—10:30/11:00	Review notes from the previous evening's class. Make flashcards for law.
11:00—11:30	Break—go for a walk or any kind of exercise.
11:30—1:00	Work through 15 to 20 MBE questions in the subject you have just studied.
1:00—1:30	Lunch break.
1:30—3:00	More multiple choice practice, one to two essays from a released bar exam, or an MPT, depending on your study needs.
3:00—3:30	Take a break; have a snack.
3:30—5:00	Review materials for next day's bar review session; review notes from one subject covered earlier in the bar review period.
5:15	Leave for bar review class.
6:00—10:00	Bar review class.
10:30/11:00	Home at last.
11:00/12:00	Relax. Watch *Law and Order.* Pass out.

Note: Evening review classes eliminate a regular dinner hour. Have a snack before class or pack a sandwich to eat during class. Learn which works best for you and make sure you have healthy snack foods available.

DEFINE YOUR INDIVIDUAL STUDY SCHEDULE

Create a schedule that works for you:

Time	Activity

DURING THE BAR REVIEW PERIOD

Next 2 Weeks of Bar Review

Goal: To avoid burnout and boredom and maximize retention of the black letter law

☐ Is the study schedule you set at the beginning of your bar review course still working for you by

    ☐ Keeping you engaged so you can focus?

    ☐ Allowing adequate time to review your bar review notes and practice questions?

    ☐ Ensuring sufficient time for study breaks?

    ☐ Enabling you to memorize the black letter law?

If your answer to any of the above is "no," then consider *revising your schedule* to:

☐ Vary the sequence of your study activities

☐ Change your study location

Or consider *revising your approach* to:

☐ Alternate your review materials to take up the topic in another form—anything that keeps you interested and adds to your understanding of the subject

    ☐ Read a different outline from your bar review materials

    ☐ Go back to your law school outline

    ☐ Consult a hornbook

☐ Shift the balance of study vs. practice time to allow more time for practicing questions (Chapter 7)

☐ Are you acclimating yourself to the "time zone" in which you'll be taking the bar exam by getting up in the morning and beginning your studies at the same time in which you'll be taking the bar exam?

☐ Are you going to sleep at a reasonable hour so you have enough rest?

☐ Are you finding your stress level starting to increase and interfere with

    ☐ your ability to concentrate?

    ☐ your ability to sleep?

If so, consider:

    ☐ Revising your study goals to make them more consistent with what you can realistically achieve each day

    ☐ Varying your routine

    ☐ Increasing your study breaks to a minimum of 10 minutes for every 90 minutes of study

    ☐ Including a regular exercise period every other day, even if it is only a 30 minute walk

    ☐ Scheduling an entire afternoon or evening away from your studies

    ☐ Making sure that you are eating properly

☐ Have you identified your strong and weak subject areas so you can target your study efforts effectively? (Chapter 7)

☐ Have you been reviewing subjects covered earlier in the bar review period, selecting a different one each day?

☐ Have you been steadily increasing the number of questions you practice each day to complete the following by the bar exam:

    ☐ All the released MBE questions and hundreds more for a total of at least 2000 questions?

    ☐ A minimum of three MPTs and more if you have a problem with timing?

    ☐ Most, if not all, of the released essay questions available in your jurisdiction?

☐ Have you received your Admission Ticket from the bar examiners?

☐ Have you received your Test Center Assignment?

☐ If possible, have you visited the Test Center location?

- ☐ Will it be a big room?

- ☐ Will it be noisy? If so, will you need earplugs?

- ☐ Will there be distractions?

- ☐ Will there be somewhere for you to go on your lunch break?

- ☐ Will you need to bring all of your own food? If so, be sure to bring something high in protein and easily digested!

☐ If you'll be traveling to the test location on the days of the exam, have you planned a trial run to know exactly where you're going and how long it will take to get there?

☐ If applicable, have you checked the Security Policy for your Test Center to verify

- ☐ The required form of personal identification?

- ☐ What personal items you may or may not take with you to the test site?

- ☐ If you are typing your exam, have you loaded it with the approved software and verified its operation?

Notes:

_____

_____

_____

_____

_____

_____

DURING THE BAR REVIEW PERIOD

Final 2 Weeks of Bar Review

Goal: to solidify your knowledge of the black letter law and improve your timing

☐ Have you confirmed your hotel reservations?

☐ Have you packed what you need to take with you?

    ☐ For staying at a hotel?

        ☐ Your most comfortable clothing?

        ☐ An alarm clock (or will the hotel give you a wake-up call)?

        ☐ Snack foods?

    ☐ For taking to the test site?

        ☐ Admission Ticket?

        ☐ Personal Identification?

        ☐ A watch?

        ☐ Adequate supply of pencils, pens, highlighters?

        ☐ "Quiet" food?

☐ Have you taken a simulated exam, either with a bar review course or on your own?

    ☐ Was your timing within range for the MBE? for the MPT; for the essays?

    ☐ Were your scores within range?

☐ If you simulate a portion of the exam on your own, are you able to

    ☐ Complete 17 MBE questions in 30 minutes; 34 MBE questions in an hour?

    ☐ Complete an essay in the time allotted for your jurisdiction?

    ☐ Complete an MPT in 90 minutes?

☐ Are you now practicing MBE questions in random order instead of one subject at a time as in earlier weeks?

☐ Have you been reviewing subjects covered earlier in the bar review period, one each day, to keep them fresh in your mind?

☐ Based on the results of simulated exams, can you identify where to focus your attention for the next two weeks:

    ☐ By specific subject areas?

    ☐ MBE subjects?

    ☐ Jurisdiction-specific law?

    ☐ By specific exam components?

        ☐ The essays?

        ☐ The MBE?

        ☐ The MPT?

☐ Now that your bar review course has ended, have you increased your study time and directed most of the additional time to *practicing* questions?

Notes:

_____

_____

_____

_____

_____

_____

THE DAYS OF THE BAR EXAM

☐ Have you put your books away the night before the exam and tried to relax by watching television or a movie?

☐ Have you set your alarm or left a wake-up call with the hotel?

☐ Are you dressed in layers so you will be comfortable during the exam whether it's warm or cold in the exam room?

☐ Have you packed snack foods and lunch?

☐ Are you planning to get to the test site approximately 30 minutes before the starting time, yet stay away from the crowd?

☐ If you will be with friends, have you agreed not to talk about the exam, either before or after the exam?

☐ Will you listen carefully and follow all instructions from the test proctors?

☐ When you are told to begin the exam, will you allocate your time for each question and set a timetable on scrap paper?

☐ When a session is over, will you leave the test site promptly and go home or to your hotel?

☐ Will you try and get a good night's rest between the days of the exam, knowing that you have done everything possible to prepare?

Notes:

_____

_____

_____

_____

_____

_____

AFTER THE BAR EXAM

☐ Have you made plans to:

    ☐ Get together with friends?

    ☐ See family?

    ☐ Have some fun?

    ☐ Do something you were not able to do during bar review?

☐ Do you find you need some time to simply de-compress? If so, this is perfectly normal and you should give yourself time—

    ☐ to be absolutely alone

    ☐ to "veg out" in front of the television

    ☐ to do absolutely nothing

☐ Do you find yourself reliving the exam or rethinking your answers?

Invariably, you will find yourself thinking about the exam. It will be difficult, but you must stop yourself. You have no idea how you did on the exam and thinking about it won't change the results. It will only drive you crazy! Instead, as soon as you find your mind wandering in this direction, stop yourself and do something— listen to music, call a friend, watch a movie—anything to redirect your thinking.

☐ Do you find that you are physically exhausted yet have trouble sleeping?

If so, you are most likely overtired from the weeks of concentrated study and it will take time to get back to a normal routine. Consider exercising every day—even if it is only walking for half an hour.

☐ Do you find that you are have difficulty staying focused on even simple activities?

This too is a result of the hundreds of hours you have just spent in preparation for the exam. Because of the intensity of the effort, it will take time for you to feel normal again!

☐ If you have received the Application for Character and Fitness from your jurisdiction, have you begun to fill it out?

Notes:

_____

_____

_____

*

CHAPTER 3

Lifestyle Considerations

A critical part of your preparation for the bar exam is to clear the way for you to concentrate solely on the bar exam for the entire bar review period—or as much of it as possible. There will always be life's little emergencies that come up along the way so if you've done your best to eliminate the major ones, you'll be able to deal with the unexpected ones as they arise and minimize their impact on your studies.

In this chapter, we'll consider the other essential aspects of planning for the bar exam:

- Setting aside the time

- Organizing your study area

- Managing finances

- Advising your family

- Attending to basic health issues

Making Time to Study

"Making the time" you need to study for the bar exam is the first step in your study plan. You must plan ahead to give yourself enough study time. To a considerable extent, success on the bar exam is a function of the actual time spent in concentrated study.

And concentrated study requires a mind free from distraction and worry.

This sounds funny—free from worry—when all you're going to do is worry about the exam, but I mean free from the basic concerns of money, family obligations, living arrangements, and the countless other demands on your time and attention. These major life considerations must be addressed as early as possible so that you won't be distracted when you need to concentrate. It's hard to focus on the elements of crimes and learn the Rule Against Perpetuities when you're worrying about the rent and childcare.

The key is to make these arrangements well before the bar exam period. The optimum period would be eight weeks of uninterrupted, concentrated study time. Certainly candidates have passed the bar exam while relying on less study time, but the stakes are high and you want to do everything in your power to maximize the likelihood that you'll pass the first time around. Whatever your personal situation, you will want to "free up" as much time as possible.

How do you "make" the time you need?

You knew the bar exam was lurking as soon as you began law school. Still, it was easy enough to put it out of your mind since there is no real need to deal with it before you are ready. But sometime during your last year of law school, you need to start thinking about it and planning for it—especially if you are a working student. have family obligations, or both.

1. Accumulate all your available vacation and sick time and use it in the final weeks before the bar exam if you must work during the bar review period.

    It is preferable to have several weeks of uninterrupted time towards the end of the bar review period rather than a day here and there. The idea is to have concentrated study time when you will benefit most from it—the bar review course will be over and you can devote all of your energies to your studies.

2. Rely on your friends and family.

Don't be shy about asking for help. Now is no time to be a martyr and insist on doing everything yourself. Let others help you. They can assist in a variety of ways, making them feel useful and a part of the process. They can baby sit, prepare meals, run errands, and provide much needed moral support.

Choosing Your Study Place

During the bar review period, your life will be rather limited and confined. You need to realize that simple fact right now. For the most part, your day will be spent in a bar review course and a study area. Your study area should be that place where you can concentrate for long periods without distraction. By now, you should know whether that place is at home or the school library. In either case, you'll want to make sure it's fully ready to meet your study needs.

Consider, as well, packing away any papers, books, or magazines that might distract you from studying. Clean out your closet and take care of leaking faucets—whatever could possibly keep you from concentrating. You do not want underlying irritations to distract you from your goal.

Arranging Your Finances

Once again, you cannot be focused on your studies if you are worried about paying the rent and grocery bills. Whatever your financial situation, you are best prepared for the bar exam if you have made arrangements for all aspects of your financial life during this time so the most you have to think about is getting to the ATM machine when you need cash. Everything else should have been planned for and arranged. Here's how:

1. If necessary, take a loan to meet all your basic needs. There are bridge loans available to cover your expenses during

the bar review period. Chances are you have taken loans to get you this far in your education; now is not the time to shy away from loans. If you consider the alternatives—as a true lawyer would do—you'll realize that the sooner you pass the bar, the sooner you get your license, the sooner you practice law, and the sooner you earn some money.

2. Consider paying all the usual bills that come due during this six-week period before you settle down to your bar studies. Pre-pay the rent or mortgage or anything else that can be paid ahead of time for this period.

3. If you can't do this—and most of us can't—then prepare all the paperwork and then just mail things out as they come due. This should obviate the need to go through all of your usual time-consuming bill-paying procedures.

4. If you can delegate this task to another, then do that. The less you have on your mind, the more room you have for the law!

Advising Friends and Family

You'll need the people in your life to realize how critical this time is for you. You may not be available to them in the same way you may have been in the past. If you prepare your family and friends for your unavailability during this time, they will be more understanding when you have to refuse invitations because you must study.

Most importantly, the people in your life can be understanding of your situation—if you let them know what you are doing, how long it will last, and what it requires from them. Get them on board with what you are doing and it will be easier on all of you.

Child-care arrangements

If you are a parent—of children of any age—you'll need to plan for them. Of course if your children are younger, this probably means making actual child-care arrangements. Do this as far ahead of time as possible and have a back-up plan in place as well.

However, even if your basic child-care needs are met, you must plan for time to be with your children. They need you and you need them. This time may be as little as half an hour every morning before you leave for bar review or an hour after dinner. Or it may be able to wait for the weekend if your children are older. But whatever the case, factor this time into your study schedule.

Caring for Your Health

If possible, get a complete physical exam before you begin your bar review course. Now is the time to see to basic medical needs. Have your vision checked. While you read a lot during law school, you'll be pushing it to the limit during bar review. You want to make sure that you're using the right prescription. Also, go to the dentist. Don't wait. Toothaches don't go away. They get worse and you can't study when you're in pain.

During bar review, plan to take vitamins, exercise, get enough sleep, and watch what you eat. While now is not the time to go on a killer diet or give up smoking, you must take care of your basic health. You can put off any promises to quit smoking and give up chocolate until after the bar exam. Now is not the time to add any more stress to your life!

PLANNING AHEAD

1. Have you arranged for the time you need to study for the bar exam?

    The optimum would be to have eight weeks of uninterrupted, concentrated study time but if that is not possible because you must work, then

    ☐ Have you considered speaking with your employer to minimize your workload or postpone major projects until after the bar exam?

    ☐ Have you asked to take all of your available vacation and sick time in the weeks prior to the exam?

☐ Can you revise/arrange your schedule to allow for maximum study efficiency by working work four 10–hour days and have three day weekends?

☐ Can you get up earlier and study for an hour or two before going into the office?

2. Have you put your "financial house" in order?

    ☐ Have you considered taking a bridge loan if you need assistance in paying for bar-related fees and living expenses during the bar review period?

       ☐ From your law school?

       Some law schools offer loans to their students to help them pay for their bar review course and living expenses.

       ☐ From a commercial lender?

       ☐ From a family member?

       If you are lucky enough to have someone willing and able to lend you the money, take it and pay it back with interest with your first paychecks as a practicing attorney!

☐ Have you prepared the bills for payment that come due during this period so that all you have to do is sign the check and drop it in the mail?

    ☐ Rent/mortgage?

    ☐ Utilities?

    ☐ Car payment?

    ☐ Credit cards?

    ☐ Insurance?

    ☐ Child care?

☐ Have you selected your study area?

    ☐ Do you plan to study in the library?

    If you are used to studying in the school library, then continue to do so. Its familiarity will be comforting and you should be able to acclimate quickly to your new study routine.

Even so, you will want to check the following:

☐ What are the library's hours?

Sometimes law schools extend their hours during the bar review period. Make sure you are aware of the hours.

☐ Do I have another place to study if the library is not available on a particular day?

Even if the library has extended hours, they may not be sufficient to meet your needs. In that case, make sure you have a back-up plan. Usually, your local library can serve the same purpose of providing a quiet, distraction-free place to study.

☐ Do you plan to study at home (either yours or someone else's?)

If you plan to study at home, then you may need to take certain precautions to make sure you spend the time studying and not doing other things—like watching television, doing the laundry, or cleaning the house.

☐ Do you have a specific work area?

Even if you studied for law school finals at home, you will find studying for the bar exam a different experience. It is more intense and takes over your life for a much longer period. You will need a dedicated space for your materials. Even if it is only part of a room, make that part yours, where all your study aids are kept. Try not to scatter them all over the house. This is annoying to others as well as to yourself—when you finally take a break from your work, you don't want to find bar review materials everywhere you look!

☐ Have you defined a study schedule?

While we'll take up the specifics of scheduling your study time in a subsequent chapter, you need to know that a schedule is critical for keeping your life balanced. Since you are studying at home and not a library, there is no "closing time." You will have to set the closing time.

☐ If you will be living and studying at someone else's home, then make sure you define your living arrangements well before the bar review period. Have you discussed and agreed upon:

☐ Your financial contributions?

☐ Cooking and cleaning arrangements?

☐ Your study schedule?

4. Have you acquired all necessary study supplies?

In addition to the "substantive" materials which we'll address in a later chapter, you need to consider basic supplies. A trip to the local office supply store is probably in order. Nothing is more time-consuming and energy sapping than having to run out to get something when you are studying.

☐ Do you have a reliable computer?

If you are planning to type your bar exam or type your bar review lecture notes, then make sure your computer is up to the task. Now is not the time to suffer a "memory loss" or downtime, if at all possible. Too much is at stake.

☐ Do you have a printer or access to one?

☐ Do you have an adequate supply of paper and printer cartridges?

You'll need to be able to print out the notes you take and the practice essays you write. You may not be able to continue using your law school's resources since you are now a "graduate." Please don't assume anything and check with the Dean of Students.

☐ A sufficient supply of pens, pencils, and highlighters?

☐ Two large binders?

After typing and printing each day's notes, you should put them in binders. You'll probably need at least two 3 ring binders.

☐ Index cards?

Consider getting a couple of packages of index cards—they are terrific for making your own flashcards for memorizing the black letter law.

5. Have you prepared the people in your life?

It is essential for your well-being and that of your significant others to let them know exactly what they can expect from you during the bar review period. Get them on board with what you will be doing so they will understand if you are not as available as you used to be. Plan to meet with them before your bar review classes begin and explain:

☐ How challenging the bar exam is and how important it is to pass

☐ How much their support means to you

☐ Your study schedule for the period

☐ What they can expect from you during this time

☐ What you would like from them

On another note:

☐ Do you know of any family or social events planned for the next few months?

The general rule is that you should not be taking time away from your studies for social events during bar review. However, just because your life is on "hold" during this period, it does not mean that everyone else's is as well. If you receive invitations during this time, you will have to make some careful decisions. An afternoon or evening of fun with family or friends can be a welcome break. If you've been working diligently each day, you can afford the time. Besides, such major events as engagements and weddings do not suddenly appear on the horizon. Chances are you'll know weeks in advance so plan accordingly and enjoy!

6. Have you made plans for your children?

☐ Have you made childcare arrangements, including a back-up plan?

☐ If you have young children at home, have you set aside a short time every day to spend with them?

Young children have no conception of time. They don't understand that you will be available to them again in a couple of months. Besides, there is no need to rob yourself of this small bit of happiness. I suggest you set aside some time each day to be with your children—either get up a bit earlier in the morning or forgo something else during the day—but make time to read to your child or play a game. This time will be well spent.

☐ If you have older children, have you considered letting them in on the study process?

Here you might consider such a simple thing as taking a walk together while your child tests you with your flashcards. Your son or daughter might enjoy the role reversal. After all, you are usually the one doing the testing! Or you can choose an area of law of interest—usually Criminal Law or Constitutional Law—and explain some aspect of the law. Teaching something to someone else is the best way to teach it to yourself.

☐ Have you considered designating an afternoon every week or every other week to visit with family or friends and including it in your study schedule?

Sometimes it helps to schedule a "family and friends" day. It's often easier on everyone to know when they will be getting together because it takes the pressure off. If you plan for it, the time away from your studies will let you return rested and energized.

☐ Have you considered using an "Away" message for non-essential email contacts?

This is a tough call: you need access to your email to receive critical messages but you can't allow it to become a distraction. In any case, set up a schedule where you check your incoming messages at most twice a day and respond only to the most urgent.

7. Are you taking care of your health?

Remember how at the beginning of each school year you had to give the school nurse a signed form from your doctor and dentist to verify your yearly check-up? There was something to that. You need to be in reasonably good health to focus on your studies.

☐ Have you had a recent medical exam?

    ☐ Are you taking any medications? If so, be sure to continue your regimen. Now is no time to make changes. It is also a good idea to have a check-up and make sure that you have the right prescriptions.

    ☐ Do you have any questions about managing stress and anxiety? It is best to discuss these concerns with your doctor before you begin the bar preparation process.

☐ Have you been to the dentist for a check-up and taken care of all necessary dental work? Toothaches do not go away so if you've been living on aspirins, take care of this before your bar review class begins.

☐ Have you had your vision checked recently?

While you read a lot during law school, you'll be pushing it to the limit during bar review. You'll want to make sure that you're using the right prescription. The last thing you need when studying for the bar exam are daily headaches from eyestrain.

    ☐ If you wear glasses or contact lenses, make sure you have a spare pair on hand.

☐ Do you follow a reasonably sensible diet and exercise plan?

You should take a multi-vitamin, exercise (even if it's just a 30 minute walk three or four times a week), get enough sleep, and watch what you eat. While now is not the time to go on a killer diet or give up smoking, you must take care of your basic health. You can put off any promises to quit smoking and give up chocolate until after the bar exam.

*

CHAPTER 4

Procedural Matters

Selecting the State for Your Bar Exam

Typically, the matter of where you will "sit" for the bar exam is determined by where you received a job offer or where you want to live. Often you know the answer to this question—or have a pretty good idea—before you graduate and so selecting the state in which to apply for bar admission is not a major consideration.

Sometimes you are not so sure—maybe you attended an out-of-state school and are considering a move away from your hometown or perhaps you received a clerkship and will be in a temporary location for a year or two. In any case, you need to select a licensing jurisdiction and you need to do so carefully. Since the expenses involved in taking the bar exam are high—physically, emotionally, and financially—you want to make the right choice for you.

Taking More Than One Bar Exam

Some candidates choose to sit for more than one bar exam. Usually, this is based on not knowing for sure where they will finally settle or believing that it increases their employment opportunities. Sometimes this makes sense if you know (or there is a strong likelihood) that you will be relocating in the near future since it is usually best to take the bar exam while the habits of studying and the black letter law are fresh in your mind.

However, before you commit to taking more than one bar exam, consider the costs involved—and not just the additional application and licensing fees and time and energy spent in studying for and taking the exam, but the expenses associated with maintaining that license. Each jurisdiction has its own annual or biannual license fees and Continuing Legal Education "(CLE)" requirements. So plan carefully—if you do not intend to practice law in another jurisdiction, think long and hard before making that commitment.

The Case of Concurrent Exams

Since the MBE is given on the same day in every jurisdiction, it is possible for applicants to take a concurrent bar examination in a state which gives their essay or local section on a different day from your primary jurisdiction. For example, in New York, the essay or local day is Tuesday whereas in New Jersey it is Thursday so you can sit for bar exams in both jurisdictions during the same exam period.

It is your responsibility to determine jurisdictional requirements and whether or not it is feasible for you to take a concurrent examination. While it might seem like an excellent opportunity to take two bar exams simultaneously because you take the MBE only once, you should nonetheless consider the following:

- the added expense of application fees and subsequent licensing and CLE costs

- the physical burden of an additional day of exams

- the study time involved in preparing for another jurisdiction's exam

As you should realize, the most critical factor in making this decision is whether you can afford the time to prepare for two exams. While this is your call, you must consider whether your time is better spent in concentrating on learning the substantive law of one jurisdiction or splitting your efforts between two. Even if you can rely solely on multistate or common law for one of the exams, you still need to become familiar with the essay structure of the other jurisdiction. Weigh these factors carefully before you make your decision.

Learning What Your State Requires for Admission

Bar passage is only one of a number of jurisdictionally-set criteria you must meet before gaining admittance to the practice of law. While you are probably aware that each state determines the composition and scoring of its own bar exam, you might not realize that there are other requirements for admission besides exam passage. These include age, education, and moral character requirements. We'll discuss the specifications of the bar exam in the next chapter and we'll consider these other requirements here.

The Licensing and Application Process

Naturally, the primary source for this information is your individual licensing entity. Make sure you check licensing requirements early in the preparation process to ensure that you are fully compliant—or can become compliant—before you seek admission. Pay close attention to the following:

- **Application deadlines**: pay careful attention to all deadlines. In some cases additional fees are imposed if you miss a deadline; in other instances, you may be out of luck and there is no second chance. Note all applicable deadlines in your Bar Planner.

- **General education requirements**: general requirements include college work requirements and, in some cases, high school requirements.

- **Legal education requirements**: there are requirements for law school (i.e., ABA-accredited, provisionally accredited, or otherwise authorized by statute) or, in some cases, work-study alternatives such as supervised study in law offices or the courts.

- **Moral character qualifications**: these are typically satisfied by a passing score (as determined by the jurisdiction) of the

Multistate Professional Responsibility Exam ("MPRE") and satisfaction of a Professional Responsibility course in law school.

- Other "moral character and fitness" requirements may include:[1]

  ☐ Compliance with court ordered child or family support obligations

  ☐ Letters of reference

  ☐ Character and fitness interviews in addition to passing scores on ethics exams

  ☐ Conditional admission where there are issues of substance abuse, mental instability, debt, or criminal history

While this list is not exhaustive and varies widely among jurisdictions, it indicates that states consider more than just a passing score on a bar exam before the privilege of a law license will be granted. I strongly recommend that if you have so much as an outstanding parking ticket, you pay it as soon as you finish reading this chapter.

Test Accommodations

If you had special accommodations during exams in law school, then you will want to have them for the bar exam as well. However, each jurisdiction has its own policy and procedures with respect to test accommodations. Be sure to verify that policy well in advance of your test date to allow sufficient time to provide any requested documentation.

Test Center Location

There may be multiple test locations depending on the size of your jurisdiction. You should note where your exam will be held in case it is necessary to make hotel reservations.

---

1. Check with your individual jurisdiction for the most recent requirements. You can also refer to Chart II: Character and Fitness Determinations in the *Comprehensive Guide to* *Bar Admission Requirements* on the NCBE website at www.ncbex.org/comprehensive-guide-to-bar-admissions/.

Request for Changes

Some jurisdictions allow changes in assigned test locations but typically only in rare instances and require a showing of good cause. Be sure to comply fully with all requirements for such requests—be especially careful to check the date for submission of such requests.

Admission Tickets

Typically, you will receive your seating assignments about two to three weeks prior to the date of the examination. Depending on your jurisdiction, seat assignments may be mailed to you or made available for printing directly from the website.

Seating assignments are often used as a means of identification throughout the grading process (on MBE answer sheets and essay booklets) so it is extremely important for you to follow all directions regarding these tickets.

Security Policies

At some point prior to the date of the bar examination, you should consult and carefully review the security policy in effect in your jurisdiction, noting the following:

* What you will be allowed to take with you to the exam site (you will probably have to part from your cell phone)

* What you will need for personal identification

Using Your Laptop

Increasingly, jurisdictions are offering their candidates the opportunity to type the essay portion of their bar exam. This option is usually time-sensitive and sometimes done as a lottery among candidates so pay close attention to all directions. Also, there is special software you will need for your computer, usually at an additional cost.

PROCEDURAL MATTERS

1. Have you selected the jurisdiction where you want to take your bar exam?

   ☐ Yes. If so, write it down and include its contact information and website address. Then proceed to question 2.

   _____

   _____

   ☐ No. If not, then ask the following:

   Do you know where you would like to live, having considered:
   ☐ Career opportunities?
   ☐ Proximity of family and friends?
   ☐ Affordability?
   ☐ Quality of life?

   Do you know the type of law practice that interests you?
   ☐ Sole practitioner?
   ☐ Small to mid-size law firm?
   ☐ Large firm?
   ☐ Government agency?
   ☐ Public interest work?

2. Are you planning to take more than one bar exam? If so, then ask:

   ☐ Have I considered the additional expenses of
      ☐ Application and licensing fees?
      ☐ Time and energy spent in studying for and taking the exam?
      ☐ Continuing Legal Education "(CLE")" requirements?

   ☐ Do I have the study time and stamina needed to prepare for another jurisdiction's bar exam?

   If you will take a second exam, what is the jurisdiction and its contact information?

   _____

   _____

3. Have you requested your bar exam application?

   ☐ Date requested? _____

   ☐ Filing fees? _____

   ☐ Filing deadline? _____

4. If you are taking the MBE concurrently in another jurisdiction and wish to transfer that score, have you made a timely transfer request by using the MBE Score Transfer Form available through the National Conference of Bar Examiners (NCBE) at www.ncbex.org/multistate-tests/mbe/services/transfers/?

   Date of request:

   _____

5. Does your jurisdiction require the Multistate Professional Responsibility Exam ("MPRE")? If so,

   ☐ When must you pass it in relation to the bar exam?

   Identify the time frame:

   _____

   ☐ If you have not already taken the MPRE, when do you plan to take it?

   ☐ March ☐ August ☐ November

   ☐ What is the application deadline for the MPRE administration you will take?

   _____

6. Are there any "character and fitness" issues you need to resolve? If so, identify and take appropriate action:

   _____

   _____

   _____

7. Do you intend to request test accommodations? If so, then

    ☐ Have you checked the accommodation policy for your jurisdiction?

    Note compliance dates:

    _____

8. Do you know the Test Center Location for your bar exam?

    _____

    ☐ Do you intend to request a change in the Test Center Location? If so, have you:

        ☐ Identified the procedures for such requests in your jurisdiction?

        ☐ Noted the timeframe for making such requests? Identify the date:

    _____

9. Have you noted the date in your Bar Planner when to expect your Admission Tickets? Note the date here as well:

    _____

    ☐ How will you receive your Admission Tickets?

    ☐ By mail?   ☐ Downloadable from website?

10. Have you checked the security policies in your jurisdiction to know what you are allowed to take with you to the test site? List the items here:

    _____

    _____

    _____

    _____

    _____

11. Do you know what forms of personal identification are acceptable for admittance to your bar exam? List what you will need:

    _____

    _____

12. Will you use your laptop if your jurisdiction provides this option?

    If so, have you:

    ☐ Verified the procedures for exercising this option?

    ☐ Identified the application date? Note it here as well as in your
       Bar Planner:

    _____

                                    *

CHAPTER 5

De-constructing
the Bar Exam

Know Your Bar Exam

Each jurisdiction sets the format for its own bar exam. It determines the type of questions and sets its own policy with regard to the relative weight given to each section of the exam in calculating a bar passage score. To this extent, each state's bar exam is unique and you'll want to know everything there is to know about the make-up of your particular bar exam. Still, bar exams tend to be more similar than different in several respects. For example:

Bar exams are licensing exams that seek to test for minimum competency.

The methods of testing typically include objective questions and essay questions.

There is a state-based component that tests the candidate's knowledge of local law.

There is a national component from the National Conference of Bar Examiners.

It's Time to Meet the Bar Examiners

It is all too easy to overlook this primary source of inside information. The bar examiners give you the real scoop on the bar exam and any information they provide should figure prominently in your collection of study materials. This is true of both national and state bar examiners.

The National Conference of Bar Examiners ("NCBE")

The NCBE develops the national bar exams and provides them to the participating jurisdictions who administer them. The NCBE creates four tests which may be included as part of a state's bar exam.

1.   The Multistate Bar Exam ("MBE")

The MBE is part of almost every jurisdiction's bar exam. It is administered by participating jurisdictions on the last Wednesday in February and the last Wednesday in July of each year. The state-specific portion of the bar exam is given either the day(s) before or the day(s) after the MBE. There are a few states that offer the MBE only once a year so it is essential to consult your individual jurisdiction for precise information.

The MBE is a six-hour examination, consisting of 200 multiple choice questions. The exam is divided into two periods of three hours each: one in the morning and one in the afternoon, each containing 100 questions. Applicants are asked to choose the *best* answer from four alternatives. Since your score is based on the number of correctly answered questions, you're advised to answer every question. Even if you have no idea as to the correct answer, it's still appropriate to guess because you're not penalized for incorrect answers.

Each jurisdiction sets its own policy with respect to the relative weight given to the MBE score. If you have any questions with respect to the use made of your MBE score in calculating your overall bar passage score, you must direct such inquiries to your individual jurisdiction and not the NCBE. A regularly updated list of each jurisdiction's bar admission office address and phone number is available from the NCBE website.

The NCBE website is a comprehensive resource for current information on the MBE. It provides:

- A detailed description of the MBE

- Subject matter outlines indicating the scope of coverage for each subject with a breakdown by percentage of questions from each category

- Representative sample questions

- MBE Study Aids

Study Aids are available for purchase and include released questions from past administrations of the MBE. The most recent release is the MBE Annotated Preview, a 100–question, annotated online practice exam. The MBE–AP uses questions drawn from recent MBEs. According to the NCBE, "you can take the exam in either timed or untimed sittings, and you will receive feedback on your answers, including annotations and a customized score report that can help you identify strengths and weaknesses in your knowledge of the six MBE subject areas."[1]

The MBE–AP

The MBE–AP is delivered online. The 100 questions represent the same content distribution as seen on a full-length MBE. Both the correct and incorrect answer choices are annotated to provide guidance and explanations. Finally, the test includes a scoring component allowing you to assess your performance to some degree—both overall and with respect to each of the six MBE areas.

The test may be taken in a timed three-hour sitting or on a question-by-question basis. Taking the exam one question at a time allows you to consider the annotated answers in close proximity to answering the test question. After the exam is taken once, you may choose to take the entire exam again or retake only the questions

---

1. *See* National Conference of Bar Examiners, NCBE Study Aids Store, www.ncbex2. org/catalog/ (last visited February 10, 2007).

answered incorrectly. The NCBE expects that in addition to using the MBE–AP to gain experience and familiarity with the MBE multiple-choice format, examinees will also use it as a learning tool for substantive content.

What Subjects are Tested

Multiple choice questions are used because they allow the examiners to test a wide range of topics. The MBE includes questions from six subject areas:

- Constitutional Law

- Contracts (including Article 2, Sales)

- Criminal Law (including Criminal Procedure)

- Evidence

- Real Property

- Torts

The questions are presented in a completely random manner so both the subject matter and the complexity of the question varies from one question to the next. This means that you might go from answering a Contracts question to a Property question and on to an Evidence question. You'll also have to figure out the subject for yourself since you're not told which area is being tested for any question.

As of July, 2007, there are 190 scored questions [2] consisting of 33 questions each on Contracts and Torts and 31 questions each on Constitutional Law, Criminal Law, Evidence, and Real Property. Of the 33 Contracts questions, approximately 25% of the questions are based on provisions of the Uniform Commercial Code, Articles 1 and 2. Of the 31 Criminal Law questions, approximately 40% of the

---

2. On each administration of the exam, 10 of the 200 questions are used by the NCBE for question evaluation purposes and not included in calculating the candidate's MBE score.

questions are based on Criminal Procedure issues arising under the 4th, 5th, and 6th Amendments.[3]

The MBE is challenging for even the best students. It's a challenge because there are so many questions and so little time. It's a challenge because it tests knowledge of the substantive law, reading comprehension and reasoning skills, the ability to work quickly and efficiently, and the capacity to remain focused and functioning over a long period of time.

Still, a candidate need not expect to walk into the bar exam knowing every single rule of law and its fine distinctions—this is not only impossible, it's not necessary. Considering that a candidate can pass the bar exam even though almost 80 out of 200 questions have been answered incorrectly depending on the weight accorded the MBE in a particular jurisdiction,[4] it is evident that a candidate is not expected to know every rule to be found "minimally competent" to practice law.

2.   The Multistate Performance Test ("MPT")

The MPT has been adopted by thirty-three jurisdictions as part of their bar exam.[5] Participating jurisdictions select from the two ninety-minute problems provided by the NCBE for each exam

---

3. The NCBE provides subject matter outlines indicating the scope of coverage for each of the topics covered on the exam. There is an outline for each of the six MBE subjects. Not only is each potential test topic identified within each subject, there is also a breakdown by percentage of how many questions will be taken from a particular category. For example, of the 33 Real Property/Future Interests questions on the MBE, only 25% (8–9 questions) come from Real Property contracts and mortgages. The likelihood that there will be more than four or five actual mortgage questions is extremely unlikely. On the other hand, it is very important to know that of the 34 Torts questions, approximately one-half of them will be negligence questions which represents almost 8.5% of the entire MBE.

4. Only six states and the District of Columbia require candidates to achieve a "set" passing score for the MBE, i.e., Kentucky, Oklahoma, Rhode Island, South Carolina, Vermont, and Wyoming. Out of 39 states identifying scoring standards, only South Carolina sets an automatic failure based on an MBE scaled score of less than scaled 110. If a candidate achieved a scaled score of 110, then that candidate conceivably answered less than 50% of the MBE questions correctly. See National Conference of Bar Examiners, Comprehensive Guide to Bar Admission Requirements, www.ncbex.org (last visited February 10, 2007).

5. NCBE, www.ncbex.org (last visited February 10, 2007).

administration. It is administered by participating jurisdictions on the Tuesday before the last Wednesday in February and July of each year. Like the MBE, each jurisdiction determines its own policy with regard to the relative weight given to the MPT and grades the exam.

Just as it publishes released MBE questions, the NCBE makes previously released MPTs available on its website. Additional MPTs and Point Sheets (points sheets are the scoring guidelines suggested by the NCBE in preparing the question) can be ordered from the MPT Study Aids Order Form at the end of the MPT Information Booklet. You will want to practice as many MPT problems as possible to sample the various tasks you might encounter on the exam.

The MPT tests fundamental lawyering skills: the ability to read and follow directions, synthesize and apply law from cases, separate relevant from irrelevant facts, and complete an assigned task in the allotted time. Here you are given both the legal issue and the law because the goal is to test your proficiency in the basic skills developed in the course of a legal education and not the ability to memorize.

Designed very much like a closed-universe memo assignment, the MPT consists of a client "File" and a law "Library" and you are asked to complete a typical assignment for a first year associate. Examples of such tasks include the following:

- writing an objective memorandum

- writing a persuasive memorandum of law or trial brief

- writing a client letter

- drafting a will or contract provision

- drafting an opening or closing statement to the jury

3. The Multistate Essay Examination ("MEE")

The MEE is administered by participating jurisdictions on the state day of their bar exam. It consists of a set of thirty-minute essay questions where participating jurisdictions typically select six of the seven questions prepared by the NCBE.[6] You must check with your jurisdiction to find out whether it administers the MEE. Also, you'll want to know how many MEE questions there will be and whether you are to apply the common law or state-specific law.

Beginning July, 2007, new test specifications are being introduced and jurisdictions will be able to choose from nine questions instead of seven. Some questions may include issues in more than one area of law. The areas of law that may be covered include the following:

- Business Associations (Agency and Partnership; Corporations and Limited Liability Companies)

- Conflict of Laws

- Constitutional Law

- Contracts

- Criminal Law and Procedure

- Evidence

- Family Law

- Federal Civil Procedure

- Real Property

- Torts

- Trusts and Estates (Decedents' Estates; Trusts and Future Interests)

- Uniform Commercial Code (Negotiable Instruments; Secured Transactions)

Here, too, the NCBE provides candidates with the opportunity to work from previously released questions. Several examples

---

6. NCBE, www.ncbex.org (last visited February 20, 2007).

are included in the MEE Information Booklet and five years of MEE Study Guides are available online. Additional questions are available for purchase at the NCBE Online Store.

The MEE Study Guides contain questions and model analyses that are "illustrative of the discussions that might appear in excellent answers to the questions. They are provided to the user jurisdictions for the sole purpose of assisting graders in grading the examination."[7] This information may be given to graders to guide them in grading essays, but it is given to you to help you prepare for writing them.

4.   The Multistate Professional Responsibility Exam ("MPRE")

The MPRE is a multiple-choice examination consisting of sixty questions and is required for bar admission in all but three jurisdictions. Passing scores are established by each jurisdiction and currently vary between 75 and 86.[8] For the most current information regarding passing scores and exam policies, you must check with the jurisdiction to which you intend to apply for admission.

The exam is given three times a year in August, November, and March. It tests the law governing the conduct of lawyers, including the disciplinary rules of professional conduct as stated in the ABA Model Rules of Professional Conduct, the ABA Model Code of Judicial Conduct, and other controlling rules and judicial decisions. For this reason, many students like to take the MPRE when they have completed the course on Professional Responsibility or Legal Ethics given in their law school.

However, it is not necessary to take a course before taking the MPRE. In fact, even if you have taken a course, it might not cover the same material as is tested on the MPRE and not necessarily in the same detail. So in either case, you'll want to do the following:

---

7. See NCBE, THE MULTISTATE ESSAY EXAMINA-TION 2007 INFORMATION BOOKLET, available at www.ncbex.org/uploads/user_ docrepos/ 1999MEEQA.PDF.

8. See NCBE, www.ncbex.org/multistate tests/mpre/ (last visited February 20, 2007).

- Check with your bar review company. Most bar review courses include an MPRE component and offer a review session timed to coincide with the administration of the MPRE.

- Use the materials available to you from the NCBE. [9] In fact, however you choose to prepare for the MPRE, an essential part of that preparation includes the materials offered by the NCBE: be sure to work with its subject-matter outline identifying the scope of the exam and the MPRE Study Aids which include actual and simulated MPRE questions.

It makes sense to take the MPRE sometime during your third year of law school to complete this hurdle before sitting for the bar exam. Just be sure when checking the MPRE requirements for your jurisdiction, that you take the exam within the time frame specified. Not only does each jurisdiction set its own passing score as previously noted, but it establishes its own policy for when the exam must be taken with respect to the bar examination.

State-based Components

Like the NCBE, the individual state bar examiners make vital information available to its bar candidates. It is your primary source for such basic information as application materials, test locations and accommodations, test dates, admissions issues, and more.

Unfortunately, it's easy to overlook this primary source of inside information when you have so many bar review guides competing for your attention. But if you fail to consult this incredibly valuable resource, here's what you would be missing:

- a comprehensive and detailed list of the topics tested on your particular bar exam

---

9. *See* NCBE, www.ncbex.org/uploads /user_ docrepos/MPRE_ IB2007.pdf (last visited February 23, 2007). A wealth of information is at your fingertips: application procedures, sample questions, and guidelines for taking the exam are available in the MPRE Information Booklet.

- the exam schedule

- specific exam-taking instructions

- grading and scoring information

- guidelines for answering an essay question

- past examination questions and sample answers

1. The Subjects to Be Tested

The state bar examiners identify the specific subject areas tested on their bar exam. This information is often found in the Rules for the state's Board of Bar Examiners. By knowing the scope of the exam, you can narrow the universe of what you need to know. Even if you can eliminate only one or two topics, it makes a difference.

Florida

Like most other jurisdictions, Florida provides information regarding the precise subject matter of its bar exam.[10] It advises its candidates that Part A of the exam consists of six one-hour segments where:

"One segment shall embrace the subject of Florida Rules of Civil and Criminal Procedure and the Florida Rules of Judicial Administration Rules 2.051, 2.060, and 2.160. The remaining five segments, each of which shall embrace no more than two subjects, shall be selected from the following subjects including their equitable aspects:

Florida Constitutional Law

Federal Constitutional Law

Business Entities, including Corporations and Partnerships

Wills and Administration of Estates

---

10. *See* Florida Board of Bar Examiners, Rules of the Supreme Court Relating to Admissions to the Bar, Rule 4–20, www. floridabarexam.org/ (last visited February 24, 2007).

Trusts

Real Property

Evidence

Torts

Criminal Law

Contracts

Family Law

Chapter 4, Rules of Professional Conduct

Chapter 5, Rules Regulating Trust Accounts, of the Rules Regulating The Florida Bar"

New Jersey

New Jersey provides candidates with the following information in its Admission to the Bar Booklet, section C, the Bar Examination, subsection 4, New Jersey Essay Questions:

"The questions are based upon the subjects of contracts, criminal law, real property, torts, constitutional law, evidence, and civil procedure. An essay question may cut across two or more of the basic subject areas. In addition, these questions may be framed in the context of fact situations involving, and interrelated with, the following subjects:

Agency

Conflicts of law

Corporations

Equity

Family law

Partnership

Uniform Commercial Code Articles 2 (Sales), 3 (Commercial Paper), and 9 (Secured Transactions)

Wills, trusts, and estates

Zoning and planning

Disciplinary rules"[11]

New York

New York follows the same approach in identifying tested subject areas. Its bar examiners inform candidates that:

"The New York portion is based on both procedural and substantive law. It may deal with the six subject matters covered on the Multistate Bar Examination (MBE)—Contracts, Constitutional Law, Criminal Law, Evidence, Real Property, and Torts (including statutory no-fault insurance provisions). In addition, the questions may deal with

Business Relationships

Conflict of Laws

New York Constitutional Law

Criminal Procedure

Family Law

Remedies

New York and Federal Civil Jurisdiction and Procedure

Professional Responsibility

Trusts, Wills and Estates, and

UCC Articles 2, 3, and 9

More than one subject is tested in a single essay question. Except for questions involving federal law, the New York

---

11. *See* New Jersey Board of Bar Examin-   (last visited February 24, 2007).
ers,   www.njbarexams.org/barbook/aic4.htm

essay and multiple choice questions are based on the law of New York."[12]

California

The California bar exam has a reputation for being one of the most difficult bar exams to pass. I am not interested in discussing whether that reputation is deserved, or even if it's true—my only concern, as should be yours—is how to pass it. And California does a lot to help you in this effort, if only you choose to follow its advice.

The State Bar of California's website is easy to navigate and provides lots of useful information. A good starting point is the "Scope of the California Bar Exam." Here you will find a list of the 13 subjects from which you may be expected to answer questions as well as additional instructions from the bar examiners regarding some of the subject areas, including how and where to target your studies. For example, you are told to direct your study to specific provisions of the UCC and the California Probate Code.

Further, and even more important for your studies, you are told that when answering questions that have issues concerning the Federal Rules of Civil Procedure and the California Code of Civil Procedure, you should "be prepared to discuss the differences between the Federal Rules and the California rules, especially those California procedures of pleading and practice that have no specific counterparts in the Federal Rules."[13] You are given similar instructions with respect to Evidence questions.

This information is invaluable because it tells you exactly what the California bar examiners want you to discuss when answering these questions. Your job is to follow such instructions to the letter.

2. The Exam Schedule

An essential part of the preparation process is being familiar with the format and length of the exam. In addition to helping you

---

12. *See* New York Board of Law Examiners, www.nybarexam.org/barexam.htm (last visited February 24, 2007).

13. *See* the State Bar of California, Scope of the California Bar Exam, at www.calbar.ca.gov/calbar/pdfs/admissions/ex1000900.pdf (last visited February 24, 2007).

structure your practice sessions, knowing what to expect goes a long way toward lessening your anxiety on bar day.

While commercial bar review courses provide some of this information, your state bar examiners provide precise details. If you want to know exactly what to expect on bar day—down to the last detail—check with your bar examiners.

For example, Connecticut advises its candidates as follows:

"The Connecticut Essay Examination is a 12–question, essay-style examination. Each question should be answered in 30 minutes. Questions 1–6 are distributed in the morning and questions 7–12 in the afternoon. *Applicants must answer the questions in order. Questions are collected every hour: Questions ##1 & 2 in the first hour; Questions ##3 and 4 in the second hour, etc.* If you finish a pair of questions early, you may go on to the next question. Detailed instructions will be provided the morning of the examination. Bring plenty of black pens."[14] *[italics added]*

Here, even though all the questions are distributed at the beginning of the test session, you are required to answer the questions in order and you are not free to use your time any way you choose. If you were not familiar with these instructions, you could easily go astray since it is not the usual or ordinary test practice to collect questions every hour.

New York is equally explicit in its information to candidates but does not set the order in which you must answer the questions; this part is up to you:

"In the morning session, which begins at 9:00 A.M. and ends at 12:15 P.M., applicants must complete three essays and the 50 multiple choice questions in three hours and 15 minutes. Although applicants are free to use their time as they choose,

---

14. *See* State of Connecticut Judicial Branch, Connecticut Bar Examining Committee, Taking the Bar Examination at www. jud.state.ct.us/CBEC/examinfo.htm#How (last visited February 24, 2007).

the Board estimates an allocation of 40 minutes per essay and 1.5 minutes per multiple choice question."

"In the afternoon session, which begins at 1:30 P.M. and ends at 4:30 P.M., applicants must complete the remaining two essay questions and the MPT in three hours. Again, although applicants are free to use their time as they choose, the National Conference of Bar Examiners developed the MPT with the intention that it be used as a 90–minute test. Therefore, the Board recommends that applicants allocate 90 minutes to the MPT and 45 minutes to each essay."[15]

3. Grading and Scoring

Each jurisdiction has its own formula for calculating a passing score and makes this information available to candidates. The NCBE also includes information on each jurisdiction's grading and scoring policy in its *Comprehensive Guide to Bar Admission Requirements*.[16]

While you need not concern yourself with understanding the fine points of the procedures bar examiners use to scale and equate scores, you should know the relative weights accorded each section of your bar exam. This allows you to apportion your study time with respect to where it will yield the most return: for example, if the written portion of your bar exam is weighted twice that of the MBE, you want to be sure to spend considerable time developing your essay writing skills.

It is also important to know whether your jurisdiction sets a minimum passing score for individual components of the exam. For example, an applicant with a scaled MBE score of 110 or less automatically fails the bar exam in South Carolina.[17] However, the number of jurisdictions with individual passing scores are very few,

---

15. *See* New York Board of Law Examiners at www.nybarexam.org/ (last visited February 25, 2007).

16. *See* NCBE, Comprehensive Guide to Bar Admissions, Chart VII: Grading and Scoring at www.ncbex.org/fileadmin/mediafiles/downloads/Comp_ Guide/2007 CompGuide.pdf (last visited September 11, 2007).

17. *Id.*

seven to be precise,[18] and the overwhelming majority consider a combined score in calculating bar passage. In New York, for example, there is no passing or failing on any one portion of the exam and its bar examiners write that "a poor performance on one section of the examination may be offset by a superior performance on another section. Passing or failing is determined only on the basis of the applicant's total weighted scaled score."[19]

4. Guidelines for Answering an Essay Question

Not only do bar examiners provide a list of subjects to be tested so you'll know exactly what to study, many provide guidelines so you'll know exactly how to answer their questions. They give you the details you need to know to write point-earning essays. Let's consider two jurisdictions.

New Jersey

In its Complete Bar Book, the New Jersey Board of Bar Examiners directs its candidates to write "lawyer-like" responses that "approximate the work product of a practicing lawyer." To help in this effort, they offer the following advice:[20]

1. Read and re-read the problem carefully to familiarize yourself with the facts and circumstances. Do not assume additional facts unless directed to do so.

2. Make sure you understand the directions that appear in boldface type at the conclusion of the problem. Adhere to those instructions and plan your response accordingly. Before you begin to write your answer, outline and organize your response.

3. Do not use a "scattershot" approach; rather, structure your answer before you begin to write so that your essay will

---

18. *Id*. In addition to South Carolina, the jurisdictions which require individual passing scores include: the District of Columbia, Kentucky, Oklahoma, Rhode Island, Vermont, and Wyoming.

19. *See* New York Board of Law Examiners, www.nybarexam.org/barexam.htm (last vis-

ited February 25, 2007).

20. *See* The New Jersey Board of Bar Examiners, the Complete Bar Book, Suggestions on Answering Essay Questions, at www.njbarexams.org/barbook/barbook.pdf (last visited February 25, 2007).

demonstrate your ability to analyze legal problems and to provide an organized, logical and coherent written response.

4. When appropriate to the format of the question, discuss all sides of issues and do not let your disposition of an issue preclude discussion of other issues presented. When appropriate, discuss procedures and remedies, as well as legal rights and liabilities.

5. Allocate enough time to compose a clear and concise response. The writing ability exhibited by your response will affect your grade.

Oregon

Similarly, Oregon's State Board of Bar Examiners provides its candidates with an information booklet containing answers to questions about the entire bar admission process, including seven questions relating specifically to the essay examination. Consider the following three questions:

What is expected in an answer?

Must my answer be voluminous?

What techniques should I employ in answering the essay questions? [21]

As you can see, Oregon's bar examiners have anticipated the questions every candidate has about the bar exam. They are the same questions you had in law school. Here they are answered for you in scrupulous detail. For example, with respect to what the examiners are looking for in exam answer, they write:

"A frequently voiced complaint is that the essay questions present too many issues to permit full discussion within the time allotted. While the examiners do not seek superficial answers, they likewise do not expect law review articles. The purpose of the bar examination is to test the minimum legal

---

21. *See* Oregon State Board of Bar Examiners at www.osbar.org/_docs/admissions /06Q & A.pdf Question 13, What is expected in an answer? (last visited February 27, 2007).

competence, not to identify and rank the best legal scholars. In this respect, the bar examination differs from law school examinations."[22]

Texas

The Texas Board of Law Examiners provide an incredibly comprehensive set of guidelines tailored to each of the tested subject areas. For example, in its "Comments on Civil and Criminal Procedure Evidence/Questions," the Examiners write not only what not to do, but exactly what you should do:

READ THE QUESTION, UNDERSTAND THE "CALL" OF THE QUESTION *BEFORE* YOU ATTEMPT TO ANSWER IT.

For example, a question typically may ask the student, "Explain whether there is any proper basis for your objection *and* the proper method through which any error is preserved."

The response that "I would object with a *Batson* motion stating that the opponent . . . struck a particular race [from the panel]" without more, answers only *part* of the question. The student did not explain the proper *method* through which error is preserved, i.e., explain that before the jury is empanelled, one must offer the objection and demonstrate to the court the suspect pattern of strikes. The burden then shifts to opponent to show a race neutral reason for strikes.

E.g., "Explain whether there is any prohibition regarding the discussion of liability insurance *and* whether the trial court's ruling is reversible error (emphasis added)." The answer should include the proposition that while (1) there is a general prohibition against mentioning liability insurance before the jury (2) the mere mention of insurance is not reversible unless it caused the rendition of an improper verdict (i.e. "harm")."[23]

---

22. *Id.*

23. *See* Texas Board of Law Examiners, at www.ble.state.tx.us/Comments/comments

_ main.htm#Criminal%20Procedure%20 Evidence/Questions (last visited February 27, 2007).

While the Texas law examiners refer to these as "comments," you can see that they are much, much more: they speak directly to content and provide direction for both the scope and substance of your answers. If you plan to take the Texas Bar Exam, you should go to the Law Examiners' website, select the Examiners' Comments menu from the Main Menu, and print the Comments for each and every subject. As you study each topic, you will work with this information to guide your every step.

Connecticut

Connecticut's Bar Examining Committee is straightforward in its advice to candidates. Its website offers concrete advice on "Taking the Connecticut Bar Exam," including how to answer a Connecticut bar examination essay question. It also offers some practical advice on "what not to do": consider the following two suggestions:

"Do not anticipate trick questions or attempt to read into the question hidden meanings or facts not clearly expressed."

and

"Unless specifically called for in the question, it is not necessary to engage in an academic discussion of the applicable law or its historical basis and ramifications."[24]

Naturally, jurisdictions vary widely in approach and the level of detail they provide to candidates. Still, there is a wealth of information available to assist you in your preparation and this resource should figure prominently in your study plan.

5. Past Examination Questions and Sample Answers

Just as you studied from professors' old exams to prepare for law school finals, you'll review released essays from your state's bar examiners. Released exams should be your primary source for practice essays. While your bar review course includes a good

---

24. *See* Connecticut Bar Examining Committee, www.jud.state.ct.us/CBEC/examinfo.   htm (last visited September 11, 2007).

number of simulated practice tests and essay writing exercises, there is no substitute for the real thing—nor is there any need.

Most jurisdictions make their past exam questions available to you from their website—some even provide sample answers, either student essays or suggested analyses. In a few cases, you are told where you can access these materials. For example, the Arkansas State Board of Law Examiners advises candidates that "previous exam questions and answers are available from the Arkansas Supreme Court Library, the Law School Library at Fayetteville, and the Law School Library at Little Rock."[25] If no information about past exams is available online, then contact the licensing entity directly. This is no time to be lazy!

It is impossible to overemphasize the value of working from released bar exam essays. There is no greater authority on the bar exam than the writers and graders of the exam themselves and when they provide their questions and answers, they are doing what they can to make the test process as transparent as possible.

Consider what the following jurisdictions provide in addition to past exam questions and answers:

Alaska

The Alaska Bar Association provides past exam questions with grader's guides. Grader's guides are answers written by the examiners for the purpose of guiding grading of the exam—as the word itself indicates. However, Alaska also provides "benchmarks" answers. "Benchmarks" are actual applicant answers which are selected by the graders as being representative of points on the grading scale, with 5 being the highest, and 1 being the lowest.[26] These answers offer a window into the grading process and let you see the basis on which graders distinguish between answers.

---

25. *See* Arkansas State Board of Law Examiners, Arkansas Bar Examination Requirements and information at www.courts.state.ar.us/courts/ble_exam.html (last visited February 27, 2006).

26. *See* Alaska Bar Association, Resources: Past Exam Questions and Grader's Guides, February 2006, Exam Questions, Grader's Guides, and Benchmarks at www.alaskabar.org/INDEX.CFM?ID=6280 (last visited February 27, 2007).

Florida

Florida provides its candidates with a Study Guide. It contains general essay examination instructions, essay questions with selected answers, and sample multiple choice questions with an answer key. The essay answers were written by candidates who passed the exam and received high scores.

The Study Guide is updated with the essay questions from the last administration of the bar exam twice annually. When last viewed, there were five Guides online for a total of six complete exams.[27]

California

The State Bar of California offers questions and selected answers for the past 11 administrations of the bar exam.[28] There are two candidate answers for each question, thus showing a range of possibility in answering the question.

Texas

Texas provides its candidates with an abundance of study materials. In addition to general comments by subject, Texas bar examiners provide specific, detailed comments on past exams, indicating the common problems they encountered in grading the essays.[29] These critiques are very specific as to substance, identifying what was answered correctly and where incorrect, exactly how the answers were deficient.

For example, the following paragraph is a short excerpt from the comments on the Wills and Administration question from the July 2006 Bar Examination:

"Examinees who did poorly on this question often did not

---

27. *See* Florida Board of Bar Examiners, Frequently Asked Questions, "Does the Board offer any Study Materials?" Study Guide, at www.floridabarexam.org (last visited February 27, 2007).

28. *See* The State Bar of California at www. calbar.ca.gov/state/calbar/calbar_home.jsp (last visited February 27, 2007).

29. *See* Texas Board of Law Examiners at www.ble.state.tx.us/Comments/comments_main.htm (last visited February 27, 2007).

recognize that, in order to have the photocopy of Fred's will admitted to probate, you had to overcome the presumption of revocation of the will by Fred and that you could use the fact that the maid last saw the will in Joe's hand to overcome this presumption. Those examinees did not, however, discuss the other requirements for probating a photocopy of Fred's will as a lost will, i.e., showing due execution of Fred's will through the testimony of at least one attesting witness to his will and also proving the contents of Fred's will through the testimony of a credible witness (an attesting witness or even the lawyer who drafted the will) who had read Fred's will or had heard it read."[30]

CHECKLIST FOR NATIONAL COMPONENTS

The National Conference of Bar Examiners ("NCBE"):

1. Have you met the National Conference of Bar Examiners by visiting their website at www.ncbex.org/?

    The following questions can be answered by using the appropriate links from the NCBE website, including the *Comprehensive Guide to Bar Admission Requirements*.

The Multistate Bar Examination ("MBE"):

2. Is the MBE a part of your bar exam?

    Note: The MBE is very likely a part of your exam since only Louisiana, Washington, and Puerto Rico do not administer the MBE, but you should still verify.

    ☐ Does your jurisdiction accept the transfer of MBE scores from other jurisdictions?

---

30. *See* Texas Board of Law Examiners,   _ 0706.pdf (last visited February 27, 2007). www.ble.state.tx.us/Comments/comment

3. When is it offered? ☐   July   ☐   February

4. Have you read the MBE Information Booklet available online?

5. Have you ordered MBE Study Aids from the NCBE Online Store, including

   ☐ released questions from past administrations of the MBE?

   ☐ the MBE–AP so you can take the exam online in timed or untimed sessions and receive feedback?

The Multistate Performance Test ("MPT"):

6. Is the MPT a part of your bar exam?

7. If so, have you obtained MPT practice materials to sample the various tasks you might encounter on the exam

   ☐ by downloading available MPTS and Point Sheets from the NCBE website?

   ☐ by ordering additional MPTS and Point Sheets from the MPT Study Aids Order Form at the end of the MPT Information Booklet?

The Multistate Essay Examination ("MEE"):

8. Does your jurisdiction administer the MEE?

9. If so, have you read the MEE Study Aids and Information Guides available online at no cost:

   ☐ the MEE Information Book?

   ☐ the MEE Question and Analyses Books?

10. Have you ordered additional MEE Questions and Analyses from the online store?

The Multistate Professional Responsibility Exam ("MPRE")

11. Is passage of the MRPE required in your jurisdiction?
    Note: since the MPRE is required for bar admission in all but three jurisdictions, it is very likely a part of your bar exam.

12. What is the required passing score in your jurisdiction?

13. Have you checked with your bar review course to see if it offers an MPRE review session?

14. Have you ordered the MPRE practice materials available from the NCBE

    ☐ the subject matter outlines?

    ☐ the MPRE Study Aids which include actual and simulated MPRE questions?

15. Have you chosen when to take the MPRE?

    ☐   March   ☐   August   ☐   November

16. Are you planning to take the MPRE within the time frame specified by your jurisdiction for when the MPRE must be taken with respect to the bar examination?

Identify the time frame:

_____

17. What is the application deadline for the MPRE administration you will take?

_____

CHECKLIST FOR STATE–BASED COMPONENTS

1. Using the link to Bar Admission Offices from the NCBE website, did you locate the website for the jurisdiction(s) in which you plan to be licensed?

   List the jurisdiction(s): _____

   Website(s) _____

2. What are the parts of your bar exam?

   A. Are there essay questions?

      1. If so, how many? _____

      2. Are the essays prepared by

         ☐ your state's bar examiners?

         ☐ the NCBE where MEE questions are used?

         If MEE questions are used, will you be required to apply:

         ☐ state-specific law?

         ☐ common law principles?

         ☐ a combination of both?

         South Dakota, for example, advises its candidates: "The MEE is a two and one-half hour examination consisting of five 30–minute essay questions which will test subject areas which are available at the National Conference of Bar Examiners' website at http://www.ncbex.org/tests.htm. The MEE will test both general and South Dakota principles of law. Indian Law includes basic principles of federal Indian law, including but not limited to civil and criminal jurisdiction, the Indian Civil Rights Act, the Indian Child Welfare Act, and the Indian Gaming Regulatory Act. It does not include tribal laws or customary laws. Indian Law is tested by one 30–minute essay question."

      3. What areas of law will be tested?

         List the subjects to be tested on the essays:

         _____

         _____

_____

_____

_____

_____

_____

_____

_____

B. Are there state-based multiple choice questions?

☐ If so, how many?

_____

C. Is there an MPT?

If so, how many? ☐ One   ☐ Two

3. Grading and scoring

A. Is there a minimum passing score for individual components of your bar exam?   ☐ Yes   ☐ No

A select number of states set minimum passing scores for their bar exam which means that individual component scores are not combined to calculate a passage score; instead, you must meet the passing score for each section.

If there are defined minimum scores, what is the required passing score for:

1. The essays?   _____

2. The MBE?   _____

3. The state-based multiple-choice questions?   _____

4. The MPT?   _____

B. Are scores combined to calculate your overall bar passage score? If so, what is the weight of each of the following?

1. The essays?   _____

    2.   The state-based multiple-choice questions? _____

    3.   The MPT? _____

    4.   The MBE? _____

4. What is the exam schedule?

    A. What can you expect on day one?

Depending on the jurisdiction, the first day of your bar exam may be the state component or the MBE day.

    1. If it is the MBE day,

then the examination is divided into two periods of three hours each, one in the morning and one in the afternoon. There are 100 questions in each session.

    2. If it is the state day, then ask

      (a) What is the format of the morning session?

         1.   How long is it? _____

         2.   What is the format in terms of number of questions and time per question?

Essays	Qty _____	Time _____
Multiple-choice	Qty _____	Time _____
MPT	Qty _____	Time _____

      (b) What is the format of the afternoon session?

         1.   How long is it? _____

         2.   What is the format in terms of number of questions and time per question?

Essays	Qty _____	Time _____
Multiple-choice	Qty _____	Time _____
MPT	Qty _____	Time _____

    B. If your bar exam has a third day, what can you expect?

If your jurisdiction includes a third day of testing, it typically consists of additional essays and an MPT, although state-based multiple choice questions are always a possibility.

What is the format in terms of number of questions and time per question?

1. Essays   Qty _____   Time _____

2. Multiple-choice   Qty _____   Time _____

3. MPT   Qty _____   Time _____

5. Does your jurisdiction provide candidates with guidelines for answering questions?

Many states provide guidelines so you'll know exactly what the bar examiners expect from you in an exam answer.

If your state provides this information, have you read the guidelines to learn the following:

☐ What is expected in my answer?

☐ Must my answer be confined to the particular issues presented and not include information that is not responsive to the question?

☐ Does my writing ability affect my grade?

☐ Am I to assume additional facts or work only with those presented to me?

6. Are past examination questions and answers available?

Most jurisdictions make their past exam questions available to you from their website—some even provide sample answers, either student essays or suggested analyses.

A. Have you checked the website to see whether questions/answers are available:

1. Online

☐ Downloadable?

☐ For a fee?

2. At another location such as the state supreme court or bar association?

B. If the website does not provide this information, have you contacted the licensing entity directly?

C. Have you checked to see whether the following are available?

1. Essays
    ☐ Questions?
    ☐ Candidate answers?
    ☐ Sample analyses/guidelines from the bar examiners?
    ☐ Benchmark answers?

2. MPT
    ☐ Questions?
    ☐ Sample answers?

3. Multiple choice
    ☐ Questions?
    ☐ Answers?

*

CHAPTER 6

The Bar Review Course

Selecting the Right Course

O ne would think that three years of law school (four if you were a part-time student) would be enough to prepare you for the bar exam. It is and it isn't: on the one hand, your law school education has taught you the fundamentals of the legal system and "how to think like a lawyer." On the other hand, chances are your law school professors did not focus on imparting the "black letter law"—even though you learned a lot of substantive law—but rather on developing your analytical abilities and understanding of legal process. Successful performance on the bar exam, however, requires both an expertise in the reasoning skills you developed in law school and a comprehensive knowledge of core substance.

Here's where a bar review course plays an integral role: it puts together a master template of all the law tested in your particular jurisdiction. It structures and sequences the material, providing a comprehensive and organized approach to study. But it's no substitute for what you learned in law school and you'll need both to succeed on the bar exam.

When it comes to selecting a bar review course, there's no such thing as "one size fits all." There are lots of options and you will want to select a course that best suits your learning style, time availability, and pocketbook. Do you learn by listening? By writing? Can you study on my own or do you need a daily regimen of classes and assignments? It's your job to make the phone calls, ask the questions, and review the materials until you find a course that suits your needs. As you proceed, remember that your goal is to find a course or combination of courses that prepare you for the entirety of your exam, both its substance and its structure.

A Matter of Timing

Not only is it important to find a course that suits your learning style, it is equally important to take that course at the right time, i.e., the right time of year and the right time of day.

Would a July or February bar exam be a better "fit" for you?

It is usually best to take the bar exam as close as possible to law school graduation while the habits of study and the retention of substantive knowledge are at their peak. However, if you found it difficult to concentrate for spring semester exams because you had "spring fever," then you will find it incredibly challenging to study for almost three months in the summer. In this case, you might consider sitting for the February exam—if it is offered in your jurisdiction.

Would a day or evening bar review class be a better "fit"?

Typically, bar review courses offer day and evening sessions. Don't rule out taking an evening session just because you are available during the day—a day session is not always the most productive use of your study time. If you are a "morning person," you might be better off taking an evening bar review course and leaving your days free to study—and vice versa.

Once you've made your choice, stick with it. Don't alternate class sections unless you need to make up a missed class. You want to get used to a regular work schedule. While it may seem strange to you now, you'll find comfort in a familiar routine. Even if you fought the predictability of a routine existence all your life, give up the battle for the next two months and let your body and mind have what it needs to function at its best. Eat regularly, sleep regularly, exercise regularly, and study regularly. And don't forget to take breaks regularly.

What to Expect From Your Course

If you were expecting the type of lectures you had in law school about legal policy, principle, and theory, then you are in for a bit of a surprise. A bar review course is all about imparting the black letter law. As I mentioned earlier, such courses do an excellent job of providing comprehensive coverage for the topics tested in your jurisdiction.

However, a bar review course does not teach you how to process all the law you'll cover in the course, how to write essays, or how to analyze questions. It assumes you developed these skills in law school. And for the most part, you have. You just have to be sure not to fall into the trap of devoting all of your effort to reviewing notes and memorizing rules without spending enough time working with questions. Practicing questions is essential for developing your analytical, reading, and writing skills. An effective study schedule includes time for both.

SELECTING A BAR REVIEW COURSE

1. Where do you learn about bar review courses?

    The answer is pretty simple: you learn about bar review courses from all the usual sources:

    A. Do your preliminary research on the web and then check out each program by calling and speaking with a representative. Ask to see sample study materials and a course schedule.

    B. Speak with recent law school graduates. Ask what they liked and disliked about the programs they took and whether they thought they received adequate preparation for the bar exam.

    C. Ask your school's director of academic support or dean of students. Typically, these people are familiar with the various bar review courses offered in your area and can help you make an informed decision.

2. Have you identified the right program for your learning style?

Your individual learning style is a critical factor in the choice of a bar review course.

    A. Are you an auditory learner?

        If so, then you learn primarily by *hearing* the information. In this case, choose a lecture course over one which requires you to write extensively. A course that provides tapes as well as the usual course outlines would be very helpful to you.

    B. Are you a visual learner?

        If so, then you learn primarily by *seeing* the material. Choose a course that requires you to write—of course there will be lecture, but it will be geared primarily to having you record what you hear. Your course materials should include lots of tables and charts, and if not, creating such materials yourself will be essential.

3. Do you require structure or are you a self-learner?

    A. If you need discipline, then the structure of a traditional bar review course that requires daily attendance with a schedule of study activities should be your primary choice.

    B. In contrast, if you are primarily a self-learner, capable of setting your own study goals and schedule, then consider a home study program. Some of the traditional courses include a home study option for those unable to attend regularly scheduled sessions. This is also a viable option if you must work during the bar review period or would have difficulty reaching one of the bar review locations. But choose this option carefully—it only works if you are highly motivated and dedicated.

4. Does the course provide adequate coverage for all aspects of your bar exam?

    A. Does it provide full coverage of the law tested in your jurisdiction?

        ☐ the state-specific law?

        ☐ the multistate law?

    B. Does it provide full coverage of the specific components of your bar exam?

      ☐ the essays?

      ☐ the MBE?

      ☐ the MPT?

      ☐ jurisdiction-specific objective-style questions?

5. Should you take supplemental courses?

Depending on your own strengths and weaknesses, you might want to consider one of the add-ons to supplement your basic bar review course. Typically, these are specialty courses designed to provide additional assistance in particular areas of the bar exam, most notably in essay writing and MBE preparation. Once again, the options are numerous and you can choose from in-class or home study versions.

6. Should you take the bar exam in February or July?

In general, it's best to take the bar exam closest to your graduation date. Even if a later exam seems preferable, this does not outweigh the benefit of coming to the exam straight from the rigors of your law school education. Unless you have some extraordinary reasons for doing so, don't postpone the bar exam. Even a few months away from your studies can have a significant impact. It's much harder to get back into the routine when you've been away from it for a while. And if you think that you'll devote all the extra time you have to studying, trust me—you won't. You won't start studying in May when you know you're not taking the exam until February.

Still, you might want to consider the following questions:

    A. Did you have more difficulty studying for final exams in the spring semester than in the fall because you were distracted by the weather?

      For some, it's easier to study during the winter months, when the days are short and you don't mind being indoors. After the excitement of the holidays, there are few, if any, distractions.

    B. Did you find it difficult to study in the winter because of the dark days? If you are taking the February bar, then you might want to consider investing in special lighting to help you through this period. This problem has been linked to seasonal affective disorder.

7. Should you take a day or evening bar review course?

Since attending bar review lectures are the most "passive" part of your bar preparation, select a time that allows you to maximize your "active" study time.

A. Are you a "morning person"? If so, then you might be better off taking an evening bar review course and leaving your days free to study.

B. Are you a "night person"? If so, then your most productive study hours are in the evening and the last thing you want to do is use them to sit through lectures. However, you will probably need to reset your body clock toward the end of the review period so that you are wide awake for the actual bar exam!

C. Did you take evening courses in law school and become used to an evening schedule? If so, it may make sense to continue this arrangement.

CHAPTER 7

Learning the Black Letter Law

Bar review courses pretty much lead you to believe that you must read everything, learn everything, and do everything they tell you in the way that they tell you or you'll fail the bar exam. The result is that you can end up feeling overwhelmed and anxious.

Make no mistake: you need to master the substantive law presented in the bar review course but the way you go about it is up to you. Sometimes when you're caught up in the hysteria of bar review, it's easy to forget that you're the one in charge of your study program and you may—and probably should—change it to suit your needs. Bar review courses are designed for the "average student" but, as you know, not everyone learns the same way or at the same rate. An effective study program is based on your individual strengths and weaknesses. This chapter will show you how to create such a program.

Studying the Law

A solid knowledge of the law is required to answer bar exam essays and objective short answer questions. Preparing for the bar exam simply by attending lectures and reading through bar review outlines, even if read several times, does not allow for the type of internalization of the material necessary to respond to these questions.

"Knowing the law" means that you internalize the material in such a way that you truly "own" it. This is not the same as thinking you know something because a term or concept seems familiar. There's a big difference between recognizing something because you've seen it before and really knowing it. The bar exam requires you to know the rules with precision and specificity: it also requires a solid understanding of those rules.

Consequently, it is essential that your study plan include time for memorizing the rules and time for practicing them. Let's begin with how you memorize the law.

The Need for Memorization

Memorization is essential to success on the bar exam. As you proceed through your bar review course, make it a priority to memorize basic definitions and the elements of rules. Here are some suggestions:

- Focus on the basic vocabulary in each subject area.

- Create your own condensed study outline of key concepts in each subject area.

- Make your own flash cards.

  Remember when you were in grade school and had to learn the multiplication tables? You used flash cards and repeated the tables over and over again until you knew them cold. The same principle applies here.

- Create a short hypothetical for each rule.

  Play around with the facts of the hypothetical. Ask yourself whether the change affects the outcome. Apply different rules to the same scenario. What if you apply the common law to this set of facts? What if you apply the rule in your jurisdiction? Same result or different result? This type of practice provides the context you need for understanding as well as memorizing the rules of law.

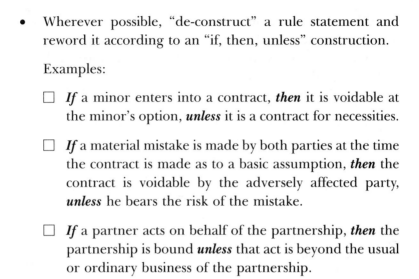

- Wherever possible, "de-construct" a rule statement and reword it according to an "if, then, unless" construction.

Examples:

☐ *If* a minor enters into a contract, ***then*** it is voidable at the minor's option, ***unless*** it is a contract for necessities.

☐ *If* a material mistake is made by both parties at the time the contract is made as to a basic assumption, ***then*** the contract is voidable by the adversely affected party, ***unless*** he bears the risk of the mistake.

☐ *If* a partner acts on behalf of the partnership, ***then*** the partnership is bound ***unless*** that act is beyond the usual or ordinary business of the partnership.

The Who, What, and When of Practicing Questions

Studying to learn the material is one activity; practicing with it is quite another. Memorizing rules from flash cards and outlines won't guarantee that you'll recognize them when they're tested in a fact pattern. Instead, you must learn the rules in the context in which they're likely to appear.

There is a method to learning from practice exams and you may be surprised to discover that it's not just about sitting down and answering the questions. That's what you'll do on bar exam day but not when you're studying. The difference is between answering the questions and using the questions to learn.

One of the most important things you can keep in mind as you study is that the only test that counts is the one you take on exam day. All the rest is preparation.

Whose Questions to Practice

Work with the "real thing": just as you studied from your professor's old exams to prepare for law school finals, you'll review released exams from the National Bar Examiners and your state's bar examiners. While your bar review course includes a good number of simulated practice tests and essay writing exercises, there is no substitute for the real thing. It is essential that you become familiar with the structure, style, and content of the test questions you can expect to see on bar day. Since the ultimate authority on the bar exam are the bar examiners, their questions should be the primary source for your practice questions.

Fortunately, the NCBE knows this is the most effective way to prepare for the MBE and offers candidates the opportunity to purchase past exams. The Information Booklet contains an MBE Study Aids Order Form and makes previously published MBE questions available to you for purchase at a small fee. The order form is also available on the Bar Examiners' website. Periodically, as old MBE questions are retired, the bar examiners release them and make them available to you. Such questions are a treasure trove to the candidate preparing for the bar exam.

Most jurisdictions have made their past essay exam questions available to you from their website—many even provide sample answers, either student essays or suggested analyses. If released bar questions are not accessible online, then contact the licensing entity directly. It is well worth the extra effort to find out if questions are available. If your jurisdiction uses the Multistate Essay Exam or "MEE", then contact the NCBE directly for sample questions.

What Questions to Practice

While you must practice questions in all subject areas tested on the bar exam, you can focus your energies in two ways: where you need the most work and where it will do you the most good.

1. How do you know which subjects require the most work?

    All subjects are not created equal—not with the bar exam and not with you. This means that you can target your energies where you need them the most.

    If you completed the Checklist in Chapter 1 to determine whether you would benefit from an early bar preparation program, then you have already identified your subject strengths and weaknesses. You can also turn to the end of this chapter and refer to Question 2 in *What To Include In Your Study*

Schedule Checklist and rank your subject strengths.

Or you can answer the following questions:

A. What are the specific topics tested on your bar exam?

You need to know exactly what will be covered on your jurisdiction's bar exam. Refer to Chapter 4 and complete the **Checklist For State–Based Components.** This will lead you through the steps to identify the specific subjects tested on your bar exam.

B. Are you weaker in some of these subjects than others?

Be completely honest with yourself—any course where you received a grade of "C" or below means you don't know it as you should. Make a list of these subjects.

_____

_____

_____

_____

_____

_____

C. Compare the list of bar-tested subjects (which should include the six multistate subjects) with your personal subject list and highlight the subjects that appear on both lists. List them here:

_____

_____

_____

D. Are there subjects you didn't like, couldn't understand, and simply never figured out? Maybe it was Future Interests, the Rule Against Perpetuities, or Third-party Beneficiaries.

It doesn't really matter which topics they were—only that they were so challenging that no matter how much time you spent on them, they still eluded your grasp.

While I would not ordinarily suggest "writing off" any subject, I strongly recommend that you consider doing so with the one or two sub-topics that you just can't seem to master. After making a good faith effort to learn the topic, if even the most diligent efforts yield minimal results, then it's time to give yourself a "pass" and move on. Just make sure that the topic is a very small part of your bar exam—at most two or three objective questions or a sub-issue on an essay. The time you save on this subject can be redirected to where it will do the most good.

E.   Are there some subjects you like better than others? Are there some which just seem to come easier to you? If you excelled in certain subjects in law school, it's likely to be the same on the bar exam. Here's where you can "save" some study time and "spend" it on the more difficult subjects.

2. Can you identify which type of question poses more of a difficulty for you?

Once again, if you completed the Checklist in Chapter 1, you know the answer to this question. If you did not complete the Checklist, then answer the following:

A.   Did you score lower on objective, multiple-choice exams than essay exams in law school? If so, then you are going to want to allocate more practice time to working with MBE questions.

B.   Alternatively, did your professors write the comments "conclusory," "lacking analysis," or "sketchy on the law" in your exam books? If so, then you will want to budget more time for working on your essay writing skills.

When to Practice Questions

You should begin practicing exam questions as soon as you begin your bar review class. Don't make the mistake of waiting until you think you know enough law: first, you'll never think you know enough law; second, once you've attended a class and reviewed your notes on a topic, you're ready to go to work. Working with rules as you learn them by applying them in the context of new factual situations is the most effective way to determine whether you truly understand them while you still have time to find answers to questions that naturally arise as you practice the material.

Why to Practice Questions

The reason to practice questions is to learn from them. While you may find this difficult to believe, you've learned as much as you are going to learn from your notes after you've read them once or twice. You've got to put them aside and move on to the questions to apply what you've learned to actual problems. This is the only way to find out what you know and what you don't. When your studying is "question-driven," it will lead you back to any gaps in your knowledge of the rules.

The more I work with students, the more I realize that they don't know what it means to study from questions. Instead of learning from them, students are constantly testing and grading themselves. Certainly the instinct to "answer" the question and see if you've gotten it "right" is instilled in the educational process early on, but here it's more of a hindrance than a help.

This approach doesn't work because while you may have "answered" questions, you've not learned to "analyze" questions. And you must know how to reason through a question to arrive at the correct answer choice. Not only is this process essential to arriving at the correct answer, but you must be aware of how you've reasoned through a problem so you can go back and examine that thought process should you make an incorrect choice.

What you need to do is *learn how to learn* from the questions.

How do you learn from "doing questions"?

- By looking up the rule to help you work through analysis of an MBE question: this is learning through repetition and reinforcement.

- By going back to your outline and reviewing your notes to help you write an essay answer if you are not certain of the complete rule: this is learning in context.

Learning Law for the MBE

Learning the law for the MBE, a short-answer, objective exam, is not the same as learning the law for the essays. It requires not only that you memorize the rules of law but that you fully understand them. If you don't know the rules with precision and specificity and truly comprehend how they fit together, you won't be able to find the issue in the facts, apply the rule, and select the best answer from among the four answer choices in the span of the 1.8 minutes you have for each question.

Such an understanding of the law usually comes only with real experience—but in the fictionalized world of the MBE, even real life wouldn't prepare you adequately for the way that the bar examiners like to test the rules, the elements of rules, and the exceptions to the rules. In this case, the only meaningful way to prepare for the MBE is to practice from actual MBE questions. Anything else is, as they say, "close, but no cigar."

Why Contracts and Property Present a Challenge

Contracts and Property questions pose difficulty for many bar candidates. It turns out that Contracts and Property questions share some significant characteristics—characteristics which have nothing to do with the rule of law but everything to do with the construction of the questions.

1. The questions are longer and feature a series of transactions between parties. A long fact pattern generally means a greater likelihood for error—in mixing up parties, in missing significant language, and in just plain losing focus.

2. How do you deal with questions where there is a series of transactions?

   ☐ Read the call-of-the-question first. Use it to narrow the scope of the problem and focus your attention as you read.

Often, it helps to distinguish relevant from irrelevant facts, keep track of transactions, and follow the relationships between parties.

☐ Sketch the sequence of transactions in the test booklet.

Why Evidence Presents Difficulty

Evidence questions present quite a different matter. While these questions tend to be shorter and take less time to read, they nonetheless require more time to answer because they involve several levels of analysis. Each analytical step takes time and presents a possibility for error. Still, there's something to like about Evidence questions. They're shorter, so you can keep your focus. They require a no-nonsense direct application of the Federal Rules of Evidence. The MBE follows *only* the federal rules so don't make the mistake of applying the local rule or the common law.

1. No matter how it is presented, an Evidence question is pretty much always the same question: is this evidence admissible or inadmissible?

2. Identify the theory operating behind the evidentiary proffer and apply the federal rules rigorously to the facts of the question.

3. After considering the threshold questions of admissibility including relevancy and the balancing test of probative value and undue prejudice, if you find the evidence admissible, then consider,

   ☐ What form is it permitted to take?

   ☐ Who can admit it?

   ☐ When can it be admitted?

Statute-based Questions

1. Criminal Law questions

   Questions that work with a statute are a means of testing your ability to follow "the letter of the law." Such questions are a "gift" because you don't have to worry about identifying which rule of law to apply to the issue—the bar examiners are giving you the rule with the statute.

☐ Read and apply the statute to the facts. The shortest distance to the correct answer choice is a simple, direct application of the elements of the statute to the facts in the problem.

☐ Pay particular attention to the issue of "intent." While it's easy to identify the "act" the criminal defendant committed, it's not so obvious to discern the "intent." That makes it a favorite test topic with the bar examiners. Consequently, you should make learning the intent requirements for the different crimes a top priority when you study Criminal Law topics.

2. Constitutional Law questions

Statutes operate a bit differently here than in Criminal Law. Here, they're used as a vehicle to test your knowledge of federal and state powers.

☐ You'll be given a statute and asked whether it's valid. This translates to whether it's a valid exercise of the relevant state or federal power.

☐ Focus on learning the enumerated powers of Congress, the typical bases of state regulatory authority, and the limits on such authority. Pay particular attention to the Constitutional requirements of due process and equal protection, and the commerce clause.

Torts: Keep Negligence and Strict Liability "Strictly" Separate

Torts questions on the MBE are relatively "nice," rule-based questions. If you know the black letter law and apply the elements of the rules to the facts in the question without deviation, you should do well. So what are the "sticking points?"

1. Negligence accounts for one-half of the 34 MBE questions so you must really, truly know the categories of negligence, its elements, and the defenses.

2. It's usually your job to figure out whether it's a negligence claim or defense from the facts of the question because the bar examiners don't tell you.

3. You may find language of strict liability in the fact pattern and the answer choices although the issue in the question is one of negligence. What should you know?

    ☐ Remember that the major difference between negligence and strict liability is one of "intent." An actor can be held liable in strict liability even though he did not intend to bring about the undesirable result and even though he behaved with the utmost care.

    ☐ Be alert to words in the fact pattern that refer to "intent" and "care" and evaluate such language carefully against the stated cause of action. For example, if you're told that an actor "carelessly knocked a lighted Bunsen burner into a bowl of chemicals," or acted with "all reasonable care," but the suit is based in strict liability, then whether the actor was careless or careful is purely irrelevant.

Defining Your Study Schedule

A schedule is essential for making sure you study "actively" by covering all the necessary material with the right mix of class time, study time, and practice time. Typically, your bar review course will provide a daily and weekly schedule of study activities. However, this is only a general guide and you'll probably need to make some changes to make it responsive to your needs.

The Checklists that follow will guide you in defining a personal study schedule, one that takes account of when you study, the way you study, and what you need to study. After considering the factors for an effective schedule and identifying your personal strengths and weaknesses, you'll be ready to create your own schedule.

FACTORS TO CONSIDER IN PLANNING YOUR SCHEDULE

1. What is your study personality?

    Your study personality is an important factor in planning a schedule that works for you. Be honest as you consider the following questions.

    A. Are you the "gung-ho" type?

        Do you plunge wildly into the fray, vowing to study 14 hours a day, complete every bar review assignment, read every outline, and do at least 100 multiple choice questions a day? While there is much to be said for enthusiasm, you won't survive a week at this frantic pace. Not only is this kind of schedule impossible to maintain, it's guaranteed to lead to burn-out.

    B. Do you share Scarlett O'Hara's philosophy that "tomorrow is another day?"

        Do you believe that there's always tomorrow to get serious about studying? Do you think it's no big deal if you miss a bar review class or two because there is a tape backup? The problem with this mind-set is that there's no time to waste. You can no more "ease into" bar review than you could "ease into" law school. Each day counts; there's no making up for lost time.

    My advice is to strike a balance between the overly aggressive approach and the overly complacent approach. You can do this by setting realistic goals for yourself. If you know that there's no way you're going to get through 50 multiple choice questions a day, don't set such an unreasonable goal. Why set yourself up for failure? You must be able to sustain the effort over the entire review period, up to and including the bar exam itself. It's no good if you burn out too soon. Besides, as we'll discuss shortly, the objective in practicing multiple choice questions is not the "doing" of numbers but the learning of law and the process of analysis.

2. Do certain types of exam questions pose more difficulty for you than others? Are multiple choice questions or essays your weak area? Consider your performance in law school:

A. Are multiple choice questions a problem area?

- ☐ Do you tend to score lower on objective tests than essay tests?

- ☐ When it comes to choosing between two answer choices, do you always seem to make the wrong choice?

If you answered "yes" to either of the above, then you need to devote more of your study time to learning how to analyze objective questions.

B. Are essays a weak area?

If your professors made such comments in your exam books as "conclusory," "lacking analysis," "sketchy on the law," or "disorganized," then you'll need to spend more time on developing your essay writing skills.

3. Are you stronger in certain subject areas than others?

Here is where you can use expertise in certain subjects to your advantage by allocating your study time accordingly. While you must cover all the topics tested on the bar exam, you do not need to study them all with equal intensity.

- ☐ How do you decide where to spend your time?

For the MBE, use the subject outlines to identify which sub-topics within each subject tend to be more difficult for you. You will want to devote more of your study time to these subjects than to the ones where you have a pretty solid understanding.

Here is where you will adjust your study schedule: if your bar review course devotes but one lecture to contract remedies and this is your weak spot, then you'll spend more time with it than the review course might allocate and make up the time in an area where you are stronger.

- ☐ Do you find some subjects easier to learn than others?

Since the MBE does not treat all topics equally in terms of their significance on the exam, neither should you. Why spend precious study days on a topic that is particularly difficult for you when it might be at most one or two questions on the bar exam? This is penny wise and pound foolish.

Here's some information to help you decide where to focus your efforts:

☐ If mortgages happen to be your most dreaded topic, it's unlikely that you'll see more than four or five actual mortgage questions since of the 33 Real Property/Future Interests questions on the MBE, only 25% (8–9 questions) come from real property contracts and mortgages.

☐ On the other hand, it's very important to know that of the 34 Torts questions, approximately one-half of them will be negligence questions. With 17 questions, which represents almost 8.5% of the entire MBE, you can't afford to treat negligence issues lightly when you study.

4. Did you suffer burnout and boredom when you studied for law school exams?

If you found it difficult to maintain your focus for the typical two-week final exam period, then you will find the six-to-eight week bar review period a true challenge. Here's what to do:

☐ Maintain a realistic work schedule, one that allows for lecture time, review time, practice time, and relaxation time.

☐ Once you've decided whether to attend a morning or evening bar review session, stay with your choice. Avoid alternating sessions unless you must make up a missed class.

☐ If you find yourself losing momentum and stuck in a study rut, then it's time to make some revisions. A few weeks of the relentless routine of going to bar review class, reviewing your notes, and practicing questions will make you feel as if you are reliving the same day, much like a scene from the movie "Groundhog Day." Here's what you can do:

☐ Change your study location. If you've been studying in the same spot in the library, you might consider moving to another floor in the library. Or you might try studying at home. Sometimes a change in venue works wonders.

☐ Vary the sequence of study activities. If you always review your notes right after the bar review lecture, try beginning your study sessions with working through MBE questions. Or try writing out an essay. Answering questions requires that you study "actively" as opposed to the passive process of reading notes.

☐ Study from different materials. Not only can your notes lose their appeal after the second read, but they can also lose their ability to engage your mind simply because you're familiar with them. It's like listening to a song on the radio. The first time you hear the song, you pay attention and listen carefully. The next time you hear it, you pay less attention because you've heard it before. Your mind drifts and you think of other things. Well, the same is true when you study. You think you're studying but you've stopped paying attention because it's already familiar to you. What you need to do is change to new study materials. Take up the topic in another form—read a different outline from your bar review materials, go back to your own outline from law school, or consider a hornbook—anything that keeps you interested and adds to your understanding of the subject.

WHAT TO INCLUDE IN YOUR STUDY SCHEDULE

1. Does your study schedule include sufficient time to:

    ☐ Attend bar review lectures? (Approximately 4 hours)

        ☐ Bar review courses usually meet five days a week for about four hours per day. There may be some weekend sessions or longer days, but this is the exception. You may want to revise your schedule on a weekly basis to keep current with your bar review course.

    ☐ Review and consolidate your lecture notes? (2–3 hours)

        ☐ Allow between two and three hours each day to review and digest notes from that day's session of your bar review lecture.

    ☐ Practice exam questions? (1½ to 2 hours)

        ☐ 15 to 20 MBE questions should take approximately 1½ to 2 hours

        ☐ One or two essay questions (depends on the essay length in your jurisdiction but you should allocate 2 hours at a time; this can vary based on how long you spend with multistate questions)

        ☐ One MPT per week (approximately two hours)

    ☐ Review materials for next day's bar review session? (½ hour)

    ☐ Review notes from a previously covered subject? (45 minutes–1 hour)

    ☐ Take mini-study breaks and exercise?

    ☐ Give yourself one afternoon or evening off each week?

2. Have you allocated study times based on your individual strengths and weaknesses?

    "Borrow" time from your strengths to "spend" it on your weaknesses:

    ☐ Rank the six MBE subjects according to your strengths with "1" the strongest and "6" the weakest.

_____ Constitutional Law
_____ Contracts
_____ Criminal Law
_____ Evidence
_____ Property
_____ Torts

☐ Rank the state-specific law tested in your jurisdiction according to your strengths.

_____ _____

_____ _____

_____ _____

_____ _____

_____ _____

If there are more subjects tested on your state exam than on the MBE—which is very likely in several jurisdictions—then don't rank them all but identify three or four (at most five) of your weakest subject areas.

Now use these rankings to allocate your study time. Even though you may spend more time working on one topic than another, the skills gained from learning how to read, analyze, and answer questions in one subject area is transferable to others.

3. Are you varying your study activities sufficiently throughout the day to maintain your concentration level?

Notes:

_____

_____

_____

_____

_____

A DAY IN THE LIFE

The following are two sample study schedules. You can adapt them to suit your needs or create a schedule of your own. In either case, be as specific as possible about allocating your time and activities.

Assuming you take a morning bar prep course:

7:30—9:00 a.m.	Shower, breakfast, dress, and travel to bar review class
9:00—12:30/1:00	Bar review course
1:00—2:00	Lunch break
2:00—4:00/4:30	Review and consolidate notes from morning's session; make flashcards for black letter law
4:30—5:00	Break—go for a walk with your dog, exercise, call a friend
5:00—6:30	Work through 20 MBE questions in the subject you have just studied
6:30—7:30	Dinner break
7:30—9:30	Work through another group of 15 to 20 MBE questions, one to two essays from a released bar exam, or an MPT, depending on your study needs
9:30—11:00	Review materials for next day's bar review session; review notes from one subject covered earlier in the bar review period
11:00/12:00	Relax. Watch *Law and Order.* Pass out.

Assuming you take an evening bar prep course:

7:30—8:30 a.m.	Shower, breakfast, and dress
8:30—10:30/11:00	Review and consolidate notes from the previous evening's class; make flashcards for black letter law
11:00—11:30	Break—go for a walk or any kind of exercise
11:30—1:00	Work through 15 to 20 MBE questions in the subject you just studied
1:00—1:30	Lunch break
1:30—3:00	More multiple choice practice, one to two essays from a released bar exam, or an MPT, depending on your study needs
3:00—3:30	Break; snack
3:30—5:00	Review materials for next day's bar review session; review notes from one subject covered earlier in the bar review period
5:15	Leave for bar review class
6:00—10:00	Bar review class

10:30/11:00   Home at last
11:00/12:00   Relax. Watch *Law and Order.* Pass out.

Note: Evening review classes are difficult because they pretty much
eliminate any regular dinner hour. But you can't afford not to
eat or to eat improperly. Have a snack before class or pack a
sandwich and eat during class. Figure out which works best
for you and have some healthy snack foods available.

DEFINING YOUR INDIVIDUAL STUDY PLAN

The boldface periods are the hours engaged in actual "study." Vary these times by subject area and task according to your needs. Be sure to spend enough time in an area until you feel comfortable with your knowledge level before moving on to another subject. However, don't expect to know everything—this is not possible, nor necessary—but you should feel a level of competency in answering questions before you take up another topic. If you follow your schedule, you will have time to review each subject several times during the bar review period.

Day	Study Subjects	Time/Task	
Monday	Contracts	7:30 - 9:00	Shower, breakfast, dress, and travel to bar review class
		9:00 - 12:30/1:00	Bar review course
		1:00 - 2:00	Lunch break
		2:00 - 4:00/4:30	**Review and consolidate notes from morning's bar review class**
		4:30 - 5:00	Break — go for a walk with your dog, exercise
		5:00 - 6:30	**Work through 20 MBE questions**
		6:30 - 7:30	Dinner break
		7:30 - 9:30	**Work through 15 to 20 MBE questions, one to two essays, or an MPT**
		9:30 - 11:00	**Review materials for tomorrow's bar review class; study law from a previously covered subject**
Tuesday			
Wednesday			
Thursday			
Friday			
Saturday			
Sunday			

STUDY SCHEDULE

Week of: _____

Day	Study Subjects	Time/Task
Monday		
Tuesday		
Wednesday		

Day	Study Subjects	Time/Task
Thursday		
Friday		
Saturday		
Sunday		

*

CHAPTER 8

Practicing Essay Questions for the Bar Exam

Every state or jurisdiction includes an essay component as part of its bar exam. Some jurisdictions consider the ability to write so essential that greater weight is given to the written portion (essays combined with the Multistate Performance Test "MPT") than to the Multistate Bar Examination "MBE" in calculating the overall bar passage score—anywhere from doubling the scaled written score to counting it as much as two-thirds.[1] While there is a wide range in scoring formulas, you can count on the essays to be at least equal in weight to the MBE with a good likelihood that the total written portion will weigh even more.

This should be welcome news. It means that the written portion of your bar exam presents the greatest opportunity for you to influence your score because:

You are the one in control of the question when you write. Unlike a multiple choice question where you have to match up your

---

1. For example, the MEE/essay/MPT is weighted two-thirds in Idaho; the written portion is 65% of the total score in California; the essays are weighted 60% in North Carolina; scores on the written portion (MPT and essay) are scaled to the MBE and the scaled written score is doubled and added to the scaled MBE score in Ohio. *See* NCBE, Comprehensive Guide to Bar Admissions, Chart VII: Grading and Scoring at www. ncbex.org/fileadmin/mediafiles/downloads/ Comp_ Guide/2007CompGuide.pdf (last visited September 11, 2007).

analysis of the problem to fit one of the answer choices, here you have some flexibility. While there are limits determined by the issues set up in the facts, you can take a slightly different path and still accrue significant points.

You can write your way to bar passage—especially when what you write represents a substantial portion of your overall score.

A Dialogue With the Bar Examiners

Think of the essays as your opportunity to converse with the bar examiners. With every word you write, your goal is to tell them that you are prepared to take your place in the profession, meet with clients, analyze their problems, and represent them in court.

How do you convey this message? By using the language of the law in the format and structure of legal analysis. Presumably, after reading hundreds of cases, you sound something like a lawyer. Using the appropriate terminology in your discussion of a legal issue is what sets you apart from a layperson. When a grader reads your essay, there should be more than "a scintilla of evidence" to show that you've attended law school.

Many of you have been very successful in law school and a large part of that success can be attributed to your ability to communicate effectively in writing. For you, doing well on the essay portion of the bar exam will be mostly a matter of gaining familiarity with the types of essays on your state's bar exam and their structure. However, even if writing was not one of your primary strengths, you can still write effective bar exam essays with adequate guidance, preparation, and practice. And you can begin by taking advice from the bar examiners.

What It Takes According to the Bar Examiners

Bar examiners have the same expectations when reading an essay as did your law professors: one that demonstrates your ability to engage in legal thought and analysis. They are very clear about what they expect from you in an exam answer:

- An answer that evidences "your ability to apply law to the given facts and to reason in a logical, lawyer-like manner from the premises you adopt to a sound conclusion." The State Bar of California Committee of Bar Examiners.

- Neither a "right answer" nor a "bottom line" answer but a well-reasoned argument based on an analysis of the relevant issues and an application of the law to the facts followed by a legal conclusion.[2] New York Board of Law Examiners.

- "The ability to reason logically, to analyze accurately the problem presented, and . . . demonstrate a thorough knowledge of the fundamental principles of law and their application." Florida Board of Bar Examiners.

- A demonstration of "your ability to analyze legal problems and to provide an organized, logical and coherent written response." New Jersey Board of Bar Examiners.

Outlining the Approach

While the substantive law and the essay format differs between jurisdictions, what does not is what the bar examiners are looking for when grading an essay. Because of this shared expectation, the process outlined below will allow you to prepare successfully for a bar exam in any jurisdiction.

Always keep in mind that exam writing is a dialogue with the reader. Here, the bar examiner begins the conversation with the question. Your role is to segue to the answer and continue the conversation.

The following are the steps you'll take for writing "bar-right" essays:

1. Know your audience

---

2. The ability to reason in a logical, lawyer-like manner is so important that you can get credit for your analysis even if you technically arrive at the incorrect conclusion. The New York Board of Law Examiners advise that "[a]ppropriate credit is given in the grading of essay answers for well reasoned analyses of the issues and legal principles involved even though the final conclusion may be incorrect."

You must know your audience to write for your audience. Bar exam graders read a large number of essays and evaluate them according to strict criteria. They know what they are looking for and the easier you make it for them to find it, the more points you will accrue. Generally, you can count on writing clear, concise, and focused exam answers which conform to the basic structure of legal analysis—in other words, IRAC, but more about that later. This may require you to make certain adjustments in your style and presentation if you are more accustomed to broad, generalized discussions.

Just as you studied from your professor's past exams to prepare for law school finals, you'll review released essays from your state's bar examiners. Released exams should be your primary source for practice essays. While your bar review course includes a good number of simulated practice tests and essay writing exercises, there is no substitute for the real thing.

Most jurisdictions have made their past exam questions available to you from their web site—many even provide sample answers, either student essays or suggested analyses. If released bar questions are not accessible online, then contact the licensing entity directly. It is well worth the extra effort to find out if questions are available. If your jurisdiction uses the Multistate Essay Exam ("MEE"), then contact the NCBE directly for sample questions.

2. Know exactly what is tested and how

    As we discussed in an earlier chapter, your jurisdiction provides general information about bar admission requirements, exam dates, and the application process. However, it also provides vital information about the bar exam itself, specifically, its composition and subject coverage.

    Check for the following:

    • The components of the exam

        Know the mix of the elements and the weight accorded to each. There is usually a combination of the MBE, essays, and the performance test. Some jurisdictions include their own multiple-choice questions based on state law as in New York and Florida.

- The number of essays

Know how many questions you can expect. The number of essays determines your timing. Knowing what you'll see on your bar exam lets you practice answering questions of similar length and complexity.

Taking law school exams should have taught you that questions answerable in 30 minutes are significantly different from questions to be answered in an hour. Shorter questions typically involve only one area of law and are more focused; longer questions combine areas of law and present more issues, thus requiring greater organization on your part.

- Subject coverage

You must know the law to write the law and the first step is to identify what you need to know. Some jurisdictions test only the multi-state law; others include their own common law, statutes, and constitutional law as well. While it might seem as if you're facing the entire legal universe, you're really not since the depth of coverage tends not to be as detailed as a law school exam—but this is something you need to determine.

You can identify the boundaries of your bar exam by checking with your local bar examiner. Your jurisdiction typically provides a list to bar candidates of the state-specific subjects to be tested. Some provide rather detailed outlines of the covered subject matter which should be used as a checklist to guide your studies.

- Form of questions

Each jurisdiction has its own distinctive essay style. Some will lead you to the issues they want you to discuss and others will leave it open and require you to "issue-spot." Some include both styles in the course of the exam, but not in a single essay. Thorough preparation will let you know what to expect.

You'll find that bar essays conform to one of two general essay styles:

☐ *Single issue: outcome specific*

These tend to be structured, focused, and narrow—quite unlike the long, issue-laden narratives you've seen on law school exams. If you've not had experience answering this type of question, you'll need to practice.

For example, in New York, the essay question asks you to come to a conclusion by answering a particular question:

> *Was the court correct in granting the motion for summary judgment/ for the injunction/ to admit the testimony?*

> *Can the defendant successfully assert the defense of justification?*

This type of problem is challenging because the precise issue is not identified for you: the issue is not "whether the court was correct or incorrect" but whether the legal theory the court relied upon in coming to that decision was correct or incorrect. Identifying the particular legal theory in controversy requires a multi-step analysis of the facts. It's essential to think through the problem and articulate the precise issue in dispute before writing to produce an essay that is focused instead of one that rambles and follows a "kitchen sink" approach.

Further, this type of question requires that you *not* raise opposing arguments. While typical law school exams are structured for you to see and argue both sides of an issue, this is not the case here. You are required to reach a conclusion and argue specifically for that result. Any time you spend identifying potential counter-arguments is a waste of your time and a loss of potential points.

☐ *Multi-issue: focused response*

These questions are harder to characterize since they seem open-ended and conclude with such familiar interrogatories as "discuss the rights and liabilities of all parties" or "analyze fully." Even these general questions are unlike typical law school exams in that the bar questions are focused and limited in the actual number of issues tested in a single essay.

The challenge lies in your ability to cover the relevant possibilities with the requisite level of detail without going astray. Once again, organizing your answer around the issue and sub-issues is the key to a focused, concise answer.

For example, MEE questions typically ask you to "explain" your answer to a specific question but the "explanation" required is not an extensive dissertation of the law but a concise and succinct discussion of the relevant legal principles as they relate to the issues presented by the question. Consider Question 6 from February 1998:

> *"On what basis, if any, can the injured persons hold Transport liable for tort claims resulting from the HotTrucks accident? Explain."*

While the call-of-the-question contains the usual language indicating an open-ended query *"on what basis, if any"* and *"explain,"* you can't be deceived into a general listing of possible causes of action. You would be casting too large of a net and "fishing" instead of writing the targeted, focused analysis required by the facts of the problem. ***Only practice with reading and writing such questions would allow you to proceed to the relevant discussion.***

Whether your state's bar essays are narrow and focused or present more of an open-ended inquiry, you must answer the question asked and only the question asked. In some jurisdictions, the bar examiners will ask you to come to a conclusion. What's critical when you're asked to provide a conclusion is that you take a position and argue it. Unlike a typical law school exam, here you are not supposed to argue in the alternative and present both points of view. In conclusion-based jurisdictions, you're suppose to be an advocate and demonstrate how you marshal the facts to the law.

3. De-construct exam questions and sample answers

    *   De-constructing exam questions

    You might be wondering how "de-constructing a question" differs from "reading a question." Generally, your focus when reading a question is to determine what is required of you to answer it. You are concerned with the information relevant to your task—evaluating whether the defendant committed felony murder, whether the statement was admissible, whether a contract was formed, and so forth.

    But when you are studying and trying to learn from the questions, your purpose in de-constructing a question is to analyze its organization and content for patterns and consistencies. This kind of scrutiny lets you see:

    ☐ How different areas of the law are combined in a single essay

        Unfortunately, bar essays do not come with neat little labels to let you know which is the Contracts essay and which is the Torts essay. Further, most questions combine areas of law in a single essay—quite unlike what you've experienced in law school where you knew exactly what to expect because exams were class-specific.

Still, there is a natural connection between certain topics and with preparation, you will become familiar with the questions and able to recognize the issues. Although it is not likely you'll find more than two substantive topics in a single essay, you may find ethics or procedural issues woven into any of the questions.

The following are the more common substantive combinations you can expect to see:

☐ Contracts with Business Organizations (Corporations, Agency, Partnership) Remedies, Damages

☐ Torts with Agency principles and Conflict of Laws, Damages

☐ Criminal Law with Criminal Procedure or Evidence or any combination of the two

☐ Family Law with Property or Trusts and Estates—or any combination of the two

☐ Constitutional Law with Criminal Law or Evidence—or any combination of the two

☐ Civil Procedure: in some jurisdictions, this topic may present as its own question (for example, New Jersey) but procedure issues are more likely to be integrated with substantive ones

☐ How procedural issues are combined with substantive issues

Bar examiners are adept at weaving procedural questions with substantive issues in ways you might hardly notice— that is, unless you were looking for them. Of course, sometimes procedural questions are "open and notorious" such as,

"Al duly filed a notice of removal in federal district court to remove the action to that court, and Dot promptly moved in federal district

court for remand of the action to the state supreme court. The court (1) granted Dot's motion. After issue was joined, Al moved, upon proof of the foregoing pertinent facts, for summary judgment dismissing the complaint on the separate grounds that . . . . . "
(New York July 2001 Question 4)

Here it's obvious that you must evaluate the procedural standard for summary judgment before discussing the underlying substantive law. However, it's not so obvious when procedural matters are woven into the fabric of the facts as sub-issues. Some jurisdictions are so subtle in the presentation of procedural questions that unless you're completely familiar with the style and substance of their questions, you could easily overlook the procedural question.

Consider the following interrogatories from past New York bar exams:

1. *"Apple* **moved to dismiss** *Willie's complaint . . . "* (New York July 2003 Question 4)

and

2. *"Harold* **brought a separate action** *against Wilma . . . "* (New York February 2005 Question 3)

with

3. *"Move–It Inc.* **moved to dismiss** *the action on the grounds that (a)* **as a matter of law**, *it could not be held liable in strict product liability for the cost of repairing the conveyor system . . . "* (New York February 2002 Question 1)

and

4. *"Frank* **moved to dismiss** *Sean's complaint as to him for* **failure to state a cause of action** *and the court (1) granted the motion"* . . . (New York February 2004 Question 4)

Examples 1 and 2 do not present procedural questions even though the language may seem suggestive. Without more information, there is no procedural standard to evaluate. On the other hand, Examples 2 and 4 refer to a standard with respect to the motion and now you have work to do.

☐ How issues present in the facts

As you found with law school exams, certain facts give rise to certain legal issues. The more essays you read, the more familiar you will become with seeing causes of action in the context of the facts in which they arise.

☐ How bar examiners use vocabulary to signal issues, most notably adverbs and adjectives

Bar examiners are incredibly efficient at using a single word or short phrase to convey enormous meaning. Only careful reading of essay questions—lots and lots of essay questions—will allow you to recognize key words and phrases. It's not that the words are unusual or even buried in the text, but they are easy to overlook in the heat of the exam unless you know to look for them.

For example, consider the phrases "walking peacefully" and "without provocation or warning." Such phrases convey enormous meaning. Consider a Criminal Law problem where you're told the plaintiff was "walking peacefully" or the defendant acted "without provocation or warning." You'll know that a claim of self-defense is not viable because it is not grounded in the facts.

Another good example of a loaded phrase is "public place." Just think of the possibilities for Property and Constitutional Law questions. Here a single word can make all the difference in your analysis.

The same is true for such words as "written" and "oral" and all the possible phrases used to convey their meaning. Consider e-mails, telexes, and letters for writings; think of telephone conversations for oral discussions. These words figure prominently in Contracts and Property questions. Learn to look for them.

☐ How bar examiners use vocabulary to identify non-issues

Bar examiners are similarly adept at using language to signal non-issues. Only the careful, observant reader will know not to discuss such matters, saving time and effort for the real issues.

For example, when the hypothetical contains such phrases as,

"Signed and duly acknowledged"

"Proper written consent"

"Duly executed"

"Duly commenced"

it's your signal **not** to discuss the matter. For example, if you are told that "the will was duly executed," then the issue is not a problem with one of the elements required for execution. Accept what the bar examiners are telling you and move on to address the real issue in the problem.

☐ How topics tend to repeat

Working through past exams lets you see how often particular topics are tested. While I am not suggesting you will be able to predict the precise questions you will see on your exam, it's very likely you will be able to control the surprise factor and on bar day, the questions will seem distinctly familiar.

• De-constructing sample answers

Now that you have de-constructed exam questions, it's time to de-construct exam answers—an equally important part of your preparation. Here, rather than studying past exams to see what *you* can expect from the bar examiners, your goal is to learn what *they* expect from you.

By examining each part of a sample answer, you will learn:

☐ How important a statement of the issue is to the development of the answer

☐ How much rule you need to write to address the issue

☐ How a complete and concise statement of the rule differs from a treatise-like discussion

☐ How to incorporate "distinctions" into your statements of the rule, both state and federal, and statutory and common law

☐ How analysis of the facts differs from a recitation of the facts

In addition to observing the heavy dependance on IRAC construction in candidate answers and bar examiners' grading sheets, you will discover such other critical information as:

☐ The need to state the "obvious"

For example, in working with a Sales question, many a bar candidate neglects to make such a basic statement as

> *"This was a contract for the sales of goods because computers are goods."*

but such a sentence is essential to a solid analysis because it completes the nexus between your statement of law that the Uniform Commercial Code governs transactions involving sales of goods and your facts which discuss the sale and delivery of some computers.

Equally obvious, equally necessary, but equally absent from too many answers is a reference to the particular jurisdiction when stating the controlling law

> *"**Under Florida law**, a Settlor can create a trust by. . . . "*

> *"**Under New York's** Domestic Relations Law,. . . . "*

☐ There may not always be a "right answer"

As you review sample candidate answers, you will find examples of answers that reach opposite conclusions. This is proof that it's the reasoning that counts and not the bottom line conclusion. Of course the argument had to be based on the relevant law and solidly grounded in the facts—good writing alone will not save an answer that is wrong on the law and misapplies the facts.

☐ The heavy reliance on signal language to lead the reader through the steps of an IRAC analysis

"The issue is whether . . . . *when* . . . . . "

"Under the [*statement of the controlling law: common law, federal rule, state-specific statute etc.]"*

"Here, the [buyer accepted the goods *because* . . . .]"

"Therefore,

☐ The use of "because," "since," "as," and "when" in the analysis section of the essay to connect rule with fact

4. Follow a formula: write IRAC

It should be clear from the de-construction process that your answers will follow a basic IRAC structure and it's okay to be obvious about it. There's no need to worry that you're boring the grader. He or she will be very grateful to find the issue in your essay so easily. Also, there's no need to try and impress the grader with your originality. Save the sparkling prose for your law review articles and proceed swiftly through your paces on the bar.

IRAC allows you to organize your response and remain in control, whether addressing a narrow issue-driven essay or a general question. With slight variations to account for the type of questions in your jurisdiction, you can make IRAC your blueprint for answering any essay question.

Consider the following guidelines for writing your essay:

• *When writing the issue:* rely on the *"whether, when"* construction

The "whether, when" construction leads you to connect the legal question with the specific facts in controversy. When you use this approach to formulate an issue, you avoid overly general statements and provide a path to follow in your analysis. This leads to an essay that connects the rules with the questions presented rather than one that rambles and follows a "kitchen sink" approach.

Begin with,

"The issue is whether"

then identify and state the legal conclusion you want the court to reach,

Ben committed a battery, (or a contract was formed, or the court can assert personal jurisdiction over the non-resident defendant)

and connect to the facts in controversy which determine the outcome,

when he threw the vase at Amy and hit Jill (or when the acceptance contained additional terms, or when the defendant rented office space and opened a checking account in the forum state)

You end up with the following issue statements

"The issue is whether Ben committed a battery when he threw the vase at Amy and hit Jill instead."

"The issue is whether a contract was formed when the acceptance contained the additional term of charging interest on late payments."

"The issue is whether the court can assert personal jurisdiction over the non-resident defendant when the defendant rented office space and opened a checking account in the forum state."

- *When writing the rule:* think in terms of *"context and consequences"*

The first rule when writing the rule for the bar exam is to write about the law of your jurisdiction. Even if you could answer the question using the common law, if there is a state rule on point, you want to be sure to apply that law. Never forget that you are seeking admission to practice in a particular jurisdiction: you want the bar examiners to know that you know the applicable state law.

The next "rule" to follow when writing the "rule" is to include a sufficient discussion of the law to provide an adequate context for your analysis of the facts in controversy. But what is an "adequate context"?

Just as you need a context to make sense of what you hear—just imagine hearing only one side of a telephone conversation—a reader needs a context to understand what you write. You provide it as follows:

- ☐ By stating the general rule before turning to the specific exception brought into controversy by the facts of the problem

- ☐ By identifying the general cause of action and listing all of its elements before focusing on the specific one in controversy

Now consider the following building blocks for constructing a solid statement of the relevant rule:

- ☐ *Definitions*: build on your general statement of law by writing a definition for each of the legal terms of art you've identified. A basic definition can be written in a sentence or two. What you must do is avoid going beyond the scope of the question and writing a treatise on rules not in controversy.

- ☐ *Exceptions*: exceptions to the general rule are the stuff of which bar exam essays are made. In fact, you can pretty much count on the questions to force you to deal with exceptions because that's where the problems typically arise in the real world.

- ☐ *Distinctions:* often you will have a question where the state law differs from the federal rule or the common law from the statutory law. Be sure to identify such distinctions to show how application of one rule as opposed to the other would yield a different result.

It's time to consider and discuss the consequences of applying the rule. Ask yourself the following questions,

"What happens if the rule is applied to these facts?"

"What is the likely result?"

By identifying the consequences of applying a particular rule to your set of facts, you will write a more thoughtful analysis.

- *When writing the application:* use "because"

How you set up the rule now drives the structure of the analysis. Your statement of the rule provides a blueprint to follow for your discussion of the facts. Work from your articulation of the rule to guide your application of the facts. Match up each element/factor you've identified in the rule with a fact, using the word "because" to make the connection between rule and fact. This ensures that you write facts "plus" the significance of those facts. Think of writing the application portion of your analysis in terms of a formula:

Application = Rule + Fact, where "+" is "because"

(A = F + R)

Consider the following examples:

1. Jess may have committed a "trespass "*(rule)* **because** (+) she "walked onto Farmer Dell's cornfield to pick corn without his permission" *(facts)*.

2. Ted acted in "bad faith" *(rule)* **because** (+) he "counted on the good price he was paying for the raw materials when he decided to increase operations" *(facts)*.

3. Sam the shareholder has a basis to "pierce the corporate veil" *(rule)* of Carl Corp. **because** (+) Carl was "the

sole shareholder and freely intermingled funds, used corporate funds to pay both corporate and personal expenses, maintained only one set of accounting books, and never held any corporate meetings" *(facts)*.

- *When writing the conclusion:* be definitive

If the call-of-the-question asks for a specific answer, then be definitive. State your conclusion as to that issue.

If there are multiple issues, then once you've completed your analysis of one issue, move on to the next. And it's as simple as that—begin a new paragraph and write,

> *"The next question is whether Spencer's offer was accepted when Ben said he'd take two cartons but delivery had to be September 15, not the 20th."*

5. Automate the process

One of the primary purposes of taking practice exams is to make the process of reading and answering the questions so routine that you'll follow it instinctively on exam day. **Your main focus will be on what you write, not how you write it.** Aside from allowing you to focus on substance, having a plan saves time and prevents panic because you know exactly what to do.

> **Note:** *When you first start working with essays, you will not be timing yourself. At this point, your goal is gaining familiarity with the structure and content of the questions and using them to help you learn the law in the context in which it is tested.* **Only in the last few weeks before the bar exam should you time your responses.**

Beginning with your practice sessions and then on the bar exam, follow these steps each and every time you approach a question:

a. Allocate your time for each question and set your timetable.

Since you know the precise composition of questions for your exam, figure out how much time you have for each question. Create your own "clock" by writing down the starting and ending times for each question. Follow this clock throughout the exam to stay on track.

Budgeting your time and working within that time is the only way to ensure that you'll complete the exam—or come as close as possible. You begin working toward this goal the minute you start studying for the bar exam. Every practice essay is a dress rehearsal.

b. Scan the exam but answer the questions in order.

You want to get a sense of the entire exam but it's usually best to simply follow the order of questions when answering them. If you start to read each question before deciding which one to answer, you'll waste precious minutes and dilute your concentration. Instead, take one at a time as you find them.

On the other hand, you need to be flexible. For example, if you begin a question and find that no matter how hard you try, you can't make any progress, then give yourself a couple of minutes and move on to the next question. You don't want to waste valuable time when you could be working productively elsewhere. Chances are that when you return to this question later, it will come to you.

c. Start at the end of the question with the call-of-the-question.

The interrogatory, or "call-of-the-question," lets you know what is required of you. This informs your subsequent reading of the fact pattern and ensures that you read "actively" for the information you need.

d. Based on the call-of-the-question:

1. Determine whether it's a "general" or "specific" style essay. A "general" style essay will leave the question

open-ended. The following are particular favorites of bar examiners:

- *"Analyze fully."*

- *"Identify all possible claims and defenses. Explain fully."*

- *"Discuss the cause(s) of action and possible defense(s)."*

On the other hand, a "specific" essay will present a precise question to be answered:

- *"Was the court correct in granting Plaintiff's motion for summary judgment?"*

- *"Did the Surrogate correctly admit Ben's will to probate?"*

- *"Does Wanda have a right to maintenance?"*

- *"Were the numbered rulings correct?"*

2. Identify the subject area from the call-of-the-question, if possible.

   This helps you focus on the relevant facts and disregard any non-issues as you read the hypothetical.

3. Note any instructions to follow in writing your response.

   Before you demonstrate your analytical skills with what you write, you'll want to show that you can follow basic directions. If you're asked to write on only one side of the paper or skip every other line, then you must do so. If you're asked to assume a role—law clerk or judge—then be sure to play the part. If you're asked to draft a memo, begin your response with a mock memo heading. If you're asked to reach a conclusion, then by all means answer the question. In addition to your knowledge of the substantive law, your ability to read and follow directions is a vital lawyering skill being tested on the bar exam.

e. Read the entire question for the first time:

1. Skim through the problem, spending no more than a couple of minutes to acquaint yourself with the general story and the parties.

2. Re-read the call-of-the-question and set your focus.

f. Read the question for a second time, but this time read "actively":

1. Identify the area of law and the legal relationship between the parties.

2. Circle amounts of money, dates, locations, quantities, and ages.

3. Note the words "oral" and "written."

4. Identify issues as they appear by writing the words which characterize the legal principle, i.e., "merchants," "excited utterance," etc., instead of underlining. If you underline, you might not recall why you did so and you'll have to reread the passage, wasting valuable time.

g. Outline your answer.

Resist the impulse to start writing immediately—it doesn't matter what others around you are doing—it's worth a few minutes to think through the problem and plan your response. After you've completed your second read, and before you write your answer, organize your ideas into an outline based on a consideration of the relevant issues.

Note: If there is more than one interrogatory in the question, read all of them before you begin writing: chances are the bar examiners have "divided" the issues into separate questions and you need to do the same.

Now I can hear you thinking:

- *What do I put in an outline?*

- *How do I outline effectively without wasting precious exam writing time?*

The answer is to outline *only* the rule of law. Usually, it's all you need as a guide to writing a complete answer. The process of outlining lets you see things you might otherwise miss. By using "thought triggers," you proceed through the analytical steps necessary to write a complete answer.

Refer to the Checklist for *Outlining the Rule Section* as you review the following steps:

1. If appropriate to your jurisdiction's essay style, use each interrogatory to set up your numbering scheme and organize your answer.

2. For each interrogatory, identify the issue in controversy. The issues come from one of two possible sources, depending on the particular form of the essay:

    In the specific-style essay, use the interrogatory to guide your articulation of the issues.

    In the general-style essay, determine the issues directly from the fact pattern.

3. For each issue, consider the "building blocks of the rule" relevant to addressing your problem:

    (a) procedural elements (i.e., standard for summary judgment)

    (b) the general rule

    (c) elements/factors

    (d) exceptions to the general rule

    (e) distinctions

    (f) defenses/limitations

    Your thought process may not be this organized. It's far more likely you'll jump to the specific rule necessary to answer the issue in dispute—usually the exception—and neglect to consider the rest. Here's where an outline can help by prompting you to consider all the parts of the rule.

4. For each rule, match it to the relevant facts. Here, "charting the rule" with respect to the facts is helpful in writing a solid analysis.

I strongly recommend that you work with the Checklists for *Outlining the Rule Section* and *Charting the Rule* until it becomes automatic for you to think and write this way.

The *Rule Outline Worksheet* that follows provides an example using the Checklist to outline the rule from an actual bar exam essay.

OUTLINING THE RULE SECTION

1. Use the following questions to prompt your thinking.

2. Write only words or phrases—just enough to guide you when writing your answer.

3. If necessary, reorder the steps before you write so your answer flows from the "general to the specific."

4. If you have difficulty starting with the *specific rule*, then begin with the *general rule* and work your way from there.

5. *Not all questions will apply to any particular problem*.

State the issue: _____

_____

Step 1: What is the *specific rule* brought into controversy by the facts?

_____

Are there *legal terms* of art to define?

_____

_____

Step 2: What is the *general rule*?

_____

Build the general rule of law:

A. Are there *legal terms* to define?

_____

_____

B. Are there *exceptions* to the general rule?

_____

_____

_____

C. Are there *elements/factors* to be identified?

_____

_____

_____

Step 3: Is there a *procedural element* to consider? A motion? What is the standard? (i.e., summary judgment)

_____

Step 4: Is there a *relevant distinction?* (i.e., between the common law and the UCC or state law/ between federal and state law?)

_____

_____

Step 5: Does the party have a relevant *defense*? is there a *limit* to the reach of the rule?

_____

_____

Step 6: What are the *consequences* of applying this rule to the facts?

For example, should evidence be excluded under the *exclusionary rule*?

_____

Is the party entitled to damages? If so, what kind? Punitive? Economic? Equitable?

_____

_____

Step 7: Is there a *procedural element* to consider? A motion? What is the standard? (i.e., summary judgment)

_____

RULE OUTLINE WORKSHEET

Suppose you are answering Question 4 of the February, 2007 New York Bar Exam:

> The police received a tip from an anonymous source that Bernard had been murdered. A day later, Bernard's dead body was found behind the steering wheel of his own parked car. In the back seat of the car, the police found a jacket that had Archie's full name sewn in the collar. Inside one of the jacket pockets was a sealed blank envelope. The police opened the envelope and found a note from Archie to Bernard in which Archie demanded that Bernard tell him the location of some money that the two had stolen together, "or else".
>
> The police took a statement from Carol, who said she knew Archie and Bernard. She saw them leave a neighborhood tavern together and ride off in Bernard's car on the night Bernard was reported to have been murdered. Carol also reported to the police that Archie called her the next day and said that he was getting out of the country.
>
> The police went to Archie's home without an arrest warrant and found the front door slightly ajar. They entered and searched the house. Archie was found inside a closet and was arrested for the murder of Bernard. At that time, he was given his Miranda warnings.
>
> Over his objection and without counsel, Archie was then placed in a line-up, where he was identified by Darlene. Darlene lives near where Bernard's car was found. She said she saw Archie running from Bernard's car just after she heard a shot fired.
>
> After his arraignment, and outside the presence of his assigned counsel, Archie, after signing a waiver of his right to counsel, was questioned by the police. He gave a statement to them admitting that he shot Bernard.
>
> Archie's attorney moved to suppress (1) the note found in Archie's jacket; (2) the line-up results; and (3) Archie's statement. The court denied the motion in all respects.
>
> (A) Assuming the police had probable cause, was the arrest of Archie lawful?

(B) Assuming the arrest was lawful, were the court's rulings on (1), (2) and (3) correct?

We'll work with question (A):

"Assuming the police had probable cause, was the arrest of Archie lawful?"

First we'll frame a working issue statement:

"The issue is whether Archie's arrest violated his Fourth Amendment rights when the police arrested him in his home without an arrest warrant."

Now we are ready to consider the relevant rule. Here is where the Rule Outline can help—it provides a sequence of questions to guide your thinking so you will write a complete rule statement and not just the bare bones.

Writing only words or phrases to guide your writing of the essay, here's what your outline might look like:

Step 1: What is the ***specific rule*** brought into controversy by the facts?

"Exigent circumstances" exception

_____

Are there ***legal terms*** of art to define?
Exigent circumstances and evanescent evidence

_____

Step 2: What is the ***general rule***?
4th Amendment to Constitution

_____

Build the general rule of law:

A. Are there ***legal terms*** to define?

Search and seizure, warrant requirement, probable cause, Aguilar–Spinelli test

_____

B. Are there ***exceptions*** to the general rule?

Exigent circumstances

_____

C. Are there *elements/factors* to be identified?

NOT APPLICABLE

Step 3: Is there a *procedural element* to consider? A motion? What is the standard? (i.e., summary judgment)

NOT APPLICABLE

Step 4: Is there a *relevant distinction*? (i.e., between the common law and the UCC or state law/ between federal and state law?)

NOT APPLICABLE

Step 5: Does the party have a relevant *defense*? or is there a *limit* to the reach of the rule?

NOT APPLICABLE

Step 6: What are the *consequences* of applying this rule to the facts? For example, should evidence be excluded under the *exclusionary rule*? unlawful arrest because without warrant

---

Is the party entitled to damages? If so, what kind? Punitive? Economic? Equitable?

NOT APPLICABLE

Step 7: Is there a *procedural element* to consider? A motion? What is the standard? (i.e., summary judgment)

NOT APPLICABLE

If you were to chart the facts for this problem, it might look something like this:

Chart for subpart (A): *"Was the arrest of Archie lawful?"*

Rule	Fact(s)
Exigent circumstances	Anonymous tip night before body found—had time to get warrant Archie told Carol he was getting out of the country—no time for warrant
Warrant	Police entered house without warrant—door ajar
Seizure	Arrested Archie in his home
Probable cause; Aguilar/Spinelli	Bernard's body in car with Archie's jacket in back seat; statement from Carol

h. Write the essay

When you write, you'll follow your outline, referring to each point to prompt your thinking. This will lead you through the issues and sub-issues as they naturally unfold and assures that your answer will be well-organized.

1. Use sub-headings

The purpose for using sub-headings is as much for the writer as it is for the reader. They promote organization— both of thought and expression. Your choice of sub-headings should be simple and direct. Often, you need look no further than the interrogatory for your sub-head: i.e., "Motion for Summary Judgment," "Identification of Damages," "Easement by Prescription." Sub-headings are very useful when answering multi-issue hypotheticals to keep parties and causes of action separate. Consider such possible sub-headings:

Dan v. ABC Company

Buyer's Remedies

Jon's Defenses

2. Write IRAC

(a) Write the issue using the "whether, when" construction to combine rule with fact. Each issue is the focal point around which you'll write your analysis.

(b) Identify the controlling rule of law with, "***Under the*** [state the controlling law: common law, federal rule, state-specific statute, etc.].

(c) Write a complete paragraph of law for each issue by working from the general to the specific and defining each legal term of art.

(d) Introduce your analysis with "***Here***" or "***In this case.***"

(e) Match each rule of law with a "fact" using "because" to link the two.

(f) Conclude and continue: offer a conclusion with respect to the issue and repeat the process where each issue and sub-issue forms the basis for a separate IRAC analysis.

i.   When time is up, move on to the next question.

You must follow your timetable faithfully. You simply cannot "borrow" time from one question for the next. This never works. Instead, you must continue on and keep within your "clock." If you have time remaining when you've finished all the questions, then you can go back. You'll probably only have time enough to jot down a few words but if you use your outline, this should be sufficient to guide you to the key points.

6.   "Be in the moment"

No matter how much you've studied, how many practice exams you've taken, and how carefully you've outlined and considered what's likely to be tested, once you get to the exam, you must be prepared to let go and "be in the moment." This means that you respond to what the bar examiners ask of you and not what you want to tell them. The questions are carefully crafted to test you on certain material; if you turn the questions around or avoid answering them, you're thwarting their agenda and substituting your own. Trust me—there's no better way to ensure a poor or even failing grade than to ignore what's asked of you. Answering the bar examiners' questions is the only way to show what you know.

LEARNING TO WRITE BAR–RIGHT ESSAYS

Have you followed the steps for learning to write "bar-right" essays?

1.   Have you identified your audience?

☐   Are you familiar with the guidelines and information for bar candidates provided by your state's bar examiners?

☐   Do you understand what they expect in an essay answer in terms of tone, specificity of detail, and style?

2.   Do you know what subjects will be tested?

3.   Do you know the composition of the questions on the state portion of your bar exam with respect to the following?

☐   The number of essays?

☐ The number of state-based multiple choice questions, if any?

4. Based on the composition of the exam, do you know how much time to allocate for each question?

5. Have you "de-constructed" sample exam questions from your jurisdiction to see:

☐ Whether to expect a *"single issue, outcome specific"* style essay, a more general, *"multi-issue"* style essay, or a combination of both?

☐ How different subject areas are combined within a single essay?

☐ How procedural issues are combined with substance issues?

☐ How bar examiners use vocabulary to signal issues?

☐ How bar examiners use vocabulary to identify non-issues?

☐ Patterns in questions and how often particular topics are tested?

6. Have you "de-constructed" sample answers from your jurisdiction to learn:

☐ Whether they follow the steps of a basic IRAC analysis?

☐ How to use the "whether, when" construction to state an issue that combines rule with fact?

☐ How to incorporate "distinctions" into statements of the rule?

☐ How to use "signal" language?

☐ How to use "because," "since," "as," and "when" to write a solid analysis that combines law and fact?

AUTOMATING THE EXAM WRITING PROCESS

Have you internalized the process of reading and answering essay questions so it will be automatic on bar day? Do you know to:

1. Allocate your time for each question and set a timetable on scrap paper?

2. Scan the entire exam but return to the beginning to answer the questions in order, while remaining flexible to answer out of sequence if you need to?

3. When you start to read, do you:

   ☐ Begin with the interrogatory at the end of the question?

   ☐ Check to see whether it's a *"single issue, outcome specific"* style essay or a more general, *"multi-issue"* style essay?

   ☐ Note any instructions to follow in writing your response?

4. On reading the entire question for the first time, do you:

   ☐ Read through the fact pattern to get a sense of the problem and the parties?

   ☐ Return to the end to re-read the interrogatory and set your focus?

5. On reading the question for a second time, do you read "actively" to:

   ☐ Identify the area of law and the legal relationship between the parties?

   ☐ Circle amounts of money, dates, locations, quantities, and ages?

   ☐ Note such key words as "oral" and "written"?

   ☐ Characterize legal issues in words rather than underlining?

6. Do you outline your answer before writing and:

   ☐ Articulate an issue for each interrogatory?

   ☐ Build a rule of law for each issue by following the Rule Outline?

   ☐ If necessary, "chart" each rule with the relevant fact(s) for your essay's application section?

7. When writing an essay, do you follow an IRAC-based analysis and:

☐ Use the "whether, when" construction to combine rule with fact when writing the issue?

☐ If appropriate, begin with a conclusion that explicitly answers the question asked?

☐ Consider the rule in terms of context and consequences?

☐ Identify the controlling rule of law with, "***Under the*** [state the controlling law: common law, federal rule, state-specific statute, etc.]?

☐ Write a complete paragraph of law by compiling the building blocks for the rule of law by considering

  ☐ procedural elements?

  ☐ the general rule?

  ☐ exceptions to the general rule?

  ☐ distinctions in the law?

  ☐ limitations?

  ☐ defenses?

☐ Follow a hierarchy of concepts by

  ☐ moving from the general to the specific?

  ☐ defining each legal term of art?

☐ Introduce your analysis with "***Here***" or "***In this case***"?

☐ Match each "element" in your rule of law with a "fact" using "because" to link the two?

☐ Conclude and continue to the next issue?

CHARTING THE RULES AND FACTS

Use the following when you practice answering essay questions:

(1)   The issue is whether :_____

_____.

Rule	Fact(s)

(2)   The issue is whether :_____

_____.

Rule	Fact(s)

(3)   The issue is whether :_____

_____.

Rule	Fact(s)

EMERGENCY MEASURES OR "WHAT TO DO IF"

The bar exam presents good reason for jitters—even for those who cope pretty well with exam anxiety. After all, it's not many tests that we take with thousands of other candidates at the same time and place. The surroundings alone prove problematic for some. If you begin to feel panicky during any of your practice sessions, or you know that you have this tendency, then you'll want to consider the following measures so you'll know what to do if necessary on bar day.

1. Have I begun to panic?

    ☐ Am I holding my breath?

    If you begin to feel anxious, stop whatever you're doing and breathe deeply. You want to regain your sense of control and composure immediately.

    ☐ Now that I've relaxed a bit, what do I do next?

        ☐ Review the question.

        ☐ Start with what you know: identify the area of law again and see if it provides insight.

        ☐ Focus on the basics. See if you can provide definitions. Remember, rules are really just definitions. The next step is to see if you can build on these definitions to write a paragraph of law.

        ☐ Finally, call on the resources you developed in law school. Lawyers act; they do not react. Think deliberately and respond accordingly. Reread the interrogatory and begin again.

2. Have I forgotten the rule of law? What do I do if my mind goes blank when I read the question?

    ☐ Ask: *"What is the issue?"*

    You can formulate the issue from the question you are asked to answer. Focusing on identifying the issue will allow you to regain your composure and lead you back to the process of thinking like a lawyer.

    ☐ Write the issue, whether or not you "know" the rule of law you need to apply. Formulating the issue will get you points from the grader because it shows that you can identify the legal problem from the facts.

☐ Next ask: *"What principle of law is implicated by this issue?"*

Now you're thinking like a lawyer. This will either lead you to the rule from the recesses of your memory or you'll have to improvise. When you improvise, rely on your knowledge of general legal principles and standards to guide you.

☐ What do you know about the law in general to build a specific rule for your problem?

Can you identify the general legal concept implicated in the problem? Some questions you can ask to get you thinking include:

☐ Has there been a breach of a legally recognized duty?

☐ Does this court have jurisdiction to hear the case?

☐ Is this the proper party to bring the case?

☐ Has there been a violation of a fiduciary obligation?

☐ Are the standards of due process/equal protection implicated?

☐ Has the requirement of good faith been breached?

☐ Are the "best interests of the child" at stake?

These questions become your starting point. As you study, you'll find more basic questions that you can rely on to trigger your thought process. Add them to your mental checklist.

3. How do I use what I know about a topic to build on it?

If you're asked about recoverable "damages" in a particular case, rely on what you know about "damages" in particular areas of the law and proceed from there.

☐ If it's a contracts problem, you know every breach of contract entitles the aggrieved party to sue for damages. The general theory of damages in contract actions is that the injured party should be placed in the same position as if the contract had been properly performed, at least so far as money damages can do this. Ask,

☐ Is plaintiff entitled to his "expectation interest" or "the benefit of his bargain"?

☐ If not, can plaintiff seek reliance damages?

☐ Can plaintiff recover in restitution?

☐ Does an action lie in specific performance? Was the contract for a sale for real property or a unique piece of personal property?

☐ Suppose you can't identify the issue or principle of law. Even so, you can break down the problem into the elements common to every case and proceed from there.

The following questions allow you to gain access to the problem when your initial read is fruitless. From any one of these topics, it is but a short step to finding the principle of law implicated in the question. It might be a very good idea to memorize these topics and use them to "jump-start" your thought process:

☐ Identify the parties and the nature of their relationship.

Is it that of employer/employee, landlord/tenant, buyer/seller, parent/child, teacher/student, husband/wife?

☐ Identify the place(s) where the facts arose.

Did the events occur in a public area, a private home, a school, a waterway, a farm?

☐ Identify whether objects or things were involved.

Was there a transaction involving the sale of goods?

Is the ownership of land or chattel in dispute?

☐ Identify the acts or omissions which form the basis of the action.

Was there a robbery, a breach of contract, an assault, an act of discrimination?

☐ Determine whether there is a defense to the action.

Is there a basis for self-defense, justification, privilege?

☐ Characterize the relief sought.

Are the parties seeking damages?

Are they monetary or equitable damages, or both?

RELEASED BAR EXAM ESSAY QUESTIONS

The practice materials which follow are released bar exam questions and answers and were downloaded from the websites of their respective jurisdictions. The questions and answers were selected to show a range in approach, substance, and format. For additional practice questions, consult the website for your jurisdiction or the NCBE website.

New York State

    February 2007, Question 4

    Sample Candidate Answers

    Answer De-construction

New Jersey

    July 2005, Question 3

    Sample Candidate Answers

    Answer De-construction

California

    July 2006, Question 1

    Sample Candidate Answer

    Answer De-construction

Florida

    February 2006, Question 2

    Sample Candidate Answer

    Answer De-construction

Multistate Essay Exams

    July 1998, Question 5

    Model Analyses

NEW YORK STATE

February 2007 Bar Examination

Question Number 4[3]

The police received a tip from an anonymous source that Bernard had been murdered. A day later, Bernard's dead body was found behind the steering wheel of his own parked car. In the back seat of the car, the police found a jacket that had Archie's full name sewn in the collar. Inside one of the jacket pockets was a sealed blank envelope. The police opened the envelope and found a note from Archie to Bernard in which Archie demanded that Bernard tell him the location of some money that the two had stolen together, "or else."

The police took a statement from Carol, who said she knew Archie and Bernard. She saw them leave a neighborhood tavern together and ride off in Bernard's car on the night Bernard was reported to have been murdered. Carol also reported to the police that Archie called her the next day and said that he was getting out of the country.

The police went to Archie's home without an arrest warrant and found the front door slightly ajar. They entered and searched the house. Archie was found inside a closet and was arrested for the murder of Bernard. At that time, he was given his Miranda warnings.

Over his objection and without counsel, Archie was then placed in a line-up, where he was identified by Darlene. Darlene lives near where Bernard's car was found. She said she saw Archie running from Bernard's car just after she heard a shot fired.

After his arraignment, and outside the presence of his assigned counsel, Archie, after signing a waiver of his right to counsel, was questioned by the police. He gave a statement to them admitting that he shot Bernard.

---

3. This is a released New York State bar exam essay available at www.nybarexam .org/Q&A207.htm. Copyright © 2007, all rights reserved.

Archie's attorney moved to suppress (1) the note found in Archie's jacket; (2) the line-up results; and (3) Archie's statement. The court denied the motion in all respects.

(A) Assuming the police had probable cause, was the arrest of Archie lawful?

(B) Assuming the arrest was lawful, were the court's rulings on (1), (2) and (3) correct?

February 2007 Bar Examination—New York

As stated by the Board of Law Examiners in its release of questions and answers to bar candidates, "the following answers have been selected . . . as representative of better than average submissions. They are reprinted without change, except for minor editing, and no representation is made that any answer identifies or correctly responds to all of the issues raised by the question."[4]

Question Number 4

Sample Candidate Answer 1

A. The issue is whether the police violated the Fourth Amendment when they arrested the defendant at his home without first procuring a warrant.

The Fourth Amendment to the Constitution, made applicable to the state through the Fourteenth Amendment, protects against "unreasonable searches and seizures." In interpreting this command, the Supreme Court has held that when the police seek to arrest a suspect at his home (thereby constitution [sic] a seizure), they must first procure a search warrant. There are a number of limited exceptions to this requirement. Among these exceptions are exigency—when an emergency exists at such a level as to justify not procuring a warrant. Another exception allows the police to occasionally act without a warrant in order to preserve "evanescent" evidence—evidence that might be destroyed if the police were to wait to obtain a warrant.

Here, it appears the police did have probable cause to arrest the defendant. Even under the more stringent *Aguilar-Spinelli* test that New York continues to apply, Carol's tip was reliable and would probably have justified the issuance of a warrant by a detached and neutral magistrate, on a finding of probable cause—as would be required by the Constitution.

---

4. *See* New York Board of Law Examiners   visited September 12, 2007).
at   www.nybarexam.org/Q&A207.htm   (last

This probable cause does not mean, however, that the arrest was lawful without a warrant. Because they arrested Archie in his home without a warrant, the police conduct would have to fall within one of the limited exceptions to the warrant requirement.

One of those exceptions is for evanescent evidence. Where the police fear that evidence may be destroyed, they may sometimes act outside the boundaries of the warrant requirement. Here, it is true that Carol indicated to the police that Archie told her he was leaving the country (hearsay requirements, of course, do not apply to this type of inquiry). The police might attempt to argue that the evanescence exception is triggered. However, a court would be unlikely to agree. The police could have lawfully monitored Archie's home from outside in order to monitor his comings and goings. Indeed, once he left his home, they would have been able to arrest him without a warrant merely because probable cause existed. Moreover, even with the possibility of Archie's fleeing the country, the police ostensibly had time to obtain a warrant. New York allows officers to apply for a warrant via electronic or telephonic means, and this was an option available to the officers.

The police might also try to justify the arrest on the grounds that there existed some exigency—some urgent emergency—that would take the arrest outside of the Constitution's warrant requirement. However, the facts do not seem to justify this conclusion. It is true that the police wanted urgently to arrest Archie, whom they suspected of being a murderer. But this alone cannot justify the warrantless arrest. The Supreme Court and New York courts have justified exigency exceptions to the warrant requirement in cases where public health was imminently threatened, where children's lives were imminently threatened, and similar life-threatening emergencies. There do not appear to be facts to make this case fall within that line of cases.

Finally, the fact that the door was slightly ajar does not materially alter this analysis. Once they entered the suspect's home in order to make an arrest without a warrant, the police violated the Constitution's prohibition on unreasonable searches and seizures. It is important to note however, that an illegal arrest will not of itself necessarily give the defendant a meaningful remedy. It is true that evidence obtained as a result of the warrantless arrest may be excluded under the "fruit of the poisonous tree" doctrine. Yet as the Supreme Court announced in the 1950's case of *Frisbee v. Collins* and reenunciated in the 1990's in the *Alvarez-Machain* case, the mere fact that the defendant's presence was obtained unlawfully does not act to deprive the court of the ability to try him.

B. (1) The issue is whether Archie has standing to challenge the search of Bernard's vehicle.

The Fourth Amendment protects against "unreasonable searches," but this right extends only to the extent that the person challenging the search has standing to do so. Standing means that the person had a reasonable expectation of privacy in the thing searched, such that he is a proper party to challenge the search in court.

As a general rule, people have an expectation of privacy in property that [sic] own or possess. The Supreme Court and the New York courts have extended this doctrine somewhat, and permit for instance, an overnight guest to challenge the results of a warrantless search in the home in which he or she was staying.

Here, it was not Archie's car that was searched, but rather Bernard [sic]. It does not appear that the warrantless search was unreasonable (given that the thing searched was a car parked in view of the public with a dead body in plain view). Even if it were, however, Archie would not be able to assert the constitutional rights of another in order to exclude the evidence under the exclusionary rule, which calls for the exclusion of evidence where it is illegally obtained. Consequently, Archie did not have a reasonable expectation of privacy in the car generally.

The issue then becomes whether the police unlawfully searched the jacket itself or the envelope. A court would likely reason that because Archie had no expectation of privacy in the car itself, he had no reasonable expectation of privacy in the things within the car. Even if a court were to entertain the idea that things within the car were illegally searched even without an expectation of privacy in the car as a whole, it appears the police acted reasonably. The jacket itself may have read "Archie" but the police had no way of knowing that "Archie" was not in fact the owner of the car or the dead individual within it. Archie might argue that this exception cannot extend to the envelope itself and that the police should have obtained a warrant to open it. Yet again, however, the issue probably would go back to whether Archie has standing to challenge the search in the first place.

Thus, because he almost certainly lacks standing to challenge the search, the court's ruling with respect to suppression of the note was correct.

(2) The issue is whether a suspect is entitled to counsel at a pre-charge lineup.

The general rule, and the federal constitutional requirement, is that the Sixth Amendment right to counsel does not ordinarily attach before the imposition of formal charges against the defendant. The New York approach is somewhat broader than the federal requirement. New York protects the "indelible" right to counsel whenever: 1) the police engage in activity overwhelming to the layperson and the defendant requests counsel; 2) after the imposition of formal judicial process; 3) at arraignment; and 4) anytime there is significant judicial activity in the case. Accordingly, even in New York, the general rule is that before the defendant is formally charged with a crime (thereby bringing with it the protections of the Sixth Amendment right to counsel), he has no right to counsel at a pre-charge lineup. There is an additional narrow exception in New York to this rule: where the police are aware that the defendant is represented by counsel and he makes a request for counsel, the police must provide it.

Here, the defendant had not yet been charged with a crime. The police were unaware that he was represented by counsel (nor does it appear that he was), and in any event, the defendant made no request for counsel prior to the lineup. Thus, it does not appear that his Sixth Amendment right to counsel.

Nor does the lineup invoke the defendant's right to counsel under the Fifth Amendment. While there is a right to counsel protected under that constitutional provision, it applies only where the suspect is subject to custodial interrogation. While appearing in a line-up may be incriminating, it is not testimonial. Thus, there was no violation of the right to counsel, nor any other apparent constitutional infirmity. The court was correct to deny the motion to suppress the line-up results, and the witness should be entitled to make an in-court identification (and consistent with the hearsay exception, testify to the original identification, as well).

(3) The issue is whether the police may obtain a valid waiver from a suspect post-charge and without the presence counsel.

As noted above, both federally and in New York, the right to counsel attaches once formal judicial proceedings are begun against the defendant. Moreover, in New York, a valid waiver of one known to be represented by counsel may not, post-arraignment, be obtained outside the presence of that counsel.

Archie was known to be represented by counsel (for counsel was assigned). The questioning occurred outside the presence of counsel. Though a waiver was obtained (which will generally cure constitutional defects if it was knowing and voluntary), it was not obtained in the presence of counsel.

Thus, Archie's right to counsel, as protected here by both the Fifth and Sixth Amendments was violated, and the court was incorrect to deny the motion to suppress. The court should have granted that motion, for under the exclusionary rule, an illegally obtained confession may not be used by the state.

Question Number 4

Sample Candidate Answer 2

A.   Assuming the police had probable cause, Archie's arrest may be lawful if the court finds exigent circumstances present. The issue is when the need for an arrest warrant is required. Under the Fourth Amendment, a person cannot be lawfully arrested unless the police first obtain an arrest warrant. An arrest warrant must issue from a detached, neutral magistrate on a finding of probable cause. There are certain exceptions to the requirement of an arrest warrant. For example, if there are exigent circumstances, or if the arrest is in a public place, then police can make the arrest without first obtaining a warrant. In this case, if the police can prove that there were exigent circumstances present such that taking the time to obtain an arrest warrant would result in Archie having the time to flee, then they may be able to overcome the warrant requirement. However, the facts suggest that the circumstances were not of an immediate nature. To begin with, the police received the anonymous tip the night before they actually found the body. Then, when they found the body and came across evidence suggesting Archie's involvement in the crime, they did not go straight to a magistrate but continued to investigate. Once they received corroboration from Carol, the police proceeded to Archie's house. That being said, based on Carol's testimony of Archie "getting out of the country," the police may be able to demonstrate that that fact gave them the emergency situation that would allow an officer to forego the warrant requirement for the sake of making an actual arrest of Archie. In other words, the police will argue that any minute spared to obtain a warrant would have been time wasted in arresting Archie. If the court finds this argument persuasive, then Archie's arrest will be lawful. Notably, the fact that Archie's door was open is likely not enough to allow the police to overcome the requirement for a warrant. Whereas in a fully public place, police can generally proceed to arrest on just probable cause (not a warrant), Archie's house was not a public place nor were the police invited in. The fact that the door was open will not affect the lawfulness of the warrant-less arrest.

   B.   (1) The court's ruling on the note found in Archie's jacket is correct. The issue is whether Archie has standing to object to the note found in his jacket pocket. Under the Fourth Amendment, a person is granted protection from government searches and seizures of things where there is a reasonable expectation of privacy. Whereas someone's personal property might be inherently private in nature, the fact that Archie's jacket here was found in Bernard's car takes it out of the realm of privacy that is expected. In other words, because the jacket was in Bernard's car, which Archie did not own, and more importantly, because Archie was not in the car with the jacket, he cannot reasonably expect to have the jacket itself be free of any government search. Because Archie has no expectation of privacy, he has no standing to object to the jacket, and therefore it comes in as evidence.

(2) The court's ruling on the line-up is correct. The issue is whether the Fifth Amendment attaches to line-ups. Under the Fifth Amendment, a person is free from giving testimonial evidence that may tend to incriminate them. The rights under the Fifth Amendment attach after a person is in police custody—meaning when a reasonable person would not feel free to leave. Here, Archie's Fifth Amendment privileges had clearly attached as he had been arrested, and was therefore in police custody. That being said, a line-up will not violate a person's Fifth Amendment right to be free of self-incrimination because it is not testimonial in nature. Also, Archie has no claim to keep the line-up out under his Sixth Amendment right to counsel because he had not yet been formally charged. He may be able to assert an argument under New York's right to counsel (see *supra* Section 4(b)(3)). However, he would first have to prove that there was substantial governmental interference such that a right to counsel was necessary. In this case, the court's ruling was likely correct as line-ups are non-testimonial in nature and therefore the Fifth Amendment does not apply.

(3) The court's ruling in regards to Archie's statement was likely incorrect. The issue is whether Archie's waiver was valid. Under the Sixth Amendment, a person's right to counsel attaches once a formal charge has been brought against the defendant. In this case, Archie's right to counsel likely attached after his arraignment. Under the federal rules, a waiver is valid if it is knowing and intelligent and voluntary. This means that the defendant knew the right he was giving up and did so voluntarily–without any coercion by the police. Under the federal rules, Archie's confession here would likely be admissible as he gave a knowing and intelligent and voluntary waiver of his right to counsel. Therefore, the police were allowed to question him in regards to the alleged crime. However, New York has a much more defendant-protective right to counsel. By statute, New York provides for an indelible right to counsel which attaches not just when

there is a formal charge, but whenever there is substantial government interference such that a defendant may benefit from the presence of counsel. Clearly, an arraignment qualifies as such an instance and therefore New York's right to counsel attached in Archie's case. One protection under New York's right to counsel is that a voluntary and knowing and intelligent waiver must be made in the presence of counsel. Thus, in order for Archie's confession to be valid, it would have to have been made while his counsel was still present. Here, it was not; therefore it is invalid. Indeed, Archie's waiver, the police questioning, and his subsequent confession were all made outside the presence of counsel. As such, his confession can be said to be a fruit of the poisonous tree and should therefore be excluded under the exclusionary rule. The court was therefore incorrect in denying Archie's motion to suppress.

ANSWER DE–CONSTRUCTION

NEW YORK STATE

February 2007 Bar Examination

Question Number 4

Candidate Sample Answer 1

As you review this sample answer, note the following:

☐ Adherence to IRAC construction

As we discussed earlier in this chapter, New York essays follow the "single issue, outcome specific" format. Note the candidate's use of the "whether, when" construction in writing the issue:

*"The issue is **whether** the police violated the Fourth Amendment **when** they arrested the defendant at his home without first procuring a warrant."*

The statement of the issue leads directly to articulation of the rule, followed by analysis of the relevant facts. This construction is followed for answering each subpart of the question.

☐ Development of the rule section using the "building block" approach

You should recognize this essay question from the example in the *Rule Outline Worksheet*. Here, the candidate's answer works from the general rule (the Fourth Amendment to the Constitution) to the specific exception (exigent circumstances) where each legal term is defined ("seizure," "exigency," "evanescent evidence," "probable cause").

☐ Identification of relevant distinctions between the federal and New York rule

Note answer to A:

"Even under the more stringent Aguilar–Spinelli test that New York continues to apply, Carol's tip was reliable and would

probably have justified the issuance of a warrant by a detached and neutral magistrate, on a finding of probable cause—as would be required by the Constitution."

Note answer to B(2):

"The general rule, and the federal constitutional requirement, is that the Sixth Amendment right to counsel does not does not ordinarily attach before the imposition of formal charges against the defendant. *The New York approach* is somewhat broader than the federal requirement. New York protects the "indelible" right to counsel whenever: 1) the police engage in activity overwhelming to the layperson and the defendant requests counsel; 2) after the imposition of formal judicial process; 3) at arraignment; and 4) anytime there is significant judicial activity in the case. Accordingly, *even in New York, the general rule* is that before the defendant is formally charged with a crime (thereby bringing with it the protections of the Sixth Amendment right to counsel), he has no right to counsel at a pre-charge lineup. *There is an additional narrow exception in New York to this rule*: where the police are aware that the defendant is represented by counsel and he makes a request for counsel, the police must provide it."

☐ One-to-one application of rule to fact for a solid analysis section

Note answer to B(3):

Rule paragraph:

"As noted above, both federally and in New York, the right to counsel attaches once formal judicial proceedings are begun against the defendant. Moreover, in New York, a valid waiver of one known to be represented by counsel may not, post-arraignment, be obtained outside the presence of that counsel."

Application paragraph:

"Archie was known to be represented by counsel (for counsel was assigned). The questioning occurred outside the presence of counsel. Though a waiver was obtained (which will generally cure constitutional defects if it was knowing and voluntary), it was not obtained in the presence of counsel."

ANSWER DE–CONSTRUCTION

NEW YORK STATE

February 2007 Bar Examination

Question Number 4

Candidate Sample Answer 2

As you review this sample answer, note the following:

☐ Adherence to IRAC construction

Candidate 2 follows the same IRAC format as Candidate 1. The statement of the issue is followed in each case by articulation of the rule, moving from the general rule (*"under the Fourth Amendment"*) to the specific exception at issue (*"there are certain exceptions to the requirement of an arrest warrant. For example, if there exigent circumstances. . . . "*)

☐ Extensive use of "because" in writing the analysis

Note answer to B(1):

> "In other words, *because* the jacket was in Bernard's car, which Archie did not own, and more importantly, *because* Archie was not in the car with the jacket, he cannot reasonably expect to have the jacket itself be free of any government search. *Because* Archie has no expectation of privacy, he has no standing to object to the jacket, and therefore it comes in as evidence."

RELEASED BAR EXAM ESSAY QUESTIONS

NEW JERSEY

July 2005 Bar Examination

Question Number 3[5]

Paul, a smuggler, has a cargo van filled to capacity with illegal aliens. While leaving the highway, he realizes he does not have enough change for the toll. Paul decides to go through the EZ–Pass lane even though he does not have an account.

Tollbooth Operator ("Operator") notices Paul go through the EZ–Pass lane without paying, but does not see his license number. The very next driver, however, tells Operator, "I just wrote down the license number of that cargo van! He was driving like he had something illegal in there!" The driver then hands the note to Operator. Operator writes the license number down as well as the driver's statement.

Operator notifies the State Police, who later stop Paul. As the officer approaches the van, he hears hushed voices saying, "Paul's a great smuggler, but he drives way too fast." The officer then arrests Paul and takes the illegal aliens into custody. The federal government charges Paul with smuggling.

At a hearing held at the Department of Homeland Security, the illegal aliens state they are unwitting victims of Paul. Homeland Security, however, determines the entire group consists of enemy-combatants to be held at the United States Naval Base in Guantanamo Bay.

Unable to post bail and awaiting trial in jail, Paul has an epiphany and calls Guru—a mysticist he saw on TV. During their telephone conversation, Paul tells Guru he wants to talk about his situation. Guru tells Paul, "The spirit always listens to calls for

---

5. This is a released New Jersey bar exam essay available at www.njbarexams.org /exam/oldexamsjuly2005.htm. Copyright © 2005, all rights reserved.

forgiveness." Paul then confesses to smuggling the aliens. Unfortunately, the government was listening and recording the entire conversation.

At Paul's trial, Operator testifies as to the contents of his note, explaining he is unable to remember the license number or the witness' comments he wrote, but he would have written the information correctly at the time. The State Police officer testifies about the vehicle stop, including what statements he heard coming from the van. The prosecution seeks to read to the jury the transcripts of the aliens' statements against Paul made at the Homeland Security hearing, claiming it is too dangerous to transport them to the trial. Finally, the prosecution plays Paul and Guru's telephone conversation in which Paul confessed to the crime.

The defense objects to all the evidence proffered by the prosecution and admitted by the judge. The defense seeks to introduce the testimony of Paul's former army commander, who would have stated Paul was a decorated soldier and would never commit any crime. The judge denies the request. The defense then calls a seasoned ex-FBI agent as an expert to testify that Paul's actions did not fit the profile of a smuggler according to the "FBI's Guide to Profiling Smugglers" and to enter the book in evidence. The judge also denies this request.

The jury convicts Paul, who timely files an appeal. You are the appellate judge's law clerk assigned to write a memorandum analyzing all of the trial court's evidentiary rulings, citing the factual bases and all applicable rules of law.

Prepare the MEMORANDUM

July 2005 Bar Examination—New Jersey

Question Number 3

Candidate Sample Answer 1[6]

OPERATOR'S TESTIMONY

The court's ruling admitting the operator's testimony was correct. The operator's note could be used to refresh the recollection of the operator on the witness stand, as long as it is shown to opposing counsel. The information the operator recounted came from a driver, and the driver's statements are both admissible as hearsay exceptions. The license plate number is a present sense impression, and the statement about Paul's driving is an excited utterance.

POLICE OFFICER'S TESTIMONY

The court's ruling admitting the police officer's testimony was correct. He had probable cause to stop the van, after hearing the operator's information. The statements he heard coming form the van is an exception to hearsay as a statement against penal interest by an unavailable witness. The aliens are legally unavailable because they are in military custody as "enemy combatants." The statement is against penal interest because it identified them as either accomplices in smuggling or the objects of smuggling.

TRANSCRIPTS OF ALIENS' TESTIMONY

The court's ruling admitting the transcripts of aliens' hearing testimony was erroneous. As noted, the aliens were legally unavailable to testify at trial. However, their statements at the hearing were not against penal interest, nor do they fit within another hearsay exception. To admit the transcripts would also violate Paul's 6th Amendment right to confront the witnesses against him, because Paul's counsel had not opportunity to cross-examine them when their original testimony was given.

---

6. New Jersey provides two sample candidate answers for each question. *See* www.njbarexams.org/exam/oldexamsjuly2005.htm (last visited September 13, 2007).

RECORDED TELEPHONE CONVERSATION

The court's ruling admitting the recorded telephone conversation between Paul and Guru was correct, assuming the police obtained a warrant before tapping the line. Tapping a phone line and listening in or recording constitutes a search for 4th Amendment purposes, so a valid search warrant based on probable cause is required. Since Paul had already been arrested, the police most likely had not [sic] trouble presenting probable cause and obtaining a warrant. Paul's statement in the recording, confessing to smuggling the aliens, is admissible as an admission of a party.

FORMER COMMANDER'S TESTIMONY

The court's ruling excluding the testimony of Paul's former commander was erroneous. A criminal defendant may present evidence of his good character in the form of witnesses who have personal knowledge of it. The offer of proof is sparse, but presumably defense counsel would have phrased questions to the commander in the proper way, asking him about his opinion of Paul's character for honesty and respect for the law, and about Paul's reputation in the community for these traits. Such testimony opens the door for the prosecution to offer evidence of the defendant's bad character for the same traits, using the same form of question.

EX–FBI AGENT'S TESTIMONY

The court's ruling excluding the testimony of the ex-FBI agent was erroneous. And [sic] expert may testify as to the expert's opinion, as long as the expert is first declared an expert witness by the court. Any publication or other source relied on by the expert in forming this opinion must be one that is considered authoritative in the relevant field, i.e. it is commonly relied on by experts. The ex-agent's testimony about the profile of a smuggler would have been relevant, since it would have some tendency to make the proposition that Paul smuggled the aliens somewhat less probable.

FBI GUIDE

The court's ruling excluding the FBI guide was correct. If an expert witness relied on a particular source in forming his or her opinion, relevant portions of that source may be read to the jury. However, the entire source may not be offered into evidence.

July 2005 Bar Examination—New Jersey

Question Number 3

Candidate Sample Answer 2

MEMORANDUM
TO: Judge
FROM: Law Clerk
RE: State v. Paul—Appeal

This memorandum discusses the trial court's evidentiary rulings in the above captioned case.

I.   OPERATOR'S NOTE-NO ERROR

The operator's note is hearsay. Hearsay is an out of court statement offered for the purpose of proving the truth of the matter asserted. This note that purportedly had Paul's license plate number on it is hearsay, because it was made out of court, and is being offered to prove the truth of its contents (i.e. that Paul drove through the EZ Pass lane). Hearsay is inadvisable unless an exception applies. Technically, this situation presents a double-level hearsay problem because there are two statements involved: the motorist's comments and note, plus the operator's note derived from this hearsay. Accordingly, both statements must fall within the independent hearsay exceptions to be admissible.

First, the driver's statement describing Paul's license plate number qualifies as a present sense impression. As [sic] present sense impression is a statement made during or immediately after perceiving an event. The motorists' notation of Paul's plate was a present sense impression since she had just observed him run the EZ Pass lane. Thus it is admissible.

Second, the operator's notation of the motorist's note qualifies as a recorded recollection. A recorded recollection exception applies where the witness once made a writing that was truthful and accurate when made, and attempt to refresh the witness's memory has failed, and it otherwise appears trustworthy.

Operator's statement was made by him/her immediately after being told by an eyewitness what the license plate number was. Operator's present memory has failed. There is nothing to suggest that this in [sic] untruthful (in real life, this will be confirmed by the picture of your license plate that they take when you don't pay a toll)(operator said he would have recorded this info correctly). Accordingly, it was not error to permit the pros. to read this to the jury.

II. STATEMENTS OF ILLEGAL ALIENS—Admissible

The statements of the aliens are hearsay. They were made out of court and are offered to prove the truth of the matter asserted (i.e. that Paul is a smuggler). Thus, an exception must apply or it is inadmissible.

The statements by the aliens qualify as a co-conspirator exception to hearsay. A co-conspirator statement made during and in furtherance of the conspiracy is admissible.

Here, the aliens turned out to not be "unwitting victims", but rather, enemy combatants. Thus, the trial judge could have determined that a conspiracy existed. The prosecution will likely successfully argue that, at the time it was made the conspiracy still existed, and that the statement "Paul drives to fast" is in furtherance of it; i.e. he shouldn't drive so fast or he'll risk us being caught. Thus, it is admissible.

III. ALIEN'S STATEMENT AGAINST PAUL

This would violate Paul's 6th Amendment Confrontation clause. The Supreme Court recently held in Cranford v. Washington, that in order for testimonial hearsay to be admissible, in a criminal case, the declarant must be unavailable and there must have been a prior opportunity to cross. In that case, Justice Scalia defined testimonial to include, at minimum, statements in response to police interrogatories, and prior hearings under oath.

In this case, the statements by the aliens to the Homeland Security Dept. at the hearing would very likely qualify as "testimonial" for purposes of the 6th Amendment, because they were made (likely) under oath at a prior proceeding. Accordingly, they must be both unavailable and Paul must have had a prior opportunity to cross-examine them or it is inadmissible under Crawford. Since the facts clearly indicate that the aliens are presently unavailable, and Paul never had the opportunity to cross, it should not have been admitted. Note that this will not constitute reversible error if it was a harmless error beyond a reasonable doubt.

IV.   PAUL'S TELEPHONE CONVERSATION

The 4th Amendment applies when (1) there is a Gov't actor and (2) there is a reasonable expectation of privacy. (see US v. Kate). The 4th Amendment requires either a warrant issued upon probable cause or exception if it applies.

Paul's telephone conversation to Guru from the jail cell in not entitled to 4th Amendment protection because one does not have a reasonable expectation of privacy in phone calls placed from a jail. Thus, this recording is admissible on 4th Amendment grounds. Note also that it is not hearsay because Paul is the defendant and thus it is a party-opponent admission.

V.   FORMER ARMY COMMANDER

This testimony should have been admissible. In a criminal trial, the defendant has the opportunity to "open the door" to presenting character evidence for a pertinent trait. He need not wait for the prosecution to attack it first.

Here, the testimony of the Army Commander the Paul would never commit any crimes should have been admitted because it is pertinent to rebut the inference that he was guilty of smuggling. Thus, provided the defense made an offer of proof, (to preserve this objection) this should have been admitted.

VI.   FBI GUIDEBOOK

The judge erred by not admitting this book into evidence. Although it is hearsay, it qualifies under FRE 803 (18) as a learned treatise, assuming that on [sic] of the experts (or the judge by judicial notice) has recognized it as "authoritative." Assuming that it is indeed authoritative, it should have been admitted (by being read to the jury only) undo this hearsay exception.

ANSWER DE–CONSTRUCTION

NEW JERSEY

2005 Bar Examination

Question Number 3

Candidate Sample Answer 1

As you review this sample answer, note the following:

☐ The organizational scheme

New Jersey essays tend to require its candidates to "issue-spot" and this question is no exception. Since it asks for a memorandum *"analyzing all of the trial court's evidentiary rulings,"* the answer uses sub-headings based on the testimony to organize the response:

Operator's Testimony

Police Officer's Testimony

Transcripts of Aliens' Testimony

Recorded Telephone Conversation

Former Commander's Testimony

Ex–FBI Agent's Testimony

FBI Guide

☐ Responsiveness to the question asked

The call-of-the-question requires the candidate to analyze the court's evidentiary rulings, providing the relevant rule support and factual basis. Each paragraph in the answer conforms to this model.

Consider the following response regarding the admissibility of the police officer's testimony:

[Conclusion] "The court's ruling admitting the police officer's testimony was correct. *[General rule]* He had probable cause to

stop the van, after hearing the operator's information. *[Exception]* The statements he heard coming form the van is an exception to hearsay as a statement against penal interest by an unavailable witness. *[Application]* The aliens are legally unavailable because they are in military custody as "enemy combatants." The statement is against penal interest because it identified them as either accomplices in smuggling or the objects of smuggling."

ANSWER DE–CONSTRUCTION

NEW JERSEY

2005 Bar Examination

Question Number 3

Candidate Sample Answer 2

As you review this sample answer, note the following:

☐ Strict compliance with directions by adopting a memo format for the answer

This answer begins with a memorandum heading addressed to the Judge from the Law Clerk as required by the call-of-the-question:

"You are the appellate judge's law clerk assigned to write a memorandum analyzing all of the trial court's evidentiary rulings, citing the factual bases and all applicable rules of law. Prepare the MEMORANDUM"

Interestingly, Sample Answer 1 did not follow this format although it was still selected as a sample answer. While "format" is not a substitute for "substance," it is essential to follow all directions. The inclusion of Candidate Sample Answer 2 illustrates the need to be responsive to the question asked.

☐ A similar organizational structure to Answer 1

☐ Substantive differences between Answer 1 and Answer 2

These sample answers have an important message for bar candidates: there is more than one "right" way to answer the question and that an answer need not be "perfect" to be "point-worthy." This supports the bar examiners' claim that what counts is a well-reasoned analysis of the relevant facts and law, and not necessarily the conclusion reached.

This principle seems operative here because there are several points on which the answers differ:

☐ Answer 1 discusses the admissibility of the ex-FBI agent's testimony as expert testimony whereas Answer 2 fails to mention it at all.

☐ Both Answer 1 and Answer 2 reach the same result with respect to the admissibility of the Operator's note into evidence, but do so by following very different reasoning. Compare them:

Answer 1:

The court's ruling admitting the operator's testimony was correct. The operator's note could be used to refresh the recollection of the operator on the witness stand, as long as it is shown to opposing counsel. The information the operator recounted came from a driver, and the driver's statements are both admissible as hearsay exceptions. The license plate number is a present sense impression, and the statement about Paul's driving is an excited utterance.

Answer 2:

OPERATOR'S NOTE—NO ERROR The operator's note is hearsay. Hearsay is an out of court statement offered for the purpose of proving the truth of the matter asserted. This note that purportedly had Paul's license plate number on it is hearsay, because it was made out of court, and is being offered to prove the truth of its contents (i.e. that Paul drove through the EZ Pass lane). Hearsay is inadvisable [sic] unless an exception applies. Technically, this situation presents a double-level hearsay problem because there are two statements involved: the motorist's comments and note, plus the operator's note derived from this hearsay. Accordingly, both statements must fall within the independent hearsay exceptions to be admissible.

First, the driver's statement describing Paul's license plate number qualifies as a present sense impression. As [sic] present sense impression is a statement made during or immediately after perceiving an event. The motorists' notation of Paul's plate was a present sense impression since she had just observed him run the EZ Pass lane. Thus it is admissible.

Second, the operator's notation of the motorist's note qualifies as a recorded recollection. A recorded recollection exception applies where the witness once made a writing that was truthful and accurate when made, and attempt to refresh the witness's memory has failed, and it otherwise appears trustworthy.

Operator's statement was made by him/her immediately after being told by an eyewitness what the license plate number was. Operator's present memory has failed. There is nothing to suggest that this in [sic] untruthful (in real life, this will be confirmed by the picture of your license plate that they take when you don't pay a toll)(operator said he would have recorded this info correctly). Accordingly, it was not error to permit the pros. to read this to the jury.

Answer 2 recognizes the operator's note as a double-level hearsay problem whereas Answer 1 identifies the hearsay issue by discussing the admissibility of a present sense impression—without ever defining hearsay. Further, Answer 1 discusses the present sense impression and excited utterance exceptions to hearsay while Answer 2 identifies the qualifying exceptions as the present sense impression and the recorded recollection.

☐ Answers 1 and 2 differ as well regarding the admissibility of the statements of the illegal aliens and the FBI Guide.

RELEASED BAR EXAM ESSAY QUESTIONS

CALIFORNIA

California applicants are given three hours to answer each set of three essay questions; if you intend to write an answer to the following question, give yourself one hour in which to do so.

July 2006 Bar Examination

Question Number 1[7]

After paying for his gasoline at Delta Gas, Paul decided to buy two 75–cent candy bars. The Delta Gas store clerk, Clerk, was talking on the telephone, so Paul tossed $1.50 on the counter, pocketed the candy, and headed out. Clerk saw Paul pocket the candy, but had not seen Paul toss down the money. Clerk yelled, "Come back here, thief!" Paul said, "I paid. Look on the counter." Clerk replied, "I've got your license number, and I'm going to call the cops." Paul stopped. He did not want trouble with the police. Clerk told Paul to follow him into the back room to wait for Mark, the store manager, and Paul complied. Clerk closed, but did not lock, the only door to the windowless back room.

Clerk paged Mark, who arrived approximately 25 minutes later and found Paul unconscious in the back room as a result of carbon monoxide poisoning. Mark had been running the engine of his personal truck in the garage adjacent to the back room. When he left to run an errand, he closed the garage, forgot to shut off the engine, and highly toxic carbon monoxide from the exhaust of the running truck had leaked into the seldom used back room. Mark attributed his forgetfulness to his medication, which is known to impair short-term memory.

Paul survived but continues to suffer headaches as a result of the carbon monoxide poisoning. He recalls that, while in the back room, he heard a running engine and felt ill before passing out.

---

7. This is a released California bar exam essay available at www.calbar.ca.gov/calbar /pdfs/admissions/GBX/sf_ 0607_ Essay- Selected _ Answers.pdf. Copyright © 2006, all rights reserved.

A state statute provides: "No person driving or in charge of a motor vehicle shall permit it to stand unattended without first stopping the engine, locking the ignition, removing the key from the ignition, setting the brake thereon and, when standing upon any perceptible grade, turning the front wheels to the curb or side of the highway."

1. Can Paul maintain tort claims against (a) Clerk for false imprisonment and (b) Mark for negligence? Discuss.

2. Is Delta Gas liable for the acts of (a) Clerk and (b) Mark? Discuss.

July 2006 Bar Examination—California

Question Number 1

Answer B[8]

1)

I. *Can Paul maintain tort claims against Clerk for false imprisonment?*

In order to prevail under a claim of an intentional tort, such as false imprisonment, the plaintiff must show an action of the defendant, made with requisite intent, causation and damages. False imprisonment specifically requires the following: (1) an act or omission of the defendant that causes the plaintiff to be restrained to a bounded area. This can be done through a physical act or under an imminent threat. There must be no reasonable means of escape. (2) The defendant must have acted with specific intent to confine or general intent, meaning he acted with substantial certainty that he was acting in the proscribed manner. (3) It was the actions of the defendant that caused the harm to the plaintiff. The action must have been at least a substantial factor. (4) Damages. The plaintiff had to suffer some harm so he must have known of the restraint or suffered damage because of it.

Action of the defendant (C)

In this case, C did ask P to go with him to the back of the store, which P did. Though C may argue P was free to leave, P should argue that he only went to the back room under threat of having trouble with the police. He knew C had taken down his license number, and P arguably was willing to go into the back room so he could have a chance to explain himself. P was put into the room and C closed, though did not lock[,] the only door to the room, which contained no windows. This should be enough to meet the

---

8. The California Committee of Bar Examiners selected two sample answers for this question as it does for many of its questions. Only one answer is reprinted here. You can visit the website at www.calbar.ca. gov/calbar/pdfs/admissions/GBX/sf_ 0607_ Essay-Selected_ Answers.pdf to read Answer A. (last visited September 13, 2007).

requirement that there be no reasonable means of escape. Even though P could have physically opened the door and may have been able to walk out, he was being held there under threat of having to deal with the police.

M may argue that the threat of calling the police should not be considered to be a threat that confined the P. If P was truly innocent, all he would have to do is give his story to the police. Plus, P should have known that his money was still on the counter, and if he could convince C or the police to look for [it], this story would be shown to be true. Therefore, C would argue, P did not really have to stay in this back room[;] it was only P's desire to avoid dealing with the cops that caused him to be back there. This is probably not going to work because the [sic].

Intent

Here, P should argue that C acted with the specific intent to hold P in the bounded area. The facts do support this argument, because C did specifically tell P to go into the back room to wait for Mark, the store manager. C also intentionally made the statement that cause P [to] feel that he had to stay in the back room. Therefore, this element is met.

Causation

The causation element is also met because there is a direct link from C's actions to P being held in the store room. The facts state that P went into the back room after hearing C threaten to call the police.

C may try to argue that, while his action may have caused P to be bounded to the room, it did not cause P's harm because of the intervening force of M. This is discussed below in the section on defenses.

Damages

The facts state that as a result of being held in the back room for 25 minutes, P was knocked unconscious from carbon monoxide poisoning. Therefore, he did suffer actual physical harm at the time. He also continues to suffer headaches as a result of that, so he has ongoing damages. He also may have suffered damage even before being knocked unconscious. The facts state that he recalls feeling ill even before he passed out, so he may have been afraid or suffered emotional distress.

Defenses

Because P does not seem to have met the above elements for a claim of false impri[s]onment against C, C will need to offer up some defenses if he is to shield himself from liability. The following defenses should be considered by C:

Storekeeper privilege

Tort law does permit storekeepers to retain customers suspected of shoplifting. The idea is that storekeepers are permitted to try to recapture their chattels by using reasonable means and holding the suspected thief for a reasonable amount of time. The shopkeeper is protected against making reasonable mistakes as to whether or not the suspect actual stole anything.

In this case, C should argue that he was reasonable to suspect P of shoplifting. There are facts to support this claim[.] C did witness P pocked [sic] the candy and was not aware that P had paid. It is true that P had tossed money on the counter to cover the cost of the candy, but it was reasonable for C not to have seen this. This is because it is customary for customers to pay for items by going up to the cash register and being rung up by the cashier, and giving money directly to the cashier. Clerks are not used to having to look for money dropped on counters to be sure if someone has paid or not. Therefore, C was reasonable to think P was shoplifting, so he was covered by the privilege.

However, P has a very good claim to shoot down this defense. The detention by a shopkeeper asserting this privilege must be reasonable. Here, C hold [sic] P in the back room for 25 minutes while he was waiting for Mark (M) to arrive. Arguably, this is too long to hold someone in a windowless back room by themselves to discuss stealing a candy bar that cost $1.50. C will of course argue it was reasonable for C to make P wait for the manager, and that 25 minutes really is not that long. However, he was held in the back room and was never once checked on to be sure he was okay. This is arguably unreasonable. Also the harm that came to P as a result of being in the room was clearly not reasonable. Therefore, C was outside the bounds of the storekeeper privilege and this defense is not available to him.

Superseding force

As discussed above, C may also want to argue that it was not his tortious act that caused the harm, but rather it was Mark's supervening actions. C would argue that if M had not left his truck running in the garage for so long, the exhaust would have not leaked into the back room and P would not have suffered any damages. Therefore, it is M's negligence (either in merely running the engine or in failing to take his medication) that was the real cause of the harm).

The rule for causation in tort cases is that the defendant's act was a substantial factor. P should easily be able to show that C was a substantial factor in the harm, because C left him there by himself for long [sic]. Therefore, the superseding force will not absolve his liability.

Consent

C may also try to argue that P consented to the imprisonment. Consent is a valid defense against intentional torts. C would argue that P went to the back room of his own volition, because he made the choice to go back there rather than have the police be called by C.

The problem with this defense, P will argue, is that consent must be given voluntarily, and the actions of the defendant must not exceed the bounds of the consent. Here, the consent was not voluntary, because P was acting under threat of having the police be called, even though he did pay for his item. Also, even if P did arguably consent to going into the back room, he surely did not consent to being held for 25 minutes by himself and to suffer such physical harm.

Conclusion

Based on the above, it appears that P does have a tort claim against C for false imprisonment. Though there are defenses that C will try to argue, he will probably not succeed on any of them.

II. *Can P maintain a tort claim against M for negligence?*

A basic cause of action for negligence requires a showing of the following elements: (1) existence of a duty with an accompanying standard of care; (2) a breach of that duty; (3) defendant's actions were the but [-] for and proximate cause of the plaintiff's injury and (4) the plaintiff was actually damaged. Therefore, P must show all of these elements in order to prevail against M for negligence.

Duty and Standard of Care

A duty of care is not owed to all. However, a duty of care is owed to all people who can foreseeably be injured by the actions of the defendant. In this case, the vicinity of P to the area of where M was running his engine would make him a foreseeable plaintiff. M may argue that no duty of care is owed to P because M had no idea P was back there, and had no reason to know because the store room was seldom used. However, this probably will not absolve M of his duty of care, because it is foreseeable that someone will be in the back of the store or garage at some point, and that leaving an engine running for so long in a closed area will cause harm to someone.

The standard of care owed is usually that of a reasonable person acting under similar circumstances and with ordinary prudence. This will be the standard of care applied in this case.

Breach

Now it must be determined if M's conduct fell below the standard of care. There are several ways that P can argue that it does. First, P could argue that M was negligent merely in leaving the engine running for so long in the closed area. Certainly, reasonable people know that they should not allow highly toxic carbon monoxide to fill a small space, especially when the small space is so close to a public business where it is certain people will be found. Second, P could argue that M was negligent because M failed to take his medication. A person who knows that they are likely to forget doing things that would make their actions safe (like, in this case, turning off [the] engine of his truck) arguably should not be engaged in those actions. Here, M must have known of his likelihood of forgetting such things, since he has a prescription for short-term memory impairments. Therefore, he was negligent in failing to remember to take the medication in the first place that would have allowed him to avoid putting P at risk. P should be able to show breach on both of these points, since no reasonable person would leave their car on when it[']s confined to such a small place.

Finally, P may argue that M's action is negligence per se. Negligence per se may arise when there is a statute that provides for penalties, that states the conduct that is required, that is meant to address the sorts of injuries caused [by] the defendant, and that is meant to protect peo[p]le in the plaintiff's position. In this case, P would argue that the state statute is meant to protect people from suffering carbon monoxide poisoning, by requiring everyone to shut off their car before leaving it unattended. Therefore, M's action was covered by the statute, and P's injury was meant to be addres[s]ed by the statute. However, M should be able to strike down this argument fairly easily. M should argue that the point of such statute is to prevent vehicles from causing accidents because the vehicle rolls while being unattended. The language of the statute makes it pretty clear that this is the injury the statute is meant to protect against, since the statute specific[a]lly addresses setting the brake on the vehicle and curbing wheels so the vehicle does not roll. Nothing indicates the statutes is meant to protect against carbon monoxide poisoning.

Causation

C will have to show M's actions were both the but[-]for cause and the proximate cause of his harm. It is the but[-]for, or legal, cause, because were it not for the negligence of the defendant, P clearly would not have suffered any injury. Nothing indicates that he would have suffered such harm just by being in the room. Also, it is the proximate cause. There is a direct link from the actions of the defendant to the harm suffered by P.

M will certainly try to argue that there were superseding forces that were the actual cause of P's harm. His best argument would be that it was C's false imprisonment of P that was the true cause of P's injury. However, superseding forces will not absolve a defendant of negligence unless they are unfor[e]seeable. Here, it should have been foreseeable [to] M that someone, at some point, would go into the back room or even into the garage. The facts do state that the back room is seldom use, which may seem to support M. However, this does mean that the back room is sometimes used. Therefore, the superseding force was foreseeable and will not break the chain of causation.

Damages

As discussed above, P did suffer damages. These damages can be attributed to M's actions just like they can be attributed to C's intentional tort. The likely result is therefore that P will be able to collect from both C and M, as joint and several tortfeasors.

III. Is Delta Gas (DG) liable for the acts of (a) Clark and (b) Mark?

Though the facts do not specifically say it, C and M both appear to be employees of DG. Therefore, if DG is liable for the acts of C or M, they would be liable under the theory of vicarious liability. Vicarious liability states that an employer is liable for the torts of an employee if that employee is acting withing the scope of the employment. The court will consider the time and place of the employee's act, and will also consider if the employee is acting for the benefit of the employer. In general, the scope is broad.

Liability for the tort of C

In this case, DG would argue that C was not acting within the scope of the employment. Certainly, DG would not authorize its employees to commit intentional torts, such as false imprisonment, against its customers.

However, the mere fact that DG did [not] authorize this action will not get it off the hook. All P would have to show to hold DG liable for C's act is that C was acting in the interests of the employer. It is clear that C held P only because he thought P had stolen something from DG. Therefore, C was acting to held [sic] the employer. This is going to be consider[e]d within the scope of employment, even though it was not specifically authorized. Therefore, is [sic] C is going to be liable, so too will DG. P should also point out that C was on the clock and was at the place of employment when the tort occur[r]ed, strengthening the argument that this is within the scope.

Liability for the tort of M

The same rules will apply to determine if DG is liable for the torts of M. M's tort occurred when he was running the engine of his personal truck in the back room of the garage. Nothing indicates that M was on the clock at this time. Also, nothing indicates that M was doing this with any intention of helping employer. Rather, it appears he was doing this only for himself. Therefore, it is unlikely that DG will be liable for the act of M.

The best argument P could make to hold DG liable would be the close proximity of M to the place of employment. However, this probably will not overcome the facts that he was not on the clock and was not acting to benefit the employer.

Independent contractors?

If for some reason C and M are ICs and not employees, then a different standard would apply. Employers of ICs are generally not liable for the torts of ICs. However, they are liable if the tort involves a non-delegable duty, such as the duty of care owed to an invitee. In this case, P would be an invitee of the business, so he would be owed a very high standard of care. The employer would be charged with warning him of any latent dangers that the employer knows or should have known about. Clearly, carbon monoxide is a latent danger, since it is one that is not immediately apparent and cannot be seen. Also, P would argue that the defendants should be charged with knowing when there are gas leaks in the store. It would not matter that they did not have actual knowledge. The standard is that they should have known. Failing to warn of the latent danger would therefore be a breach, and DG would be liable for the torts of M and C, even if they are construed as independent contractors and not employees.

ANSWER DE–CONSTRUCTION

CALIFORNIA

July 2006 Bar Examination

Question Number 1

Candidate Answer B

As you review this sample answer, note the following:

☐ Extensive use of sub-headings

It is helpful to both reader and writer to use sub-headings when answering a question with multiple issues and parties. This candidate did so very nicely, making it easy for the reader to follow the discussion. This would also make it easy for the grader to assign points!

☐ Thoroughness of the response

All possible theories relevant to the question presented are answered in their entirety. Each cause of action is identified and its elements listed and defined. Furthermore, while the question only asks whether Mark might be found liable in negligence, the answer addresses the issue of negligence per se as well since a state statute is cited.

☐ A detailed level of analysis

Not only is each fact in the problem analyzed in light of the relevant rule, but competing interpretations are considered as well. The level of analysis is sophisticated, not superficial. For example, consider the candidate's discussion of the storekeeper's privilege, noting the permissible inferences drawn from the facts:

> "In this case, C should argue that he was reasonable to suspect P of shoplifting. There are facts to support this claim[.] C did witness P pocked [sic] the candy and was not aware that P had paid. It is true that P had tossed money on the counter to cover the cost of the candy, but it was

reasonable for C not to have seen this. This is because it is customary for customers to pay for items by going up to the cash register and being rung up by the cashier, and giving money directly to the cashier. Clerks are not used to having to look for money dropped on counters to be sure if someone has paid or not. Therefore, C was reasonable to think P was shoplifting, so he was covered by the privilege.

However, P has a very good claim to shoot down this defense. The detention by a shopkeeper asserting this privilege must be reasonable. Here, C hold [sic] P in the back room for 25 minutes while he was waiting for Mark (M) to arrive. Arguably, this is too long to hold someone in a windowless back room by themselves to discuss stealing a candy bar that cost $1.50. C will of course argue it was reasonable for C to make P wait for the manager, and that 25 minutes really is not that long. However, he was held in the back room and was never once checked on to be sure he was okay. This is arguably unreasonable. Also the harm that came to P as a result of being in the room was clearly not reasonable. Therefore, C was outside the bounds of the storekeeper privilege and this defense is not available to him."

RELEASED BAR EXAM ESSAY QUESTIONS

FLORIDA

The following question and answer was reprinted from the March 2007 Study Guide released by the Florida Board of Bar Examiners. The answers selected by publication "received high scores and were written by applicants who passed the examination." The Study Guide is updated with the essay questions from the last examination twice annually.[9]

Florida applicants are given three hours to answer each set of three essay questions; if you intend to write an answer to the following question, give yourself one hour in which to do so.

February 2006 Bar Examination

Question Number 2—Florida Constitutional Law

After an extensive study of juvenile crime, the City of Tampa adopted a municipal ordinance that imposes a mandatory curfew on minors between the hours of 1:00 a.m. and 6:00 a.m. The ordinance provides for criminal penalties, including incarceration. The ordinance states dual purposes of preventing criminal activity by minors and preventing criminal activity upon minors.

At 2:00 a.m., Juvenile, a sixteen-year-old Tampa resident, was driving home from a political rally when a tire on Juvenile's car went flat. Juvenile parked the car along the roadside. A passing motorist saw the disabled car and concluded that the driver might need assistance. The motorist called 911.

Within minutes, Officer, a Tampa police officer, arrived at the scene. Officer found Juvenile standing next to a parked car and asked, "What happened?" Juvenile responded, "I have a flat. I don't have any pot, either."

---

9. The Florida Board of Bar Examiners Study Guide is copyrighted and is repro-duced under the express written permission of the Florida Board of Bar Examiners.

Officer placed Juvenile under arrest for violating the curfew. Before placing Juvenile into the rear of the patrol car, Officer searched Juvenile and discovered a baggie containing marijuana in Juvenile's pocket. Officer then arrested Juvenile for both possession of marijuana, a misdemeanor under Florida law, and violating the curfew, a municipal ordinance.

You have been retained to represent Juvenile. Discuss the challenges and defenses that Juvenile may make under the Florida Constitution. Do not discuss whether the City of Tampa is located within a chartered or non-chartered county and the impact such factor may have in a challenge to the ordinance.

February 2006 Bar Examination—Florida

Question Number 2

Candidate Sample Answer [10]

In Florida, municipalities are vested with house rule powers such that they can regulate and exercise traditional municipal powers. These powers include the ability to pass municipal ordinances which affect people in the municipality. Such ordinances may not conflict with the laws of the Florida legislature or impinge upon the Florida Constitution (of course the same applies for the U.S. constitution and federal laws). The supremacy clause restricts overreaching ordinances.

Juvenile (J) has several grounds of complaint under the Florida Constitution. First, Florida has expressly protected its citizens right to privacy, a right which is included in the Declaration of Rights. This protection of privacy goes beyond the protections afforded by the US Constitution, and affords Floridians the right to be left alone. Of course, this right is not absolute and some activities may be regulated even though the regulation may infringe upon the right of privacy. Because the right to privacy is a fundamental right, laws and ordinances that affect it are subject to strict scrutiny. The burden is on the government to show that the regulation is narrowly tailored to achieve a compelling governmental purpose.

The curfew at issue is subject to this strict scrutiny review. The government will argue that it conducted an "extensive study" of juvenile crime and there after determined that the curfew as narrowly tailored to prevent both crime by and upon juveniles. The city certainly has a compelling interest in protecting the health, safety, and welfare of its citizens (and even more certainly, juveniles). However, J will argue that the curfew is not narrowly tailored so as to address this compelling interest. J will argue that the same purpose can be achieved by less restrictive means and that

---

10. The handwritten answers are typed as submitted by the applicant. *See* the Florida Board of Bar Examiners Study Guide at www.floridabarexam.org/ (last visited September 12, 2007).

accordingly the curfew should be struck down. The government bears the burden and thus must overcome the presumption that the curfew is suspect.

J would next assert a violation of the Equal Protection Clause. Florida's constitution prohibits laws discriminating of people based on their gender, race, national origin or physical disability, unless the law meets strict scrutiny review. Other classifications, such as age, need to meet the much more deferential rational basis test. Here, the burden is on the movant to show that the ordinance or law is not rationally related to a legitimate government purpose. This burden lends a presumption to the validity of the law and is difficult to overcome.

J will argue that the curfew fails this test. He will say that simply preventing juveniles from being out during certain hours bears no rational relation to city's interest of protecting juveniles and protecting people from juveniles. The City's "exhaustive" study is likely enough to counter this argument. Because J has the burden, he would likely fail to meet it.

J would next argue that the ordinance may be invalid on its face. The supremacy clause strikes down conflicting state ordinances. The Florida Constitution seeks uniformity of criminal laws throughout the state. This protects Floridians and all others from unknowingly being criminally liable in one place for actions that are permissible elsewhere. Accordingly, J will argue that the imposition of criminal penalties, including incarceration, may not stand. The city would argue that the criminal penalties further the City's interest in juveniles, but would likely fail. An ordinance could be permissible that did not impose such criminal penalties.

J may also argue that his right to be free from illegal search and seizure has been violated. Florida's constitution closely tracks the US constitution in this area. J will allege that officer (O) had no probable cause to search him and thus the marijuana found would be inadmissible against him. J will argue that the simple fact that he had violated the City's curfew did not give rise to a search of his person. O and the city will argue that the search was for either protective purposes (the so called stop and frisk) or that there was probable cause. Either is likely present here, especially given J's unsolicited statement that he didn't have any pot.

J will argue that his statement may not be used against him citing his privilege against self-incrimination. Again, Florida's constitution closely tracks the federal constitution here. J will argue that he should have been read his Miranda rights by O prior to any questioning. O will argue that J was not in custody and that his question ("What happened"") was not intended to, nor did O reasonably believe it would, result in an incriminating statement. Of course, J said that he did not have pot, but it would be strange to think such a statement would be made if J did not indeed have pot. In the alternative, O will argue that J's statement was unsolicited and therefore Miranda rights had not yet attached.

J may also argue that his due process rights have been violated. Florida's constitution protects its citizens from invasion of their life, liberty or pursuit of happiness without due process of law. J will argue that he has a liberty interest in being on the streets at any hour, and that the curfew impermissibly impinges on that interest. This argument is unlikely to succeed because the procedure would be examined under rational basis review. J would nonetheless argue that he should have an opportunity to be heard prior to arrest and that the "mandatory" nature of the curfew is impermissible.

Finally, J may argue his freedom of speech and the right to assembly have been impaired. Florida's constitution permits the right of its citizens to gather and speak without substantial interference. The fact that J was on his way back from a political rally would lend credence to this argument. He would assert that his fundamental rights had been infringed upon (to assemble and speak) and that strict scrutiny review should apply. The city would have the burden again, but may prevail due to the interest in health, safety and welfare.

ANSWER DE–CONSTRUCTION

FLORIDA

2006 Bar Examination

Question Number 2

Candidate Sample Answer

As you review this sample answer, note the following:

☐ Knowledge and application of Florida law

This answer faithfully tracks Florida law with respect to each of the issues raised and discussed. The opening sentence sets the tone and signals to the reader what to expect, *"In Florida, municipalities are vested with house rule powers such that they can regulate and exercise traditional municipal powers."*

Subsequent paragraphs discuss the differences between Florida law and general law, drawing the appropriate distinctions: *"Florida has expressly protected its citizens right to privacy, a right which is included in the Declaration of Rights. This protection of privacy goes beyond the protections afforded by the US Constitution, and affords Floridians the right to be left alone."*

☐ Responsiveness to the call-of-the question

The question asks candidates to limit discussion to the *"challenges and defenses that Juvenile may make under the Florida Constitution."*

The answer complies fully with this direction and each paragraph is constructed around the Juvenile's "challenge" and appropriate "defenses." The following paragraph illustrates this nicely:

"J would next argue that the ordinance may be invalid on its face. The supremacy clause strikes down conflicting state ordinances. The Florida Constitution seeks uniformity of criminal laws throughout the state. This protects Floridians and all others from unknowingly being criminally liable in one place for actions that are permissible elsewhere. Ac-

cordingly, J will argue that the imposition of criminal
penalties, including incarceration, may not stand. The city
would argue that the criminal penalties further the City's
interest in juveniles, but would likely fail. An ordinance
could be permissible that did not impose such criminal
penalties."

☐   IRAC construction

While not as obvious as the New York candidate answers with
their reliance on such signal language as *"The issue is whether"*
and *"Under the law,"* this answer nonetheless conforms to the
basic structure of legal analysis. The following two paragraphs
from the answer are annotated to identify the role of each
sentence in the IRAC equation. As you read, notice how the
organization of the "rule paragraph" sets the structure for the
"analysis paragraph":

> *[Identification of the issue]* J would next assert a violation of
> the Equal Protection Clause. *[General rule]* Florida's consti-
> tution prohibits laws discriminating of people based on
> their gender, race, national origin or physical disability,
> unless the law meets strict scrutiny review. *[Specific rule in
> controversy, i.e., classifications based on age]* Other classifica-
> tions, such as age, need to meet the much more deferential
> rational basis test. *[Rule]* Here, the burden is on the movant
> to show that the ordinance or law is not rationally related to
> a legitimate government purpose. *[Rule]* This burden lends
> a presumption to the validity of the law and is difficult to
> overcome.
>
> [Application, beginning with overall conclusion] J will ar-
> gue that the curfew fails this test. *[Application of rational basis
> rule to the facts]* He will say that simply preventing juveniles
> from being out during certain hours bears no rational
> relation to city's interest of protecting juveniles and pro-
> tecting people from juveniles. *[Counter-argument]* The City's
> "exhaustive" study is likely enough to counter this
> argument. *[Conclusion]* Because J has the burden, he would
> likely fail to meet it.

RELEASED BAR EXAM ESSAY QUESTIONS

Multistate Essay Examination

July 1998

Question Number 5—Family Law[11]

Anna and Ben were contemplating getting married. Ben had been married before and had gone through an unpleasant divorce in which he felt that he had received unfair financial treatment. Ben told Anna he would not marry her unless she signed a premarital agreement with the following provisions: (1) all property acquired prior to or during the marriage will be held separately; (2) Anna waives all rights to alimony; (3) if they divorce or separate, custody of any children will be joint and shared; and (4) in the event Anna obtains sole custody, Ben will not be responsible for child support.

Ben's attorney prepared an agreement incorporating these provisions. Ben attached a complete statement of his financial worth to the agreement and gave it to Anna. He recommended to Anna that she show it to her attorney before signing it. Anna's attorney had serious reservations about the document and suggested she refuse to sign it as drafted. However, Anna who loved Ben and wanted to marry him, signed it anyway without making any changes. Ben and Anna married each other three months after she signed the agreement.

At the time of their marriage, Ben was an investment advisor, with a stock portfolio worth approximately $100,000. Anna was a buyer for a specialty clothing store, making a sizeable salary.

Ben and Anna have now been married for ten years. Anna worked for the first seven years of the marriage. When the second of their two children was born, she left her job permanently to stay home and care for the children, who are now six and three years of age.

---

11. The MEE has been "Reprinted by Permission" from the July 1998 MEE. Copyright © 1999 National Conference of Bar Examiners. All rights reserved.

The marriage has broken down, and both Ben and Anna wish to divorce. Ben's annual salary is $150,000 and his portfolio is worth $500,000 in part due to his annually investing part of his salary during the marriage. Anna has no income. Her only asset is a $10,000 Treasure note that she inherited from her aunt.

In the divorce proceedings, Anna requests a property settlement, including a share of Ben's portfolio, as well as alimony, sole custody of the children, and child support. Ben disagrees and insists that they are bound by the premarital agreement.

How is the court likely to rule on each of Anna's requests? Explain.

July 1998 Multistate Essay Examination

Question 5 Analysis

According to the NCBE, "these model analyses to the MEE are illustrative of the discussions that might appear in excellent answers to the questions. They are provided to the user jurisdictions for the sole purpose of assisting grading in grading the examination. These models are not an official grading guide. Some states grade the MEE on the basis of state law, and jurisdictions are free to modify the analyses, including the suggested weights given to particular points, as they wish. Grading of the MEE is the exclusive responsibility of the jurisdiction using the MEE as part of its admission process."[12]

Legal Prob-   (1) For a premarital contract to be valid, what are
lems: the general requirements and were they met in
                      this case?
            (2) Is a court likely to hold the provisions involving
                      property and/or support unfair?
            (3) Is the court likely to uphold the provision relat-
                      ing to child custody and support?

Point One: (30–40%)

> *The premarital contract is valid because it is in writing, was voluntarily executed, and there was full disclosure.*

Premarital contracts are generally valid if they meet three conditions: they are in writing, they are voluntary, and they are executed after full disclosure. The contract between Anna and Ben is in writing. On the issue of voluntariness, Anna will argue that her consent was not voluntary, as Ben drafted the agreement and refused to marry her unless she signed it. However, Anna did consult with her own attorney and refused to follow his advice not to sign it. The wedding was three months later, not the next day, so she had time to reflect. Under these circumstances, it is unlikely a court would hold that there was duress or coercion sufficient to

---

12. *See* NCBE, Preface to 1998 MEE Questions and Analyses

invalidate the contract. Ben's attachment of his complete financial statement to the draft of the contract before Anna signed it would satisfy any requirement of full disclosure. Therefore, the premarital agreement is valid. The question does not state that Ben signed the agreement, nor does it address Anna's disclosure. However, since it is Anna challenging the agreement, this is not of particular importance although it may be recognized in some answers.

Point Two: (30–40%)

> *The terms of the contract regarding property and spousal support may be evaluated by a court in terms of fairness. However, courts are more likely to set aside provisions affecting support obligations than property settlements. A court may intervene to award Anna alimony.*

Anna will argue that the provisions of the contract stating that all property should be held separately and that she should receive no alimony are fundamentally unfair. Almost all of the property is in Ben's name, although, absent the premarital agreement, under the marital property rules of all jurisdictions she would be entitled to make a claim with respect to the property that was earned after marriage, regardless of title.

Regarding spousal support, at the present time Anna has no independent source of income, has not worked for several years, and has two small children. She has very little property as well.

Although Ben will argue that Anna is bound by the terms of the contract, some courts would at least set aside the provision on spousal support under these circumstances. The support obligation is a traditional and essential part of marriage and divorce, and Anna apparently has the need (and Ben the ability) since she has no other means of support. H. Clark, *The Law of Domestic Relations in the United States*, § 1.9 (2nd ed. 1987).

On the other hand, if the jurisdiction follows the Uniform Premarital Agreement Act (UPAA), then the property distribution and alimony provisions are probably enforceable. Under the UPAA, a premarital agreement will be enforced unless (a) it was not executed voluntarily or (b) it was unconscionable when executed and there was a procedural defect with respect to disclosure of financial information. UPAA § 6, 9B U.L.A. 369. The agreement was executed voluntarily (as discussed above), and there is little, if any, evidence of procedural unfairness here. UPAA, *supra*, § 6. Therefore, at the time of enforcement, even though the provisions are obviously disadvantageous to Anna, and may even be unconscionable, they would not be set aside in these jurisdictions. The UPAA does allow (but does not require) a court to order alimony, notwithstanding a premarital agreement, if the spouse would otherwise become eligible for public support. *Id.*

A sub-issue of fairness is one of timing: should the agreement be reviewed for fairness as of the time of the execution of the contract or as of the time of enforcement? Some courts look to fairness at the time of execution of the contract; others to fairness at the time of enforcement. Ben would argue for fairness at the time of execution, when each had some property and Anna was making a good salary. The UPAA provides that unconscionability should be determined as of the time the agreement was executed. UPAA, *supra* § 6a.

Anna of course would argue that fairness at the time of enforcement is the only realistic measure. It is ten years after the contract was signed. Circumstances have changed and Anna has a need for spousal support, which was not present at the time of execution. She left a well-paying job in order to stay home with the children. If a court is willing to look at fairness (or unconscionability) as of the time of enforcement, Anna is in a good position to have the provision set aside. However, in a jurisdiction which has adopted the UPAA, Anna will be unsuccessful.

Point Three: (30–40%)

> *Provisions in premarital contracts concerning child custody and child support are probably unenforceable and, therefore, these sections of the contract would not be binding on a court.*

It is highly unlikely that provisions in a premarital agreement regarding child custody and child support would be enforceable. Although the ability to contract with respect to child custody is not entirely clear in the UPAA, most courts would hold that child custody should be determined by the court according to the best interests of the child at the time of the divorce or custody hearing, rather than by agreement of the parties prior to marriage. Therefore, a court could and probably would hold that it is not bound by a premarital custody provision. The court hearing Anna and Ben's divorce might decide that they should have joint custody, but this conclusion would be based on a consideration of the children's best interest, not because the contract so provided.

Finally, parents have an absolute obligation to support their children. The UPAA § 3 states that a child's right to support cannot be adversely affected by a premarital agreement. Moreover, federal law requires that each state have child support guidelines which set out a rebuttable presumption with respect to the amount of child support that will be ordered. Deviations from the guideline must be justified by the court through specific findings of fact. The conclusion regarding child support is clearly not enforceable.

CHAPTER 9

Practicing Questions For The Multistate Bar Exam ("MBE")

Learning the black letter law is one activity; practicing with it in preparation for the bar exam is quite another. It's not enough to memorize and understand elements and rules of law without some idea of how the issues present and will be tested. Unless you know what to expect and practice applying what you've learned in the format in which it will be presented, you will not be able to perform as well as you should on exam day.

Preparation for the MBE requires that you combine your knowledge of the theoretical with the practical. Your goal is twofold: to acquire a detailed understanding of the substantive law and to master the specific manner in which it is tested. This chapter will show you how to practice questions for the multistate portion of the bar exam, a major component of nearly every jurisdiction's bar exam. Although the examples and explanations use MBE questions, the suggested approaches are applicable as well to preparing for multiple choice questions that may be part of the state-portion of your exam.

First, you'll need to know what will be tested. Second, you'll need a good source for practice questions—lots and lots of questions. And finally, you'll need a process for working with them.

What Subjects Are Tested

The National Conference of Bar Examiners identify the subjects that are tested and exactly how many questions are presented in each area in its Information Booklet. They are:

- Constitutional Law: 33 questions

- Contracts (including Article 2, Sales): 34 questions where approximately 25% of the questions are based on provisions of the Uniform Commercial Code, Articles 1 and 2.

- Criminal Law and Procedure: 33 questions where approximately 40% of the questions are based on issues arising under the 4th, 5th, and 6th Amendments.

- Evidence: 33 questions

- Real Property: 33 questions

- Torts: 34 questions

Primary Sources for Multiple-Choice Questions

1. Your bar review course

In addition to study materials on the substantive law, bar review courses include hundreds of practice questions. You'll want to use them as you complete sections of the course to help you assess your progress in learning the material.

2. The National Conference of Bar Examiners

The bar examiners are an important source of questions. Periodically, as old MBE questions are retired, the bar examiners release them and make them available. The experience in working with actual MBE questions is invaluable in helping you gain familiarity with the bar examiner's specific use of language and framing of issues.

Working With Multistate Questions

The MBE presents a particular challenge for many students. In addition to testing your knowledge of the substantive law, the

MBE tests reading comprehension and reasoning skills, the ability to work quickly and efficiently, and the capacity to remain focused and in control as you move from one question to the next—all in the span of 1.8 minutes. You can see how preparing for the MBE will be very different from preparing for the essays.

It's important for you to answer as many practice questions as possible during your preparation period. Issues tend to repeat on the MBE and there are only so many ways a particular topic can be tested. Consequently, the more questions you answer, the more likely you are to encounter all the possible issues and the more prepared you will be for them on bar day. Ideally, you should answer thousands of questions. But just "doing questions" is not enough. There is a right way and a wrong way to "do" questions and you need to know the difference.

What Not to Do

Suppose you were to sit at your desk and answer as many multistate questions as you could in 60 minutes. At the end of the hour, you check your answers and tally your score. Then you proceed to do another set of questions, once again tallying the number of correct responses at the end of the session. Assuming you have put in a couple of hours and have "done" about 65 questions or so, you call it a day. You pack up your books and commend yourself for studying for the MBE. But did you?

Let's say you answered half of the questions correctly.

1. Does this mean that you "know" 50% of the material?

2. Can you be sure your correct responses were "correct" for the right reasons?

3. Do you know why your incorrect responses were wrong?

4. Did you select an incorrect answer choice because you didn't know or failed to identify the controlling rule of law?

5. Did you identify the correct rule but apply it incorrectly to the facts?

6. Did you misread the call-of-the-question?

7. Did you misread the facts?

Unless you can answer these questions, the hours you've just spent "doing" questions was pretty much a waste of time. This approach doesn't work because while you may have "answered" questions, you've not learned to "analyze" questions. And you must know how to reason through a question to arrive at the correct answer choice. This means that you must follow a process in answering questions, one that enables you to remain focused, in control, and conscious of your thought process.

This is necessary for still another reason when you are studying: if you answer a question incorrectly, you must go back to that question and reread it, recreating your thought process, retracing your steps, and comparing your reasoning in the two instances to find the flaw in your analysis.

A Two–Part Process for "Doing It" Right

It is important to recognize that there is a major difference between taking the MBE on bar day and preparing for that day. On the actual exam, you'll work at optimum speed and efficiency because you're in the "exam zone." This is uniquely true for MBE questions because there is a rhythm to working with them which can be cultivated through practice.

But this isn't what happens during practice sessions. Does an athlete set world records during practice or during the competition? Clearly, then, how quickly you can "race" through the questions during your practice sessions is of little value. What matters is what you learn when you practice and how you ultimately perform on bar day.

Now that I've told you what not to do, it's time to explain what you should do. The "right way" to work with multiple-choice questions during the preparation period is a two-part process. It's about:

•   Learning how to read and analyze questions

- Learning how to study from them

Part One: How to Read and Analyze Multiple-Choice Questions

Reading a Question

Because of time constraints, you'll have time for only one reading of the fact pattern. However, don't make the mistake of sacrificing a careful reading for a quick one. You must read carefully and actively to spot signal words and legally significant facts. Pay attention to the bar examiners' particular use of language and look for the following as you read:

- Relationships between parties that signal the area of law and legal duties: landlord/tenant, employer/employee, principal/agent, buyer/seller.

- Amounts of money, dates, quantities, and ages.

- Words such as "oral" and "written," "reasonable" and "unreasonable," among others.

- Words that indicate the actor's state of mind. These are critical in Criminal Law and Torts questions.

  Look for such language as:

  intended

  decided

  mistakenly thought

  deliberately

  reasonably believed

Since you may write in the test booklet, circle or highlight these words and others which "legally" characterize the behavior of the actors.

Never "Assume" Facts

The bar examiners carefully construct MBE questions to contain all the facts you need to answer the question. You must rely solely on these facts, and no others, to answer the question. Of course you may draw reasonable inferences from the facts but you cannot fabricate your own or create "what if" scenarios.

In addition to keeping to the facts, don't let yourself go off on tangents based on possible theories you see raised in the facts. Sometimes when you read a fact pattern, you'll see the potential for a number of possible causes of action. In such instances, you must refrain from anticipating what the bar examiners will ask by moving forward on your own and formulating responses based on what you "think" might be asked. This is one of the very reasons you'll read the question stem before you read the fact pattern—to keep from going astray. Potentially, this is just as dangerous as misreading or adding facts. Not only does it lead to possible incorrect answer choices but it needlessly saps your time and mental energy.

Avoid Temptation and Stick to the Law

Just as you must remain focused on the facts as presented in the question, you must apply the rule of law to the facts without hesitation or equivocation. You cannot get emotionally involved with the parties or substitute your instincts for what you know is legally correct. It's not your place to find a criminal defendant not guilty when in fact his actions satisfied every element of the crime according to the statute. Or vice versa: if an act does not violate the provisions of a given statute, then whatever you happen to think about the nature of the act (or actor) doesn't matter. It's not a crime if the jurisdiction doesn't make it one. I cannot say it often enough: your job is to follow the law and apply it to the facts mechanically.

Similarly, the bar exam is not the time or place to become "practical" and consider what you think would happen in actual practice. Many candidates have defended their incorrect answer choices by explaining "I know it couldn't happen like that in practice. That's why I didn't choose that answer." This isn't "real" life. It's the bar exam! This is not to say, however, that bar exam questions have nothing to do with the practice of law or the "real rules." It's just that on the bar exam, as in law school, we are studying and working with the theoretical rule of law and what should be, not necessarily what is. The bar exam is no time to worry about the great divide between theory and practice—simply apply the rule of law as you've learned it to answer the questions and you'll be fine.

MBE QUESTION WORKSHEET

Subject Area: _____

What is happening?

_____

_____

_____

Isolate the legally relevant facts:

_____

_____

Steps of Analysis:

(1) What is the legal issue?

_____

(2) What rule of law addresses this issue?

_____

_____

(3) What should be the outcome?

_____

_____

Identify the issue in each answer choice:

(A) _____

(B) _____

(C) _____

(D) _____

(4) What answer choice best corresponds to my answer?

Analyzing the Question

MBE questions adhere to a particular structure. There is a story or fact pattern followed by the interrogatory or "call-of-the question." While most questions follow this format, in some cases you'll have one fact setting and a series of questions based on those facts. Here, each of the questions will provide additional facts or change the facts in some way so you must be sure to read each question as if it were a new question entirely.

Perhaps because of the stringent time constraints on the MBE, the tendency to panic is greatest on this section of the bar exam. But when you panic, you're no longer in control. When you give up control, you're at the mercy of the answer choices. Then they pick you, instead of the other way around. I'm not going to let you fall into this trap. Instead, each time you answer an MBE question, you're going to "act" in response to the question presented and not "react" to the answer choices. How do you act and not react to the answer choices? *Simple: you have an answer in mind before you even look at the answer choices.*

There are four basic steps for answering an MBE question. You will follow this sequence for every question you practice and on bar day. After a bit of practice, the process will become second nature to you, although initially it will seem artificial, almost contrived, to approach a question this way. But you'll soon see that it yields results.

MBE Question Worksheet

As you practice this approach, you might want to make copies of the MBE Question Worksheet to track your reasoning process until it becomes second nature.

For each question, you will:

1. Read the *call-of-the-question* or stem and then read the fact pattern

2. Find the *issue* in the facts

3. Identify the *rule* that addresses the issue

4. Reach a *conclusion* without looking at the answer choices

5. Fill the gap from your answer to the best answer choice by translating your answer to match one of the options

Let's look at each step in detail:

(1) Read from the "bottom up"

Begin each MBE question by reading the question stem. Reading the interrogatory first serves two important functions:

- It helps to identify the area of law. Often, but not always, you can determine the subject area of the problem from the call-of-the-question. Then you can use this information to inform your subsequent reading of the fact pattern.

- It often identifies the point of view you must adopt to answer the question. For example, if you're asked to determine a party's most likely claim or best defense, then you'll want to read the fact pattern with an emphasis on that party's point of view.

(2) Find the issue in the facts

Note: While MBE questions are issue-based, analytical questions, not every multiple choice question is structured this way. Sometimes the question is straightforward and you either know the answer or you don't. If you have one of these questions, you'll eliminate the issue-formation steps.

After reading the interrogatory, you're ready to read the fact pattern and find the issue. Your ability to identify the main issue in each question is crucial to selecting the correct answer choice. For most candidates, it's not intuitive to engage in an IRAC analysis to answer an objective multiple choice question. However, MBE questions are organized around a central issue in the fact pattern and individual issues in each of the responses. The only way to distinguish between the answer choices is to identify the legal question raised in the fact pattern.

The process is the same you use to spot issues in essay questions. After you read the call-of-the-question ask, *"What is the legal theory behind this question?* As soon as you've identified the legal theory, you're in a position to articulate the rule of law that addresses that issue.

(3) Move from the issue to the rule to articulation of the answer

After you've identified the issue raised in the facts, determine the appropriate rule of law, apply the rule to the facts, and reach a conclusion—all without so much as a peek at the answer choices. By determining the appropriate outcome before looking at the answer choices, you're in control and not at the mercy of the bar examiners' distractors.

However, this approach is not practical when you have the type of question where the answer choices provide additional information which must be individually evaluated. This happens where you're asked a question such as

"Which of the following questions will NOT present a substantial issue in Plaintiff's claim for damages"

as opposed to

"Will Dan prevail?"

In the first example, you must consider the merits of each individual answer choice before you can make a decision whereas in the second you can form your own answer based solely on the fact pattern.

(4) Fill the gap from "answer" to "answer choice"

After you've decided what the answer should be, you're ready to look at the answer choices. Don't expect the bar examiners to phrase the answer in precisely the words you're looking for—these words won't be there. Instead, you'll have to "fill the gap" between your words and the words the bar examiners have chosen to express the answer. And they do such a good job of camouflage that candidates often don't recognize the correct response even though it "says" exactly what they want! *Sometimes it's a matter of determining which of the answer choices leads to the same result.*

Consider the following MBE question, where the array of answer choices nicely illustrates the dangers that await the unwary candidate:

Hydro–King, Inc. a high-volume, pleasure-boat retailer, entered into a written contract with Boater, signed by both parties, to sell Boater a power boat for $12,000. The manufacturer's price of the boat delivered to Hydro–King was $9,500. As the contract provided, Boater paid Hydro–King $4,000 in advance and promised to pay the full balance upon delivery of the boat. The contract contained no provision for liquidated damages. Prior to the agreed delivery date, Boater notified Hydro–King that he would be financially unable to conclude the purchase; and Hydro–King thereupon resold the same boat that Boater had ordered to a third person for $12,000 cash.

If Boater sues Hydro–King for restitution of the $4,000 advance payment, which of the following should the court decide?

(A) Boater's claim should be denied, because, as the party in default, he is deemed to have lost any right to restitution of a benefit conferred on Hydro–King.

(B) Boater's claim should be denied, because, but for his repudiation, Hydro–King would have made a profit on two boat sales instead of one.

(C) Boater's claim should be upheld in the amount of $4,000 minus the amount of Hydro–King's lost profit under its contract with Boater.

(D) Boater's claims should be upheld in the amount of $3,500 ($4,000 minus $500 as statutory damages under the UCC).

In this question, the issue is what, if anything, is a buyer entitled to when the buyer repudiates a sale and the seller re-sells the item but would have sold it to the second buyer anyway? It's the classic case of the lost volume seller. Application of the rule tells us that the seller is entitled to receive his lost profit on the first deal—the one he made with the repudiating seller. Under these facts, that would be $2,500 (the sales price of $12,000 minus the manufacturer's cost of $9,500). So Hydro–King would have made a $2,500 profit from Boater and is entitled to keep $2,500 of the $4,000 advance payment and Boater gets back $1,500.

Now I'm ready to find this answer among the answer choices. Of course, it's not going to appear in precisely these words. Instead, I'll have to determine which of the answer choices leads to the same result. Answer Choice (C), the correct answer, effectively states the result I've reached. Boater's claim is $4,000—less Hydro–King's lost profit. Answer Choice (B) is not completely correct because while it acknowledges Hydro–King's entitlement to its profit on both sales, it requires that Boater's claim be denied in its entirety. As we know, this need not be the case where, as here, the advance payment was in excess of the lost profit.

Analyzing the Answer Choices

It is important to recognize that analysis of the answer choices deserves as much of your time and attention as the fact pattern or story. Maybe more.

(1) Identify the issue in each answer choice

Not only is there an "issue" in the fact pattern, but there is an "issue" in each answer choice. Actually, it's more of a legal theory that's operating in each of the answer choices and unless you figure out the individual theories, you won't be able to distinguish between the answer choices. Only the issue that addresses and answers the one presented in the fact pattern can be the correct answer choice.

(2) If necessary, use "the process of elimination"

Sometimes, despite all your best efforts to work through a question according to the process outlined here, you may find that the only way to arrive at an answer choice is through the process of elimination. As we discussed, the bar examiners are particularly adept at "hiding the ball" by expressing the correct answer in a way that's less than obvious.

In these cases, you'll have to examine each of the answer choices and eliminate those that can't possibly be correct. You've already learned how to eliminate an incorrect answer choice based on whether its legal theory addresses the issue in the fact pattern. Now you'll learn some other common devices for eliminating incorrect answer choices. Even though you may be using techniques to answer the questions, you're still "acting" and not merely "reacting" to whatever sounds reasonable.

When can't an answer choice be correct?

(a) When it's not completely correct

The first rule for eliminating incorrect answer choices is that an answer choice must be entirely correct or it is wrong. For example, suppose an answer choice recites a correct statement of the rule of law but its application to the facts in the problem is flawed. Or vice versa: perhaps the answer choice is factually correct but cites an inapplicable rule. In each case, the answer choice is incorrect and can be eliminated. Don't be misled simply because the statement is partially correct.

(b) When it misstates or misapplies a rule of law

Here's where solid preparation on learning the black letter law is essential. You need to know the law to distinguish between answer choices that misstate or misapply the law.

Some common examples include the following:

- Answer choices that improperly identify the requisite elements of a crime or tort by either overstating or understating the necessary elements.

- Answer choices that rely on inapplicable principles of law.

For example, since the MBE has adopted Article 2 of the Uniform Commercial Code, you must be sure to apply its principles to questions involving transactions in goods. If you apply a common law rule to resolve the issue, you'll reach the wrong result and you can be sure it's one of the answer choices purposely included to distract you. For instance, where the common law and the UCC diverge on such points as the requirements for modifications, option contracts, and acceptances, the bar examiners find fertile grounds for test questions.

This is by no means limited to contracts. Look for similar situations to arise in other areas of law. Evidence questions are another good example. Here the potential conflict is between the Federal Rules of Evidence, the common law, and the rules of your particular jurisdiction. The MBE requires that Evidence questions be answered according to the Federal Rules.

- Answer choices that rely on the minority rule instead of the majority rule.

The rule to be applied on the MBE is the majority rule, not the minority. It no longer matters what your Contracts or Torts professor argued "should" be the prevailing view; what counts on the MBE is the modern, prevailing view. Learn it and apply it unless directed otherwise.

(c) When the answer choice mischaracterizes the facts

Once again, active reading skills will go far in detecting this type of error. Look for contradictions between the facts in the story and the facts as characterized in the answer choice. Such an answer choice cannot be correct. Nor can an answer choice that requires you to make assumptions that go beyond the facts in the fact pattern. While it's often necessary to make reasonable inferences, you should never have to add facts to arrive at the correct answer choice. If the bar examiners want you to consider additional or different facts, they will provide them.

(3) Watch out for "because," "if," and "unless"

Just when you thought it safe to answer a question, leave it to the bar examiners to muddy the waters with a single word. You'd think it would be enough to have four answer choices to test a candidate's ability to work through the details without resorting to further modification of the text of each alternative. But the bar examiners are experts at getting the most out of a question. With a single, well-placed word such as "because," "if," or "unless," they're able to transform the entire meaning of a sentence—and unless you're careful, your score!

While doable, dealing with "because," "if," and "unless" takes a bit of practice. It also takes active and careful reading. A "modifier"—whether it's "because," "if," "unless," or some equivalent—is used in the answer choice to connect the "conclusion" (the outcome to the interrogatory) with the "reasoning" in support of that conclusion. For example, an answer choice might state,

"Yes, because Dan was a third-party beneficiary of the original Smith–Jones agreement."

Here, "yes" is the "conclusion" or direct answer to the question asked; "Dan was a third-party beneficiary" is the reason that supports the conclusion; and "because" is the link between the two.

(a) Working with "because"

On the MBE, "because" is the predominant modifier and the simplest to master. The following is a typical "because" answer choice:

"Succeed, because Ben had promised her that the offer would remain open until May 15."

Such "because" statements are relatively straightforward. Simply ensure that the reasoning supports the conclusion both on a factual and legal basis. If either is incorrect, then the entire answer choice is incorrect and can be eliminated.

In addition to "because," remember to look for words that act like "because" in answer choices such as "since" and "as." These words are synonyms and serve the same function as 'because." Your analysis will be the same.

(b) Working with "if"

Unlike "because," when "if" is the answer choice modifier, you need determine only whether the reasoning could support the conclusion. It need not always be true, but only possible under the facts in the hypothetical. Be alert to possible "if" synonyms: "as long as" and "so long as." Remember, "if" is a conditional word and words of condition will be the trigger in such instances.

Consider the following example from a past MBE:

Dora, who was eight years old, went to the grocery store with her mother. Dora pushed the grocery cart while her mother put items into it. Dora's mother remained near Dora at all times. Peterson, another customer in the store, noticed Dora pushing the cart in a manner that caused Peterson no concern. A short time later, the cart Dora was pushing struck Peterson in the knee, inflicting serious injury.

If Peterson brings an action, based on negligence, against Dora's mother, will Peterson prevail?

    (A) Yes, if Dora was negligent.

    (B) Yes, because Dora's mother is responsible for any harm caused by Dora.

    (C) Yes, because Dora's mother assumed the risk of her child's actions.

    (D) Yes, if Dora's mother did not adequately supervise Dora's actions.

Let's examine the "if" answer choices employing our understanding that an "if" answer need only be plausible, based on the facts, to be correct. Remember, before you get to the answer choices, you've already formulated your own possible answer based on the interrogatory. Here, since the problem is based on an action brought in negligence, your mind should be ticking off the elements of a negligence claim: duty, breach, causation, harm.

Answer Choice (A) states that Peterson will prevail in a negligence action *if* Dora was negligent. The question stem states, however, that Peterson brought the negligence action against Dora's mother, not Dora. Thus, since Answer Choice (A) doesn't directly address the question, it can't be the best answer.

On the other hand, Answer Choice (D) addresses the issue of Dora's mother's actions. It poses the situation where Dora's mother did not adequately supervise Dora. You need to ask yourself whether in this instance a finding of negligence is possible: does Dora's mother have a duty to supervise her child and would she have breached that duty if she failed to do so? In this case, she would be negligent so (D) is the correct answer choice.

(c) Working with "unless"

In its own way, "unless" is as restrictive as "because." For an "unless" answer choice to be correct, it must present the *only* circumstance under which the conclusion cannot happen. If you can conceive of even one other way the result could occur, then the answer choice cannot be correct.

Consider the following example from a past MBE.

David built in his backyard a garage that encroached two feet across the property line onto property owned by his neighbor, Prudence. Thereafter, David sold his property to Drake. Prudence was unaware, prior to David's sale to

Drake, of the encroachment of the garage onto her property. When she thereafter learned of the encroachment, she sued David for damages in trespass.

In this action, will Prudence prevail?

(A) No, unless David was aware of the encroachment when the garage was built.

(B) No, because David no longer owns or possesses the garage.

(C) Yes, because David knew where the garage was located, whether or not he knew where the property line was.

(D) Yes, unless Drake was aware of the encroachment when he purchased the property.

Let's look at Choice A, the first of our two "unless" answer choices. Applying the "unless" strategy, you would ask yourself: "Is there any way Prudence could prevail if David was unaware of the encroachment when the garage was built?" Remember, as soon as you read the call-of-the-question, you considered the definition of trespass: one who intentionally enters the land of another. All David had to do was intend to build the garage and then build it. It doesn't matter whether he was aware or unaware of the encroachment in order to commit a trespass. Consequently, Prudence could prevail and Choice A cannot be correct.

Now let's look at Choice D. This answer choice brings Drake, the subsequent purchaser of the property, into the picture. Here's a good example of eliminating an answer choice because it doesn't address the issue in the problem. Prudence has brought the trespass action against David, not Drake. Assuming, however, that you didn't see this and instead was transfixed by the "unless" modifier, you'd come to the same result but it would take longer. You'd ask, "Is there any way Prudence could prevail if Drake was unaware of the encroachment when he purchased the property?" Now you'd see that Prudence could prevail in an action against David if Drake was unaware of the encroachment. Whether Prudence has an action in trespass against Drake is simply not the issue in this question and should not be a factor in your analysis.

Choice C is the correct answer choice. The reasoning addresses the central issue in the problem which is whether David committed a trespass. What Choice C states is right on point—both legally and factually. Legally, David would have committed a trespass if he intentionally entered the land of another. The facts tell us that David built a garage that encroached on his neighbor's property. Choice C fits all the criteria and must be correct.

(4) If you must guess, do so with a strategy

While it sounds like an oxymoron to "guess with a strategy," it's true nonetheless. You've absolutely nothing to lose by guessing since there are no penalties for incorrect answers on the MBE. Even if you can narrow the odds only slightly, you've got a decent shot at making a correct selection.

(a) Eliminate all the obviously incorrect answer choices

Usually you can safely eliminate one or even two responses as incorrect. Now that you've narrowed the field a bit, even if it's a little bit, you're ready to make the most of some informed guesses.

(b) Dismiss answer choices that address other principles or unrelated rules of law

Of course the bar examiners won't be so obvious as to include evidence principles in answer choices for contracts questions, but they will include common law rules in Article 2 sales problems and cite standards for negligence when strict liability is at issue.

Similarly, be alert to answer choices that seem to be from the applicable body of law but really are not. Such distractors are common in "cross-over" areas where the distinctions between subjects are blurred and somewhat artificial. For example, problems in Criminal Procedure may contain answer choices that draw on rules from Constitutional Law and Evidence. Remember, it's law school that imposes boundaries around the law for pedagogical purposes. The law itself does not impose such rigid demarcations.

On the other hand, do not be quick to dismiss all such cross-overs. Remember, contracts for the sale of land, while topically in property law, still require application of contract principles. And breach of warranty, while a traditional contract claim, is often asserted in products liability actions.

(c) Find your compass—the issue

When in doubt anywhere on the bar exam—the essays, the MPT, or the MBE—remember that the legal issue is your guide. It allows you to distinguish between relevant and irrelevant rules and facts, thus providing the single most effective answer choice eliminator.

Reread the question and focus solely on finding the issue in the fact pattern. Then identify the issue in each of the answer choices. One answer should be responsive to the issue in the fact pattern.

(d) Be wary of words which speak in absolutes

Assuming that the issue is disguised, then you still need to distinguish between answer choices. In this case, carefully consider statements that include such words as "always," "never," and "must." No doubt you learned as a first year law student that there are few if any certainties in the law. For practically every rule, there is an exception—if not two or three. Use this knowledge wisely and be wary of answer choices which include words of certainty. *If you can think of just one instance where it wouldn't be true, then the statement can't possibly be your best choice and you can safely eliminate it.*

(e) Finally, after you've given it your best shot, move on

With only 1.8 minutes per question, there's only so much time to allow for doubt. No matter how well you've prepared, there are bound to be questions that present difficulty. Just don't dwell on them or you'll squander precious time that could be spent on questions you can answer.

Part Two: How to Practice Multiple-Choice Questions

This part of your work is about how to study from the questions to learn the law. It focuses on developing your knowledge of the substantive law by working through targeted, subject-specific questions.

The Difference Between Studying and Taking the Exam

There is a huge difference between studying for the exam and taking it. Yet the more I work with students, the more I realize that they don't know the difference.

When studying, your primary goal is to learn the black letter law and how the bar examiners test that law. It is to use the questions to learn the material and find out what you don't know and why. At this point, it is not to test and grade yourself. However, our instinct when working with multiple-choice questions is to choose an answer, check it, and move on to the next question. Or we "do" blocks of questions and tally up the score, taking comfort if the number of correct answers choices are greater than 50%. In either case, no real knowledge is gained and genuine learning opportunities are lost.

Here's What You Should Be Doing

Suppose you are trying to answer a question and find you're not quite sure of the rule. You can't identify all the elements or you can't recall the specific language of the exception. Now is the time to look it up. It is not "cheating" to look up the rule to help you work through an analysis of the question. This is learning through repetition and reinforcement. The process of going back to your subject outlines and study notes to help you work through a specific problem is learning in context and an essential part of the study process.

Consider the following approaches when using multiple-choice questions to study the black letter law. They ensure a maximize return on your investment of time and effort.

(1) The "numbers" factor and de-constructing MBE questions

As mentioned earlier, you should be prepared to answer hundreds, if not thousands, of multiple-choice questions. Having said that, it is not so much the quantity of questions that you answer as the quality of the process involved in answering each question.

If you answer a question according to the process outlined here for analyzing a question and its answer choices, you will be reviewing four to five related rules of law each time you work your way through a single question. Not only are you working with multiple rules per question, but the rules are related by issue and presented in a factual context which aids in memory retention. You will remember the rules of law you learn in association with these multiple-choice questions because they are rooted in a factual context.

Let's see how this works. Consider the following MBE question:

Frank owned two adjacent parcels, Blackacre and Whiteacre. Blackacre fronts on a poor unpaved public road, while Whiteacre fronts on Route 20, a paved major highway. Fifteen years ago, Frank conveyed to his son, Sam, Blackacre "together with a right-of-way 25 feet wide over the east side of Whiteacre to Route 20." At that time, Blackacre was improved with a ten-unit motel.

Ten years ago, Frank died. His will devised Whiteacre "to my son, Sam, for life, remainder to my daughter, Doris." Five years ago, Sam executed an instrument in the proper form of a deed, purporting to convey Blackacre and Whiteacre to Joe in fee simple. Joe then enlarged the motel to 12 units. Six months ago, Sam died and Doris took possession of Whiteacre. She brought an appropriate action to enjoin Joe from using the right-of-way.

In this action, who should prevail?

(A) Doris, because merger extinguished the easement.

(B) Doris, because Joe has overburdened the easement.

(C) Joe, because he has an easement by necessity.

(D) Joe, because he has the easement granted by Frank to Sam.

It is easy enough to see that to answer this question, you must know the rule regarding easements. But clearly you need to know more than just the basic definition to answer this question. If used properly, this question and its four answer choices provide an opportunity for you to review the general rule of easements and four inter-related issues:

- creating easements

- terminating easements

- nature and types of easements

- transferring easements

Here's where most bar candidates fail to make use of a critical learning opportunity: instead of taking the time to analyze each of the answer choices and review the substantive law implicated in each, the candidate selects an answer and moves on. Of course this is the proper way to proceed on the exam or when practicing under simulated test conditions but not when you're studying. It's incorrect because even if you've selected the correct answer, you need to make sure you know *why* each of the other answer choices is incorrect. It's not enough to have a vague understanding of why they are wrong: you must be able to fully articulate the reason based on the applicable rule of law.

I can practically hear you thinking that there's not enough time in the world to study this way and certainly not when preparing for the bar exam. Once again, you're wrong. To borrow a very old, but appropriate expression, you're being "penny wise and pound foolish."

That's because of the way MBE questions are constructed. Answer choices are carefully crafted to represent the range of issues associated with the main issue in the question. Consequently, while it might be the incorrect answer choice for this question, it might be the right answer next time, given a different emphasis in the fact pattern. As I mentioned earlier, issues tend to repeat on the MBE and there are only so many ways a particular topic can be tested. You need to know the main issues and the related bundle of sub-issues and there is no better way to see how they come together than by de-constructing each MBE question during your study time.

Since I know you cannot read a multiple-choice question without answering it, the correct answer to this question is (D). Can you explain why? Can you explain why each of the other answer choices is incorrect?

(2) How long this takes

It should take approximately 1½ to 2 hours to answer about 15 to 20 questions if you work through them the way I've just outlined. This may seem like a very long time to do so few questions but if you consider that you've reviewed approximately 30 to 40 points of law in the process, then you'll realize just how much you've learned.

(3) The timing factor

Although we discussed the importance of incorporating timed practice exams into your study schedule in an earlier chapter, it's important to review it again with respect to practicing MBE questions.

If your goal when practicing Multistate questions (or any part of the exam) is to learn from the questions, then how long it takes to read and answer a question is not the primary concern. Rather, it's whether you absorbed anything meaningful from the exercise. It doesn't matter how long it takes to answer a question, but whether you answered the question correctly and did so for the correct reason. Even without focusing on the clock, your speed will increase naturally with practice as you become comfortable with the process of analyzing questions and more competent with the law.

Still, I strongly recommend that you include a minimum of two or three "timed" sessions when preparing for the MBE. The first session should occur about three weeks into your review period and be devoted to determining whether you can meet the general guideline of answering 17 questions in a 30–minute period. You must average 33—34 questions per hour to complete the 100 questions in the three-hour MBE sessions.

Also, you should plan to include at least one practice session to be a simulation of a complete three-hour test period covering 100 questions. This should occur about two weeks before the actual bar exam. You need to know whether you can sustain your concentration for such a long period of time. It's a very different experience to answer 100 questions than it is to answer 25 questions. It's also a different experience when the questions come at you in a completely random manner as opposed to the topical approach you've been following during your practice sessions where you know the general subject matter of the questions. Unless you've had an opportunity to perform under these conditions, you won't be able to assess your performance accurately.

Assuming your test session begins at 9:15 and ends at 12:15, the following is a timetable with appropriate milestones:

Time	Question Number
9:45	17
10:15	33
10:45	50
11:15	67
11:45	84
12:15	100

When to Practice Questions

You are not ready to work with questions until you've studied the black letter law. There is limited value, if any, in trying to answer questions before you've studied the rules. But working through questions *after* you've studied will give you a pretty good indication of what you know and what you still have to learn.

Still, this doesn't mean that you can afford to wait too long before you move from studying your notes to answering questions. Working with rules as you learn them by applying them in the context of new factual situations is the most effective way to find out what you really know. You should incorporate questions as part of your study plan as soon as you've covered a topic in your bar review course.

You are ready to begin practicing questions when you have:

- Completed the sessions of your bar review class in an area of the law, and

- Reviewed your notes with a focus on the black letter law

Note: Do not wait until you feel you have memorized the black letter law before you begin practicing questions. You will learn the law as you work through the questions.

Target a Topic

Let's assume you've attended the bar review lectures on contract formation under both the common law and the UCC. You've reviewed your notes and otherwise "studied" contract formation. You're convinced that you pretty much know what you need to know about offer and acceptance.

Now, and only now, are you ready to apply what you've learned to answering the questions.

Begin by selecting a group of questions from the specific area of law you've just reviewed. In this case, you're going to answer only questions dealing with contract formation issues.

Note: When you order sample MBE questions from the bar examiners, you're sent an actual 200–item exam. Therefore, you'll have to peruse the answer key which identifies questions by topic. Select a topic and make a list of those question numbers on your answer sheet. Follow the list when answering the questions.

By practicing groups of questions in a particular area of the law, you can:

- Identify your strengths and weaknesses

If you consistently answer questions dealing with a particular rule of law incorrectly, this means that you need to return to your notes and review that topic more thoroughly before attempting more MBE questions. You simply don't know the law well enough.

- Begin to see patterns in the facts

When you practice questions of a particular type together, you can see their common characteristics and realize that there are only so many variations of a fact pattern with respect to a single legal issue. This allows you to become familiar with the way particular topics are tested. As a result, your comfort level increases.

- Become familiar with the bar examiners' specific use of language

In addition to becoming familiar with the types of facts that invoke certain rules, by working with groups of questions in a particular area, you also become accustomed to the bar examiners' very specific use of vocabulary. Frequently, the difference between a correct and incorrect answer choice turns on the meaning and significance attached to particular language in the fact pattern. Your ability to identify such words is critical and only practice with actual MBE questions will provide the opportunity to gain this familiarity.

The following MBE question shows that you must be attuned to the signals in the language as well as the rules:

> Structo contracted with Bailey to construct for $500,000 a warehouse and an access driveway at a highway level. Shortly after commencing work on the driveway, which required for the specified level some excavation and removal of surface material, Structo unexpectedly encountered a large mass of solid rock.
>
> For this question only, assume the following facts. Structo informed Bailey (accurately) that because of the rock the driveway as specified would cost at least $20,000 more than figured, and demanded for that reason a total contract price of $520,000. Since Bailey was expecting warehousing customers immediately after the agreed completion date, he signed a writing promising to pay the additional $20,000. Following timely completion of the warehouse and driveway, which conformed to the contract in all respects, Bailey refused to pay Structo more than $500,000.
>
> What is the maximum amount to which Structo is entitled?
>
> (A) $500,000, because there was no consideration for Bailey's promise to pay the additional $20,000.
>
> (B) $500,000, because Bailey's promise to pay the additional $20,000 was exacted under duress.
>
> (C) $520,000, because the modification was fair and was made in the light of circumstances not anticipated by the parties when the original contract was made.

> (D) $520,000, provided that the reasonable value of Structo's total performance was that much or more.

Here, your ability to select the correct answer choice depends on whether you attach the appropriate legal significance to two words that appear in the fact pattern: "unexpectedly" and "accurately." If you read quickly, instead of actively, it's very easy to miss the signal language:

> First, that finding a solid mass of rock was *unanticipated* ("unexpected"), and

> Second, that Structo was acting in *good faith* ("accurately") when he told Bailey that the cost of putting in the driveway would cost more than originally contemplated.

Unless you draw the appropriate inferences from these words, you won't conclude that the parties entered into a valid modification when Structo asked for more money to complete the job which required more work than originally bargained for by the parties and Bailey signed a writing promising to pay the additional $20,000.

Instead, you'll find a lack of consideration (Answer Choice A), be led down the path of coercion (Answer Choice B), or possibly allow a recovery in restitution (Answer Choice D). Sadly, each incorrect answer choice would be for "want of a word."

While time is indeed a pressing factor, you can see that it's more important to read actively than it is to read quickly. Fortunately, it's far easier to become an active reader than it is to become a faster reader. It just takes practice.

Answer One Question at a Time

The most effective way to study from multiple-choice questions is to answer one at a time using the process outlined above. By checking your answer choice right after you've selected it, the fact pattern is still fresh in your mind and, hopefully, so is your reasoning for choosing that answer. Getting immediate feedback on your analysis of the question serves two functions: first, it reinforces your understanding of the rule if your answer choice was correct; and second, it allows you to assess quickly the flaw in your reasoning if your answer choice was incorrect.

(1) If you answered correctly

Read the explanation for the correct answer choice if explanations are available. Even if you answered correctly, you want to make sure that you did so for the right reason. Further, if you don't fully appreciate the explanation offered for the correct answer choice or can't provide one of your own, then you must return to your study materials and review the law until you can do so. These are the only ways to ensure that you fully comprehend a topic.

Many a candidate will get an answer "correct" for an "incorrect" reason and therefore can't rely on really "knowing" the material. So if you arrived at the "right" answer for the "wrong" reason, proceed as if you answered incorrectly.

(2) If you answered incorrectly

If you answer a question incorrectly when practicing multiple choice questions, you must go back to that question and reread it to recall what you were thinking the first time you read the question.

Specifically, your task is to recreate your thought process, retrace your steps, and compare your reasoning in the two instances to find the flaw in your analysis. This may be the only way to figure out how and where you made the mistake. Until you know why you select wrong answer choices, you can't make the necessary corrections. That's why it's essential—*absolutely essential*—that you answer only one question at a time. If you try to answer more than one at a time, you won't remember what you were thinking when you selected an answer choice with respect to a particular question. Self-awareness is essential to the analytical process.

How to proceed if you answered incorrectly:

If you made an incorrect answer choice, you must go back to the question and read it again, beginning with the stem. As you read, pay close attention to what you are thinking and compare what you are thinking now to the first time you read the question.

What's most important in this exercise is the real-time feedback. If I were sitting with you while you were reading, I would stop you every 30 seconds or so and ask you to tell me what you were thinking. This forces you to put into words exactly what's going on in your head at the moment, something you're probably not doing—at least not consciously— and you must do it. That's because the only way to identify if you've gone down a wrong path is while your thoughts are still fresh in your mind.

You can learn to see why a thought is the wrong one to be having at the time by answering the questions I've posed for you below. Even though I'm not with you to lead you through the steps, you can do it for yourself by asking the questions I would ask:

(1) Look at the question stem: was my first answer choice one that answered the precise question that was asked?

(2) As I re-read the fact pattern, am I noticing facts that I overlooked the first time?

(3) Did I confuse the parties and that's why I evaluated the problem incorrectly?

(4) Did I overlook such legally significant words as "reasonable," "unexpectedly," or "accurately"?

(5) Do I find my mind wandering as I read?

(6) Am I rereading the same sentence because I have trouble remembering what I've just read?

(7) Am I reading into the problem words and facts that are not there?

The problem addressed in question #7 is difficult to detect, but it is a primary reason for incorrect answer choices. You therefore must find out if this is something you do. This is how:

- Start by examining your incorrect answer choice. Re-read it and ask yourself what led you to choose that answer.

- This requires that you go back to the fact pattern and see if you can find the specific words or facts led you to that particular answer choice.

- Identify the basis for your answer. There had to be a reason—some basis you relied on for selecting that particular answer. We know it was the wrong reason, but we still need to know what it was to step in and correct it.

- Determine whether you "read into the facts" or added your own. This alters the nature of the problem. *You must never "assume" facts.* The question has been carefully constructed to contain all the facts you need to answer it. You must rely solely on these facts and no others. Of course you may draw reasonable inferences but you cannot go further.

- Do not stray from the fact pattern and go off on tangents. Sometimes when you read a fact pattern, you'll see the potential for a number of possible causes of action. Let the stem for the question guide your analysis.

- Sometimes you don't "add" facts but see implications which have no basis in the facts. This leads you astray in your analysis as well. Let the facts dictate your direction.

(8) Am I disregarding an important exception and jumping immediately to the general rule?

(9) Am I not connecting with the significance of the facts and that's why I can't identify the legal problem?

(10) Does this question require application of statutory law and not the common law? Did I disregard this before?

(11) Am I applying the minority view instead of the majority rule?

(12) Am I misapplying the rule to the facts?

(13) Am I "reacting" to answer choices instead of "acting" in response with an analysis of the issue presented?

(14) Did I get emotionally involved with the problem and substitute my instincts for what I know is legally correct?

(15) Did I become "practical" and replace the black letter law for what I thought would occur in actual practice?

Figure out what your answer means:

If you answered "yes" to questions 1 through 7, then you most likely have a reading problem.

You therefore choose the incorrect answer choices because you've misread a fact either in the fact pattern or the answer choice. This is usually the result of sloppy reading because you're intent on reading quickly rather than carefully. A hasty reader is likely to overlook the specific use of vocabulary and the significance of modifiers in the answer choices. These types of errors and omissions go directly to your reading of the problem, not necessarily to your knowledge of the substantive law or to your analysis of the legal question. In fact, your difficulties with reading may prevent you from getting to the actual problem in controversy.

If you've been able to identify your problem as one of reading, now you have a direction in which to work. You can and must learn to read questions "actively." Because of time constraints on the exam, you may have time for only one reading of the fact pattern. However, you can't sacrifice a careful reading for a quick one. You must read carefully to spot signal words and legally significant facts. *Slow down and watch what happens.*

If you answered "yes" to questions 8 through 15, then you may have a problem with either "application" or the "rule."

It's often difficult to distinguish between the two problems because they are closely related in the dynamic of answering multiple choice questions. Problems with analysis are process-oriented while problems with the rule are substance-based. But they can and do overlap as evidenced in these questions.

Analysis Problems

Conquering a problem with analysis not only involves close, accurate reading of the text, but also requires exactness in following the structure of legal analysis in the context of multiple choice questions. This requires that as you re-read the question, you focus on answering the following:

- Did you properly analyze the question?

    1. Did you begin by reading the call-of-the-question?

    2. Did you identify the issue in the fact pattern?

    3. Did you move from finding the issue to forming your answer?

    4. Did you fill the gap from "your answer" to find one of the answer choices?

- Did you properly analyze the answer choices?

    1. Did you identify the issue in each answer choice?

    2. Did you use the process of elimination by determining when an answer choice can't be correct?

        (a) Was the answer choice completely correct?

        (b) Did the answer choice misstate or misapply a rule of law?

        (c) Did the answer choice mischaracterize the facts?

What you should do

The basic remedy for reading and application-based problems is practice—lots and lots of it. ***There's no real secret:***

the more questions you work your way through, the more careful and conscious a reader you become. In some ways, answering a multiple choice question is more an art than a science but rigor in application of the method will yield favorable results.

Rule Problems

Let's face it: if you don't know the black letter law, you can't distinguish between the answer choices. The key in analyzing the question after you've identified the issue is to articulate the rule of law that addresses that issue. If you don't know the rule, you can't get to this step. Remember, it's not enough to know bits and pieces of rules or simply be familiar with the terminology. Buzz-words will not help you here. The only thing that works is complete and thorough understanding of the rule—in its entirety.

If you answered "yes" to questions 8 through 12, consider the following:

If you cannot summon to mind the relevant rule as soon as you've articulated the issue, then you must return to your notes and review the substantive law in detail. Your problem is with knowledge of the rules and you must be comfortable with answering the following questions as soon as you read a fact pattern:

- What is the legal problem presented by the facts?

- What area of law is implicated?

- What is the specific rule of law that governs under these facts?

On the other hand, if you answered "yes" to questions 13 through 15, then something slightly different may be happening and requires a different approach. Let's look at each one individually.

If you "react" instead of "act":

When you find yourself "reacting" to answer choices instead of "acting" in response to them with a careful analysis of the issue presented, then some changes in procedure are required. This type of problem is basically one of control: Because you've lost control of your thought process in analyzing the problem, you've placed yourself at the mercy of the answer choices. Then they pick you, instead of the other way around. How do you act and not react to the answer choices? *The answer is simple: formulate your own answer to the interrogatory before you even look at the answer choices.* Practice questions this way until it becomes habit and you'll see what a difference it makes.

If you ignore the rule:

If you find yourself substituting your instincts for what you know is legally correct, you're headed for trouble. You must apply the rule of law to the facts without equivocation. You can't afford to get emotionally involved with the parties and let your sympathies interfere with what you know is legally correct. It's not your place to find a criminal defendant not guilty when in fact her actions satisfy every element of the crime. And conversely: if an act doesn't violate the provisions of a given statute, then whatever you happen to think about the nature of the act (or actor) doesn't matter. It's not a crime if the jurisdiction doesn't make it one. Your job is to follow the law and apply it to the facts mechanically.

If you substitute "practice" for "theory":

If you find that you become practical on exams and replace the black letter law for what you think would occur in the real world, then you're going to end up with some incorrect answers. Instead, strictly apply the rule of law as you have learned it in your bar review course to the facts of the question and you'll find yourself making correct choices.

ANSWERING MULTISTATE QUESTIONS

Here's a checklist to follow when answering multistate questions:

1. When reading a question, do I read "actively" by noting,

    ☐ The relationship between the parties?

    ☐ Amounts of money, dates, quantities, ages?

    ☐ Words such as "oral" and "written"?

    ☐ Words that indicate state of mind such as "intended," "decided," and "deliberately"?

2. When analyzing a question,

    ☐ Do I begin by reading from the call-of-the-question?

    ☐ Do I find the issue in the fact pattern?

    ☐ Do I articulate the rule that addresses the issue?

    ☐ Do I form my own answer to the question before I check the answer choices?

    ☐ Do I "fill the gap" between my answer and the answer choices?

3. When analyzing the answer choices,

    ☐ Do I find the issue in each of the answer choices?

    ☐ Do I use the process of elimination effectively?

    ☐ Am I careful when working with questions containing the words, "because," "if," and "unless"?

4. If I have to guess,

    ☐ Do I eliminate all the obviously incorrect choices first?

    ☐ Do I eliminate answer choices that address other areas of law?

    ☐ Do I make sure to find the "issue"?

    ☐ Am I careful with words of certainty such as "always," "never," and "must"?

STUDYING FROM MULTISTATE QUESTIONS

The following checklist guides you through the process of studying from multistate questions:

1. Am I prepared to answer questions?

    ☐ Have I attended the bar review sessions in the specific area of law?

    ☐ Have I reviewed my lecture notes and outlines for the subject?

2. Have I selected a group of practice questions in the area of law I've just reviewed?

3. Do I answer one question at a time so I can learn from the process?

4. When working through a specific question, do I de-construct each of the answer choices and ask,

    ☐ Do I know why each of the incorrect answer choices is incorrect?

    ☐ Can I fully articulate the reasoning to support the correct answer choice?

    ☐ Do I check my notes if I cannot recall the specific language of the rule?

    ☐ Do I check my notes if I am not sure of related sub-issues, even if not necessary to answer the question?

5. Do I read the explanation even when I answer the question correctly?

6. If I answer incorrectly, do I go back over the question and try to determine where I made a wrong turn:

    Is it a problem with how I read the question?

    ☐ As I re-read the fact pattern, am I noticing facts that I overlooked the first time?

    ☐ Do I confuse the parties?

    ☐ Do I overlook legally significant language?

☐ Do I find my mind wandering as I read?

☐ Am I rereading the same sentence because I have trouble remembering what I've just read?

☐ Am I reading into the problem words and facts that are not there?

Is it a problem with my knowledge of the black letter law?

☐ Am I able to determine the legal problem presented by the facts?

☐ Can I identify the specific rule of law that governs under these facts?

☐ Am I disregarding an important exception and jumping immediately to the general rule?

☐ Does this question require application of statutory law and not the common law? Did I disregard this before?

☐ Am I applying the minority view instead of the majority rule?

☐ Do I ignore what I know is "legally correct" and substitute my instincts?

☐ Do I "react" to answer choices instead of "acting" in response with an analysis of the issue presented?

☐ Do I become "practical" and replace the black letter law for what I think would occur in actual practice?

☐ Am I misapplying the rule to the facts?

7. Does it take me about two hours to work through 15 to 20 questions?

8. Have I timed a practice session to see whether I can answer between 16 and 17 questions in 30 minutes?

9. Have I factored into my study time a practice session to simulate a six-hour test period of 200 questions?

ILLUSTRATIVE PROBLEMS

As this chapter has shown, there are no tricks to be learned to pass the bar exam, only the law. If there is a strategy, it is to prepare through practice and more practice. Your goal is to become so thoroughly familiar with the structure and content of MBE questions that on bar day, you'll proceed through the questions efficiently and accurately—just as you've done during your practice sessions.

Now it's time to implement the approaches I've outlined for you and work with some actual questions.

■ Problem 1. Analyzing Questions ■

Peavey was walking peacefully along a public street when he encountered Dorwin, whom he had never seen before. Without provocation or warning, Dorwin picked up a rock and struck Peavey with it. It was later established that Dorwin was mentally ill and suffered recurrent hallucinations.

If Peavey asserts a claim against Dorwin based on battery, which of the following, if supported by evidence, will be Dorwin's best defense?

A. Dorwin did not understand that his act was wrongful.

B. Dorwin did not desire to cause harm to Peavey.

C. Dorwin did not know that he was striking a person.

D. Dorwin thought Peavey was about to attack him.

Analysis

You could spend hours studying your notes on intentional torts, "know" the elements of a battery, and still answer this question incorrectly if you're unfamiliar with the way the elements are tested on the bar exam. If you're like most law students, you learned the elements of the intentional torts in a rather straight-forward manner: you read cases, identified the elements in class discussions, memorized them, and recited them back on the final in the context of an essay.

You can see that the MBE takes a different approach. Your analysis begins with the basic definition of a battery, but that's only your first step. Then you have to analyze each element with respect to the legal issue posed in the hypothetical. If you fail to identify the issue or miss the signal words in the question, you'll arrive at an incorrect answer choice even though you could probably recite the elements of a battery in your sleep!

For this first question, I'll take you through every step of the process, following the steps we've outlined. But I'll go a little further and let you in on exactly what I'm thinking as I work through the problem, beginning with the call-of-the-question. *"If Peavey asserts a claim against Dorwin based on battery, which of the following, if supported by evidence, will be Dorwin's best defense?"*

This tells us a lot: since a person is bringing the suit and not the state, it's a civil suit and not a criminal case. We're looking for Dorwin's best defense to battery, so now we know which rule of law to apply. It's time to define battery. We're also looking for some-thing that negates an element of battery or possibly self-defense because we're asked for to find his **best** defense.

Now I'll read the fact pattern "actively," looking for legally significant language in light of the rule: a battery is the intent to cause a harmful or offensive contact with the person of another. The first sentence indicates that it is a "public" and not a "private" street but since we know from the question stem that Peavey brought the action against Dorwin in battery, the state is not involved. These words are probably not relevant. On the other hand, "peacefully" goes to a question of provocation and since Peavey never saw Dorwin before, there's no past history between them.

The next few words are significant: "without provocation or warning, Dorwin picked up a rock and struck Peavey with it."

Here's the act required for the battery and I was right about the lack of provocation. Now the issue is one of intent. The facts state that Dorwin "picked up" a rock. This indicates he acted with purpose. The intent element is satisfied not only when the actor intends harmful or wrongful behavior, but if he acts with purpose or knowledge to a "substantial certainty." Dorwin need not have understood his act to be "wrongful" to have formed the requisite intent: he need only to know what would be the likely consequence of striking Peavey with a rock.

The last sentence states that Dorwin was mentally ill and suffered recurrent hallucinations. The majority view is that insane persons are liable for their intentional torts. So if Dorwin made a choice to pick up the rock and hit Peavey with it, it doesn't matter if it was an irrational or crazy choice.

Even though I've identified the rule of law and applied it to the facts, I cannot form my own answer and then look for it among the answer choices because this is the type of question where the answer choices provide additional information or a twist on the facts. Each one must be individually evaluated. Still, I'm looking for Dorwin's best defense to battery. I know the act occurred, so any defense will have to negate the intent element or provide for self-defense, which doesn't seem likely since Dorwin wasn't provoked or even knew Peavey.

Choice (A): Dorwin did not understand that his act was wrongful. This one isn't right because Dorwin doesn't have to understand his act to be wrongful to commit battery; he only has to act with purpose or knowledge to a "substantial certainty." He need only know what would be the likely consequence of hitting Peavey with a rock.

Choice (B): Dorwin did not desire to cause harm to Peavey. This is just a variation of A. Even though a battery is the intentional, harmful or offensive touching of another, Dorwin need not have intended harm to be found liable in battery.

Choice (C). Dorwin did not know that he was striking a person. This sounds funny, but if Dorwin had no idea—no "knowledge"—he was striking a person, then he could not have formed the requisite intent to do the act or to know to a "substantial certainty" the consequence of his actions. This one may be it but I need to read (D).

Choice (D). Dorwin thought Peavey was about to attack him. This sounds like self-defense, which is a defense but there's nothing in the facts to lead Dorwin to believe Peavey was about to attack him. But even assuming Dorwin believed he was about to be attacked and he needed to defend himself, this still admits that he committed the battery. The question asks for the *best* defense and that's one that says he never committed the battery. I'll go with C.

Choice (C) is the correct answer.

■ Problem 2. Analyzing Answer Choices ■

Let's return to a question we've already examined: remember our friends Structo and Bailey and the large mass of solid rock that appeared after excavation for the driveway had begun? Previously, we focused on the use of signal language to determine the difference between a correct and incorrect answer choice; here we need to identify the theories operating in each of the answer choices before we can select the correct answer.

> Structo contracted with Bailey to construct for $500,000 a warehouse and an access driveway at a highway level. Shortly after commencing work on the driveway, which required for the specified level some excavation and removal of surface material, Structo unexpectedly encountered a large mass of solid rock.

> For this question only, assume the following facts. Structo informed Bailey (accurately) that because of the rock the driveway as specified would cost at least $20,000 more than figured, and demanded for that reason a total contract price of $520,000. Since Bailey was expecting warehousing custom-

ers immediately after the agreed completion date, he signed a writing promising to pay the additional $20,000. Following timely completion of the warehouse and driveway, which conformed to the contract in all respects, Bailey refused to pay Structo more than $500,000.

What is the maximum amount to which Structo is entitled?

(A) $500,000, because there was no consideration for Bailey's promise to pay the additional $20,000.

(B) $500,000, because Bailey's promise to pay the additional $20,000 was exacted under duress.

(C) $520,000, because the modification was fair and was made in the light of circumstances not anticipated by the parties when the original contract was made.

(D) $520,000, provided that the reasonable value of Structo's total performance was that much or more.

Analysis

Answer Choice (A) raises the question of whether there was a bargained-for exchange for Bailey's promise to pay the additional $20,000. You need to determine whether Structo's promise to do more work than originally bargained for in excavating the driveway was consideration. And it was, so Choice (A) is not the answer.

Answer Choice (B) requires that you know a case of economic duress when you see one. The issue is whether Bailey was unfairly coerced into modifying the agreement. The facts do state that Bailey was expecting warehouse customers immediately after the completion date of the project but they also state that Structo "accurately" informed Bailey that the presence of the rock made the job more expensive than anticipated. Hence Structo was not making a wrongful threat but informing Bailey that the job would cost more. Bailey was free to consider other contractors.

The issue in Answer Choice (C) was whether the parties entered into a valid modification for the payment of $20,000 when Structo had to do more work in excavating the driveway and Bailey signed a writing promising to pay the additional $20,000. The answer choice reads like the rule of law itself.

Answer Choice (D) raises the question of whether Structo's recovery should be based on a theory of *quantum meruit*. This is a restitutionary theory of recovery but not a necessary one when the parties in fact had an enforceable contract.

As you can see, identifying the legal theory behind each answer choice enables you to distinguish between them and make an appropriate selection.

■ Problem 3. Working With "Because" And "If" ■

Consider the following examples from past MBE questions:

> Penstock owned a large tract of land on the shore of a lake. Drury lived on a stream that ran along one boundary of Penstock's land and into the lake. At some time in the past, a channel had been cut across Penstock's land from the stream to the lake at a point some distance from the mouth of the stream. From where Drury lived, the channel served as a convenient shortcut to the lake. Erroneously believing that the channel was a public waterway, Drury made frequent trips through the channel in his motorboat. His use of the channel caused no harm to the land through which it passed.
>
> (A) Judgment for Penstock for nominal damages, because Drury intentionally used the channel.
>
> (B) Judgment for Drury, if he did not use the channel after learning of Penstock's ownership claim.
>
> (C) Judgment for Drury, because he caused no harm to Penstock's land.

(D) Judgment for Drury, because when he used the channel he believed it was a public waterway.

Analysis

Here, the issue is whether Drury trespassed on Pennstock's property even though he "erroneously believed" it was a public waterway and he caused "no harm to the land." Once you articulate this issue, and apply the rule to these facts—to succeed in a claim for trespass, all that is required is that Drury had (1) intent to enter onto the land; and that (2) unauthorized entry onto Pennstock's land occurred—it's a quick move to the correct answer choice, which is Choice (A).

Still, let's take a moment and apply what we've learned about "because" and "if" statements to work through the answer choices.

Choice (A) states that Penstock should be awarded judgment for nominal damages "because Drury intentionally used the channel." This is a straightforward statement and all we need to do is ensure that the reasoning supports the conclusion both on a factual and legal basis. Here, the facts tell us that Drury "intentionally" used the channel because "Drury made frequent trips through the channel in his motorboat." This satisfies the elements of trespass. Since no harm need occur to commit a trespass, Drury is liable and nominal damages can be awarded. Choice (A) is the correct answer choice.

Choice (B) provides that Drury is awarded judgment "if he did not use the channel after learning of Penstock's ownership claim." This can be the correct answer only if it is a correct statement. Here we are told that Drury wins if he stopped using the channel once he learned it was Penstock's property. This statement does not "undo" the fact that Drury already used the channel. Choice (B) is an incorrect statement.

Choice (C) asks us to give judgment for Drury "because he caused no harm to Penstock's land." This statement is legally incorrect (although factually correct) because one can be liable in trespass even if no harm is caused.

Finally, Choice (D) awards judgment to Drury "because when he used the channel he believed it was a public waterway." This statement is also legally incorrect (although factually correct) because Drury's erroneous belief is irrelevant in establishing the intent requirement for trespass.

■ **Problem 4. Working With "Because"** ■

Consider the following MBE question:

> Pedestrian sued Driver for personal injuries sustained when Driver's car hit Pedestrian. Immediately after the accident, Driver got out of his car, raced over to Pedestrian, and said, "Don't worry, I'll pay your hospital bill."
>
> Pedestrian's testimony concerning Driver's statement is
>
> (A) admissible, because it is an admission of liability by a party-opponent.
>
> (B) admissible, because it is within the excited utterance exception to the hearsay rule.
>
> (C) inadmissible to prove liability, because it is an offer to pay medical expenses.
>
> (D) inadmissible, provided that Driver kept his promise to pay Pedestrian's medical expenses.

Analysis

Beginning with the call-of-the-question, we see the problem requires us to determine the admissibility of what might be an out-of-court statement. Still, without reading the fact pattern, it's too early to tell whether it will be a hearsay issue so it's critical not to make any further inferences.

After reading the story, it's possible to form a general issue: whether an offer to pay medical expenses is admissible. Under the Federal Rules of Evidence, evidence of offering to pay medical or hospital expenses is not admissible to prove liability for the injury (FRE 409). However, in this problem we cannot form our own answer before looking at the answer choices because they provide additional information.

In this example, each of the answer choices includes the modifier "because" to connect the conclusion with the reasoning in support of that conclusion. We need to evaluate the validity of each statement before we can make a choice.

Choice (A) provides that the statement is admissible "because it is an admission of liability by a party-opponent." This language implicates the Federal Rules regarding admissions: they are specifically exempted from the definition of hearsay and thus not barred by the prohibition against introducing hearsay. Here we have an out-of-court statement and if it fell within this exception, it would be a basis for admissibility. However, Driver's statement, "Don't worry, I'll pay your hospital bill" was not one of liability. Choice (A) is incorrect.

Choice (B) claims admissibility on the basis of the excited utterance exception to the hearsay rule. However, once you summon the rule regarding excited utterances—"a statement relating to a startling event or condition made while the declarant was under the stress of excitement caused by the event or condition" (FRE 803 (2))—it's easy to dismiss this answer choice. Although the facts tell you that the Driver "raced" over to the Pedestrian "immediately" after the accident, the words spoken did not relate to the accident or the Pedestrian's physical condition; instead, they were an offer to pay medical expenses, hardly the stuff of excited utterances.

Choice (C) tells us that the statement is inadmissible to prove liability "because it is an offer to pay medical expenses." This is a clear statement of FRE 409 which provides that: "evidence of furnishing or offering or promising to pay medical, hospital, or similar expenses occasioned by an injury is not admissible to prove liability for the injury." After identifying this rule, it's a quick move to select it as the correct answer choice.

Choice (D) is easy to dismiss. It is incorrect. The statement's admissibility or inadmissibility is not tied to the Driver's promise to pay Pedestrian's medical expenses.

CHAPTER 10

Practicing Questions for the Multistate Performance Test ("MPT")

The Purpose of the MPT

The MPT can be the easiest part of your bar exam. Unlike other parts of the exam where you're called upon to work solely from your memory, here you're given the rules and the test is to apply them. You're given the law because the MPT is designed to test your proficiency in the basic skills you've developed in the course of your legal education and not just your ability to memorize. According to the National Conference of Bar Examiners, the goal of the MPT is to test "an applicant's ability to use fundamental lawyering skills in a realistic situation." It seeks to evaluate your ability to complete a task which a beginning lawyer should be able to accomplish.

Now that I've told you the positive, I must be fair and share the negative: it's the time pressure. In most jurisdictions, you'll have 90 minutes to read through 15 to 25 pages, analyze the problem, outline an answer, and write a response. In other jurisdictions, you'll have two MPT problems for a total of three hours and, in California, you'll see one long MPT for three hours. You can just imagine the length of the file and the number of issues to which you must respond. Consequently, the MPT is a test of your ability to work within time constraints and remain focused and organized.

Still, the MPT remains the most "doable" portion of the bar exam. It's not difficult "legally." The challenge is to get through a vast amount of information and address only that which is required as set forth in the Task Memo. In this chapter, we'll develop the strategy you'll use when taking this portion of your bar exam.

The Skills Tested

The MPT tests the following:

1. Reading comprehension

    There's a very real difference between the type of reading you've engaged in for law school and what you'll do for the MPT. Here you must read pro-actively, with a critical eye toward solving a specific problem rather than answering a professor's questions in class. You must read carefully and quickly, all the while searching for useful information and answers to the particular issue you've been asked to resolve.

2. Organizational skills

    You must organize your time and the materials effectively to complete the required task in the time allowed. The MPT is extremely time-sensitive, perhaps even more so than the essay or multiple choice components of the bar exam in that you'll have but 90 minutes in which to read and analyze an assortment of unfamiliar materials and compose any one of the following written assignments—a memorandum of law, a letter to a client, a persuasive brief (including subject headings), a contract provision, a will, a settlement proposal, a discovery plan, or a closing argument, to list but a few of the possibilities.

3. Communication skills

    You must write concisely, coherently, and in a tone and manner consistent with the nature of the assignment. In short, you must demonstrate your mastery of the language of the law and convince the bar examiners that you "sound" like an attorney ready to begin the practice of law.

4. Ability to follow directions

It sounds so simple and basic but it's often ignored in the haste to begin writing. The MPT is task-specific: you must perform the task identified to receive credit. If you're instructed to write a letter to a client and instead write a persuasive brief, you'll have done nothing but demonstrate to the bar examiners your inability to read and follow directions.

The directions are important for yet another reason: they may ask you to identify *additional* facts that would strengthen or, alternatively, weaken a party's position. Since adding facts to a professor's hypothetical is a basic law school "no-no," you'd never think to do such a thing—not unless you had read the directions.

MPT Tasks

The bar examiners test these skills by simulating the experiences of a new attorney. You'll be given a client "File" and asked to complete what would be considered a typical assignment for a first year associate. Most likely, you'll be asked to write a legal memorandum or persuasive brief, although it is possible to be asked to draft interrogatories, a will provision, or a closing argument.[1] The bar examiners do not expect you to have performed all or even any of these tasks during your law school career. What they do expect, however, is that you'll be able to follow their Instruction Memo and rely on your basic legal training to complete the assignment.

---

1. In surveying a total of 55 MPTs from 1997 to February, 2007, the most frequently assigned task is that of the legal memorandum at 24, followed by the persuasive brief at 16. Memos and briefs are followed by letters at 11. However, letters can be either "objective"—sent to a client to explain a legal situation—or "persuasive"—sent to opposing counsel to argue a position. It is therefore essential to read the directions accompanying the task very carefully to be exactly certain of the task. *See* NCBE, www.ncbex .org/multistate-tests/mpt/ (last visited September 7, 2007).

Each task is designed to test a discrete set of legal skills in the context of one of the following settings:

1. Fact analysis tasks

    Here you might be asked to analyze a set of facts where the primary focus is to separate the relevant from the irrelevant. Such tasks include:

    • Drafting an opening statement

    • Drafting a closing argument

    • Preparing a set of jury instructions

    • Writing an affidavit

2. Fact gathering tasks

    These problems require you to be able to identify the theory of your case and what facts you must prove to make that case. Consequently, in a typical fact gathering problem, you'll be required to gather evidence. The focus will be on sifting through information to determine what's relevant to your problem and then using that evidence to defend or support your case. Typical fact gathering tasks include:

    • Drafting a discovery plan

    • Preparing a set of interrogatories

    • Drafting questions to ask a witness on cross examination

3. Legal analysis and reasoning problems

    These problems are most like law school exams but with a major difference: the MPT will articulate the precise legal issue(s) for you. You just need to follow directions carefully and answer the precise question that is asked of you. Typical legal reasoning tasks include:

    • Writing an objective memorandum

    • Writing a persuasive memorandum of law or trial brief

- Writing a client letter

- Writing a letter to opposing counsel

4. Problem-solving tasks

Here you'll be called upon to evaluate courses of action. The focus is on your ability to develop strategies for solving a problem and meeting your client's needs. You may even be called upon to suggest such non-legal solutions as mediation or counseling. Examples include:

- Drafting a will or contract provision

- Drafting a settlement proposal or separation agreement

5. Ethical issue problems

As a bar candidate, you're expected to comport with the applicable ethical standards in your representation of a client. Consequently, you may find ethical issues raised in your problem. You're expected to recognize such issues and resolve them according to the ethical standards of the profession. Conceivably, the bar examiners could raise an ethical issue without providing specific rules in the Library; in such cases, you must rely on your general knowledge of the rules of professional conduct. Be alert in your reading of the facts to potential conflict of interest issues, violations of fiduciary obligations, and breaches of attorney/client privilege.

Components of the MPT

1. The File

Here you'll find the factual information about your case in the form of:

- excerpts from deposition testimony

- client correspondence

- police reports and medical records

- invoices and purchase orders

- witness interviews

- contract provisions, a lease, or a will

While the File contains all the facts you need to know about your problem, it also contains "irrelevant information." Just as in "real life" where your client will volunteer much more information than you actually need or is relevant, and witnesses may be unreliable or have faulty memories, the File may include irrelevant or ambiguous information, unreliable and conflicting witness testimony, and inconsistent statements.

2. The "Task" Memo

This is the first memorandum in the File and the single most important piece of paper in the File: it introduces your problem and identifies your task. Your job is to answer the questions presented in the memo and perform the assigned task as precisely as possible.

3. The Instruction Memo

If the bar examiners think you need guidance in completing your task, they'll include a second memo in the File. This memo will tell you exactly what to include (and sometimes what *not* to include) in your answer.

For example, the Instruction Memo will advise you whether your persuasive brief requires a statement of facts or not. A "persuasive brief" might require a factual statement while a "trial brief" might not. You might be asked to include a "jurisdictional statement" as well as a statement of facts. Even if the Instruction Memo specifies a task you think you know well, ***do not*** skip a review of the instruction sheet. Sometimes the examiners have modified the task or require a particular format.

4. The Library

The Library contains all the legal authorities you'll need to complete the assigned task. They are the *only* legal authorities you may use to solve the problem. The Library may consist of:

- statutes, codes. and commentaries

- constitutional provisions and regulations

- rules of professional conduct

- cases

- secondary sources such as Restatement provisions

The cases may be actual cases, modified cases, or cases written specifically for the exam. So too with the "rules"— they may be actual rules or rules written specifically for the MPT. Even if you think you are familiar with a rule or a case from your law school classes, you must still read all the material in the Library. You cannot assume that the material has not been modified. There may be rules that the bar examiners have not altered, such as the UCC, provisions of the United States Constitution, the Bill of Rights, or the Federal Rules of Evidence. In these instances, the directions will so advise.

Outlining the Approach

1. Have a plan

    I've put together a set of guidelines students found helpful and subsequently used as a blueprint to guide them through the problems during practice sessions and on exam day. Following this plan saves time and prevents panic: if you know what you are going to do, and practice the routine sufficiently, it becomes second nature to you by test day.

2. Practice from actual MPTs

    Since the MPT tests your ability to extract legal principles from cases and statutes and apply these principles to solve a specific client problem, you will need to practice this skill. Work only from past MPT questions and use the grading guidelines to evaluate your answers. If your jurisdiction releases sample MPT answers, review them and compare them to your answers.

3. Allocate your time

You must complete the assignment to maximize your points. The bar examiners suggest that you allot 45 minutes to reading the materials and 45 minutes to organizing and writing your response. This is sound advice. Moreover, if you follow the strategies I've outlined below, you'll be organizing your response while you're reading the materials, thereby maximizing your efficiency.

4. Find your baseline

You have no idea how long it will take you to answer an MPT until you've actually done one. After you've read one or two of MPTs to see what they're like, answer the sample MPT at the end of this chapter according to the approach that follows in the checklist.

First, note how long it takes to read and outline the answer. This is your baseline *reading* time. Second, proceed to write the response. Once again, time yourself. This is your baseline *writing* time. Don't be surprised or disheartened if it takes longer than the suggested time to get through the materials. This is to be expected the first time you approach new material. I suggest you practice at least three to five MPTs and more if you have trouble with the timing.

Once you've established your reading and writing baselines, you can concentrate on improving your time. Learning to allocate your time is challenging but not impossible. You can do it with practice. You must practice the strategy until it becomes automatic and your approach is consistent. Don't wait until test day to see how long it takes you to dissect a case for the rule and prepare a response. *You'd never wait until the day of your road test to practice parallel parking, would you?*

5. Follow the blueprint

Practice the approach outlined below until it becomes automatic. Follow each step of the sequence for each MPT—first as you practice and then on bar day. The process will become so mechanical that you will not waste any time—you'll get to work immediately and remain calm because you always know what your next step will be.

Below is a summary of the steps you'll follow to answer an MPT:

a. Skim the Instructions

b. Review the Table of Contents

c. Read the Task Memo

d. Review the Instruction Memo (if applicable)

e. Read the Library

   Use the rule from the cases to form your outline

f. Read the File

   Add the relevant facts to your outline

g. Re-read the Task Memo to verify the task

h. Review the Instruction Memo to verify the task format

i. Write your Response

BLUEPRINT FOR TAKING THE MPT

1. Did you review the instructions?

    A. Did you skim the paragraphs to check the requirements?

      There is an instruction sheet on the back of every MPT. Read it during your preparation so as not to waste precious time on the exam. On bar day, you'll scan the instruction sheet just to make sure it's the same as the one you've read during practice—you don't want any surprises.

    B. Did you verify the jurisdiction paragraph to know what is *mandatory* as opposed to what is merely *persuasive* authority?

      The MPT is set in the fictitious Fifteenth Circuit of the United States, in the fictitious State of Franklin. In Franklin, the trial court is the District Court, the intermediate appellate court is the Court of Appeal, and the highest court is the Supreme Court. You must know the court structure before you read the cases so you can determine what is mandatory and what is merely persuasive authority.

2. Did you scan the Table of Contents?

    A. Can you identify the general area of law?

      From the listings in the Library, you can often determine the general subject area and use it to inform the rest of your reading. But don't let the area of law cause needless worry or anxiety. Bar examiners may choose an unfamiliar area of law. In such cases, the key is not to let the subject matter distract you. You'll be given all the relevant law you need to solve the problem so even if it happens to be an area of law in which you think you're weak, it doesn't matter. And if it's an unfamiliar area of law, the bar examiners know that too and the problem will be relatively basic and answerable solely on the basis of the provided materials.

    B. Can you determine whether it's a statutory or common law problem?

      For example, if you see provisions of the Franklin Commercial Code listed in the Table of Contents, it's a sure bet you have a problem involving a sales of goods. On the other hand, if all you read in the Library are case names, then it's a common law problem.

3. Did you read the Task Memo carefully and completely?

A. Did you identify the issue you're asked to resolve? Are there sub-issues?

The Task Memo reveals the precise issue you're asked to resolve. It's usually in the last two paragraphs of the memo. Read these paragraphs two or three times to be certain you have identified the issue. Write the issue on your scratch paper so that you remain focused as you proceed. Be careful not to change or vary the language of the question.

Read the directions carefully. You may be asked to identify additional facts. Also, note any exclusions.

B. Did you identify your specific assignment by

☐ Noting the precise nature of the task: memo, persuasive brief, client letter, contract provision, etc.?

☐ Identifying your point of view: is it objective or persuasive?

You want to know whether you will be advising or advocating. This informs the nature of your reading because you'll read the materials with a critical eye. For example, if you know you must write a persuasive brief with subject headings, you'll read the cases with an eye toward formulating them.

☐ Identifying your audience: is it a lawyer or layperson?

Knowing your audience allows you to adopt the proper tone in your writing.

C. Did you note any exclusions?

Sometimes you are told **not** to consider a specific issue. In these cases, the issue would most likely jump out at you when you read the problem and your first response would be to discuss it. **Your job is not to discuss it.** Fight the desire to do so because the graders are lying in wait to take off points for those who fail to follow their instructions.

4. Did you review the Instruction Memo?

The bar examiners include this memo if they think you need guidance in completing the assigned task. Read the Instruction Memos from past MPTs when you study so that you need spend only a few moments reviewing them before proceeding on bar day. You must check the Instruction Memo even if it seems familiar because it's never safe to assume it's identical to one you've seen before.

A. Is a particular format or structure required for your answer?

The memo provides guidelines for opinion letters, persuasive briefs, memorandums, etc., telling you exactly what to include and sometimes what *not* to include.

B. If a brief is requested, do you need to include

☐ A statement of facts?

☐ A jurisdictional statement?

☐ Persuasive subject headings?

The Instruction Memo will advise whether your persuasive brief requires a statement of facts or not. A "persuasive brief" might require a factual statement while a "trial brief" might not. Sometimes you might be asked to include a "jurisdictional statement" as well as a statement of facts.

C. Are there specific examples/models to follow?

5. Did you read the Library?

Although the first part of the exam booklet is the File, you're going to begin with the Library. Reading the law first informs your subsequent reading of the File. If you read the File first, with its various excerpts from depositions, client communications, and attorney notes, it would be very difficult to sift the relevant from the irrelevant information. It would not be possible to know which facts were "relevant" until you knew the law and how the cases in your jurisdiction have interpreted that law. While reading the Library first does not guarantee you won't have to review it again, it will make your subsequent reading of the File meaningful and immediately productive.

A. Did you read the cases first?

Even if there are statutory provisions or Restatements, begin your reading with the cases. Often they will explain the statutes, thus saving time.

B. For each case, did you
- [ ] Read the earliest case first and proceed chronologically?
- [ ] Verify the jurisdiction to determine whether it is mandatory or persuasive authority for your problem?
- [ ] Skim the facts to get a sense of the story?

  On the MPT, cases are constructed in a very particular order: facts, rule, and application of facts to rule. With practice, you can read the first few words of each paragraph and know exactly where you are. Consider skipping the first few paragraphs and proceeding right to the rule. If you're insecure about skipping around, then read the entire case but merely skim the facts. You can pick up the relevant facts from the court's analysis.

- [ ] Identify the statement of the rule?
  - [ ] Is it element-based?
  - [ ] Do you need to synthesize the rule from the cases?
  - [ ] Is it a "multi-part test" formulated by the court?
- [ ] Note any footnotes?

  Footnotes hold a special place in the hearts of bar examiners because they know that students ignore them. Don't. They are there for a reason. More than half the time, they contain critical information.

C. Did you adapt the rule in the cases to form your outline?
- [ ] Use the elements, the "prongs" of a rule, or the components of a statute to form the roman numerals of your outline. A general outline is then in place as you read the rest of the Library.
- [ ] Add to and refine your understanding of the rule as well as add any exceptions or limitations to the rule as you read the other materials in the Library.

☐ Be sure to leave adequate space under each section of your outline so you can add the appropriate "facts" when you read the File.

Let's see how this works. Consider the following passage from the Franklin Supreme Court in *In re Hayworth v. Wexler:*[2]

During the past 30 years, we have developed a two-pronged analysis for evaluating the validity of a premarital agreement. Under the first prong, the court must decide whether the agreement provides a fair and reasonable provision for the party not seeking enforcement of the agreement. If the court makes this finding, then the analysis ends and the agreement may be validated. If the agreement is not fair, the court must invoke the second prong and decide: (A) whether full disclosure has been made by the parties of the amount, character, and value of the property involved, and (B) whether the agreement was entered into intelligently and voluntarily on independent advice and with full knowledge by both spouses of their rights.

The following chart shows how the rule from this case can be used to form an outline for writing your answer.

---

2. See NCBE, The Multistate Performance Test: *In Re Hayworth and Wexler* [February 1997 MPT-2] available at www.ncbex. org/uploads/user_ docrepos/MPT_ 2–97_ TestsandPS.pdf (last visited September 8, 2007).

Using the Rule to Form Your Outline

I.　The agreement must be fair and reasonable for the party not seeking enforcement of the agreement.

If fair, then the analysis is complete.

[leave space to insert facts from the File]

II.　If the agreement is not fair, then ask:
A.　Was there full disclosure of the
1.　amount,
[leave space to insert facts from the File]

2.　character,
[leave space to insert facts from the File]

3.　value of the property involved
and　*[leave space to insert facts from the File]*

B.　Was the agreement entered into
1.　intelligently and voluntarily,
[leave space to insert facts from the File]

2.　on independent advice,
[leave space to insert facts from the File]
and
3.　with full knowledge by both spouses of their rights
[leave space to insert facts from the File]

D. Did you review the statutes, codes, commentaries?

Pay close attention to any "official comments" in a statute or code provision. Such comments are a means for the bar examiners to highlight an issue, draw your attention to a counter-argument, or signal a legal distinction.

6. Did you read the File?

After reading the Library and outlining the rule, you're ready to read the File and add the relevant facts to the appropriate places in your outline. Don't be surprised if you find yourself reading a fair amount of material that you believe is irrelevant. Use your outline of the issues and rules to keep focused.

A. Did you begin by

☐ Writing your issue above your rule outline?

By reading the File with the issue clearly in place, you can more easily identify the legally relevant facts from the sea of material in front of you. As you proceed, add the critical facts to the appropriate part of your outline.

☐ Characterizing the legal relationship of the parties as

☐ buyer and seller?

☐ principal and agent?

☐ teacher and student?

☐ husband and wife?

☐ employer and employee?

☐ attorney and client?

By thinking of the parties in terms of their legal relationship to each other, you'll be alert to the legal significance of the facts contained in the depositions, transcripts, and correspondence.

B. Did you identify the relevant facts based on your knowledge of the law from the Library?

C. Did you add these facts to the appropriate sections of your rule outline?

7. Before beginning to write your answer, did you

A. Review the Task Memo and ask the following questions:

☐ Has my outline incorporated or accounted for each required issue?

☐ Are the relevant facts noted?

☐ Is the applicable legal authority cited?

☐ Do I account for how the law and the facts support my theory?

☐ If appropriate, has contrary authority been cited and distinguished?

B. Review the Instruction Memo

Quickly check this memo once again to verify your task format and its required components.

8. Did you write the required response?

After completing your reading of the Library and File, you're ready to begin the task of writing. Remember, your job is to discuss the issues and the controlling rule of law. Here is where you get your points. Don't waste time "warming up" by reciting the facts or providing needless background information.

A. Did you answer the question that was asked of you?

B. Did you adopt the tone and format required for the task?

C. Did you write persuasive subject headings?

☐ Did you state the legal conclusion you want the court to reach and the factual basis on which it can do so?

☐ Is each point heading written as a conclusory statement that combines the law with the relevant facts?

☐ Is it a coherent, logical, and persuasive thesis sentence?

☐ Have you avoided abstract principles of law?

☐ Would your adversary agree with your statement?

Consider the following two examples:

I. TESTIMONY OF A HIGHLY TRAINED DETECTIVE THAT HE OBSERVED DEFENDANT SELLING WHAT APPEARED TO BE COCAINE TWO DAYS BEFORE DEFENDANT'S ARREST FOR COCAINE POSSESSION WITH INTENT TO DISTRIBUTE IS ADMISSIBLE BECAUSE IT SHOWS DEFENDANT'S STATE OF MIND.

II. OFFICER FUSCO'S TESTIMONY AS TO DEFENDANT'S ARREST AND CONVICTION FOR POSSESSION WITH INTENT TO DISTRIBUTE BUT EIGHTEEN MONTHS PRIOR TO HIS CURRENT ARREST FOR POSSESSION WITH INTENT TO DISTRIBUTE, IS ADMISSIBLE TO SHOW INTENT.

D. Did you give adequate treatment to the cases in the Library?

E. Did you avoid copying passages from cases or statutes?

F. Did you make relevant arguments on how the law and the facts support your theory?

G. Has contrary authority been cited and distinguished?

H. Did you cite to the appropriate authorities for statements of the rule?

Bluebook citation is not required but you must attribute legal authority to your statements to show you've used the Library and that you're familiar with the need for proper legal documentation. Use abbreviations and omit page references, i.e., <u>Smith</u>, is sufficient to indicate authority when citing to cases.

SUMMARY CHECKLIST

1. Did you review the instructions?

   ☐ Did you skim the paragraphs to check the requirements?

   ☐ Did you verify the jurisdiction paragraph to know what is *mandatory* as opposed to what is merely *persuasive* authority?

2. Did you scan the Table of Contents?

   ☐ Can you identify the general area of law?

   ☐ Can you determine whether it's a statutory or common law problem?

3. Did you read the Task Memo carefully and completely?

   ☐ Did you identify the issue you're asked to resolve? Are there sub-issues?

   ☐ Did you identify your specific assignment by

      ☐ Noting the precise nature of the task: memo, brief, letter, contract provision, will provision, cross examination questions, etc.?

      ☐ Identifying your point of view: is it objective or persuasive?

      ☐ Identifying your audience: is it a lawyer or layperson?

   ☐ Did you note any exclusions?

4. Did you read the Instruction Memo?

   ☐ Is a particular format or structure required for your answer?

   ☐ If a brief was requested, do you need to include

      ☐ A statement of facts?

      ☐ A jurisdictional statement?

      ☐ Persuasive subject headings?

   ☐ Are there specific examples/models to follow?

5. Did you read the Library?

   ☐ Did you read the cases first?

- ☐ For each case, did you
  - ☐ Read the earliest case first and proceed chronologically?
  - ☐ Verify the jurisdiction to determine whether its mandatory or persuasive authority for your problem?
  - ☐ Skim the facts to get a sense of the story?
  - ☐ Identify the statement of the rule?
    - • Is it element-based?
    - • Do you need to synthesize the rule from the cases?
    - • Is it a "multi-part test" formulated by the court?
  - ☐ Note any footnotes?
- ☐ Did you use the structure of the rule from the cases to form your outline?
- ☐ Did you review the statutes, codes, commentaries?

6. Did you read the File?

- ☐ Did you begin by
  - ☐ Writing your issue above your rule outline?
  - ☐ Characterizing the legal relationship of the parties?
- ☐ Did you identify the relevant facts based on the law from the Library?
- ☐ Did you add these facts to the appropriate sections of your outline?

7. After writing your outline but before writing your answer, did you

- ☐ Review the Task Memo and ask the following questions:
  - ☐ Has my outline incorporated or accounted for each required element?
  - ☐ Are the relevant facts noted?
  - ☐ Is the applicable legal authority cited?
  - ☐ Do I account for how the law and the facts support my theory?
  - ☐ If appropriate, has contrary authority been cited and distinguished?

☐ Review the Instruction Memo to verify the format of your task?

8. Did you write the required response?

☐ Did you answer the question that was asked of you?

☐ Did you adopt the tone and format required for the task?

☐ Did you write persuasive subject headings?

    ☐ Did you state the legal conclusion you want the court to reach and the factual basis on which it can do so?

    ☐ Is each point heading written as a conclusory statement that combines the law with the relevant facts?

    ☐ Is it a coherent, logical, and persuasive thesis sentence?

    ☐ Have you avoided abstract principles of law?

    ☐ Would your adversary agree with your statement?

☐ Did you give adequate treatment to the cases in the Library?

☐ Did you avoid copying passages from cases or statutes?

☐ Did you make relevant arguments on how the law and the facts support your theory?

☐ Has contrary authority been cited and distinguished?

☐ Did you cite to the appropriate authorities for statements of the rule?

MPT QUESTION

The following is a released MPT question. It is representative of the type of problem and task you might find on your exam. Answer it according to the approach outlined in this chapter.

For purposes of inclusion here, I have omitted the Preface and the test instructions which would appear on the back cover of the exam booklet. For this information, refer to the MPT Information Booklet.[3]

State v. Devine [4]

FILE

Memorandum from Peter Paulson

Memorandum regarding trial briefs

Transcript of testimony of Detective Johnny Ripka

Arrest Report

LIBRARY

Franklin General Statutes

Franklin Rules of Evidence

Milford v. State (1994)

---

3. *See* NCBE, THE MULTISTATE PERFORMANCE TEST 2007 INFORMATION BOOKLET, *available at* www.ncbex.org/uploads/user_ docrepos /MPT_ IB2007.pdf.

4. *See* NCBE, The Multistate Performance Test: *State v. Devine* [July, 1997 Test 2], *available at* www.ncbex.org/uploads/ user_ docrepos/MPT_ 7–97_ TestsandPS.pdf (last visited September 6, 2007).

Office of the District Attorney
Victoria County
145 East Harold Street
Beckley, Franklin 33331
(901) 555–1111

TO: Applicant
FROM: Peter Paulson, Assistant District Attorney
RE: State v. Devine
DATE: July 29, 1997

I am prosecuting David Devine in a criminal case in which he is charged with possession of cocaine with intent to distribute. He was arrested in possession of nearly half an ounce of high-grade cocaine. Defendant's motion to suppress the cocaine, based upon his claim that the search and seizure were unlawful, was denied at the pretrial hearing and again yesterday when his lawyer, Celia Delbert, renewed it at trial.

The defense is not contesting the possession charge, but rather is focused on that part of the charge dealing with intent to distribute. In her opening statement, Delbert hammered at the lack of evidence regarding Devine's intent.

Two witnesses have testified so far for us. The first witness to testify was Scott Crisman, a chemist with the State Toxicology Lab (because he was unavailable later, we called him first). He testified that he received a zip-lock bag from Detective Ripka that contained 13.1 grams of a white powdery substance that he determined was 70% pure cocaine. All of defendant's objections to his testimony were overruled.

The second witness was Detective Ripka, the arresting officer in the case. I have completed my direct examination, and the defense has completed cross-examining Ripka. I have attached the transcript of his testimony. The direct examination went well for us, but we were hurt on cross-examination when Ripka basically conceded that the facts were also consistent with the defense theory of possession for personal use. I now intend to conduct redirect examination of Detective Ripka to elicit his testimony that, two days before the arrest of Devine, he saw Devine selling what appeared to be cocaine in small packages from his car. The defense has objected to the introduction of this evidence.

I will call one more witness. Officer Fusco arrested Devine 18 months ago for possession of heroin with intent to distribute. Devine was convicted and served a year in prison. I want Officer Fusco to testify to the circumstances of that arrest. I've given defense counsel notice under Rule 404 of the Rules of Evidence, and the court has ruled that the notice is sufficient. Delbert has objected to the testimony of both witnesses on other grounds.

This additional testimony from Ripka and Fusco would bolster our claim that Devine intended in the present case to distribute the cocaine. It is essential, therefore, that we persuade the court to admit the testimony of the witnesses concerning the two instances of prior criminal conduct.

The judge has declared a one-day recess. This gives us time to prepare our arguments supporting the admission of this evidence. I have attached some of the Franklin Rules of Evidence (which are identical to the Federal Rules of Evidence) and a case from our Supreme Court.

I want you to write the persuasive brief requested by the court arguing for the admission of the testimony of Ripka and Fusco concerning the two instances of prior criminal conduct. The brief should also anticipate and refute the arguments the defense is likely to make in support of the objections it made yesterday just before the judge recessed the trial. Please prepare the brief in accordance with our office procedure (which I have attached).

Office of the District Attorney
Victoria County
145 East Harold Street
Beckley, Franklin 33331
(901) 555–1111

September 8, 1995

MEMORANDUM

To: Attorneys
From: Andrea Preston, District Attorney
Re: Trial Briefs on Evidentiary Proffers

This memo is for the purpose of clarifying the expectations of the District Attorney's Office and to provide guidance to Assistant District Attorneys. All trial briefs on evidentiary offers shall conform to the following guidelines.

We follow the practice of writing carefully crafted subject headings that illustrate the arguments they cover. The argument heading should succinctly summarize the reasons the tribunal should take the position you are advocating. A heading should be a specific application of a rule of law to the facts of the case and not a bare legal or factual conclusion or a statement of an abstract principle. For example, improper: THE WITNESS IS COMPETENT TO TESTIFY. Proper: A FIVE–YEAR–OLD WHO ADMITTED HER MOTHER WOULD NOT PUNISH HER FOR LYING, BUT STILL TESTIFIED SHE KNEW THAT LYING WAS WRONG, IS COMPETENT TO TESTIFY.

The body of each argument should incorporate the relevant facts, analyze applicable legal authority, and persuasively argue how the facts and law support our position. Authority supportive of our position should be emphasized, but contrary authority should generally be cited, addressed, and explained or distinguished. Do not reserve arguments for reply or supplemental briefs.

Unless specifically assigned, Assistant District Attorneys should not prepare separate statements of facts. Tables of contents, tables of cases, summaries of arguments, and indices for a trial brief on evidentiary proffers will be prepared, when required, after the draft is approved.

State v. Devine, Crim. No. 23–994

Transcript Of The Testimony Of Detective Johnny Ripka

July 28, 1997

Direct Examination by Assistant District Attorney Peter Paulson:

1   Q: State your name and occupation for the record.

2   A: I am Detective Johnny Ripka: I am employed by the Beckley Police Department at

3   the rank of detective and am currently assigned to the narcotics squad.

4   Q: How long have you been so employed?

5   A: I have been with the police department for 15 years, the last five in narcotics.

6   Q: Can you describe any special training you have had in regard to narcotics?

7   A: Yes. In addition to the training that all police officers receive in the Police Academy

8   and the normal detective training, both of which have components dealing with the

9   recognition of narcotics and controlled substances, I have attended a two-month

10   course at the State Police Academy entitled, "Detecting and Apprehending Drug

11   Dealers." I also attended a four-week course offered by the FBI in Washington on

12   working undercover.

13 Q: Have you had any experience regarding the enforcement of the laws dealing with

14   dangerous drugs?

15 A: Yes. Four years ago, I worked undercover for a period of nine months. I lived

16   among people active in the drug culture in order to investigate the drug trade in

17   Beckley. As a result of that work, 34 people were indicted and convicted of the sale

18   and possession of hard drugs in this community. I became familiar with how drugs

19   are brought into this area, prepared for sale, sold, and used.

20 Q: Detective Ripka, have you seen the defendant before today?

21 A: Yes.

22 Q: Can you describe the circumstances?

23 A: At approximately 11:15 in the evening on March 25, 1997, I was patrolling the Frog

24   Hollow neighborhood of Beckley with my partner, Eric Hellman. I observed a red

25   1990 Oldsmobile Cutlass traveling at a high rate of speed down Maple Avenue in

1   Beckley. I followed the Cutlass for three blocks, from 4th Street to 7th Street, and

2   clocked the vehicle at 53 miles per hour.

3   Q: What is the speed limit in those three blocks?

4   A: The area is posted as a 30 mile-per-hour zone.

5   Q: What did you do next?

6   A: I turned on my flashing lights and pulled the driver over. I approached the vehicle

7   on the driver's side and Detective Hellman approached it on the passenger side.

8   There was one individual in the car, the defendant.

9   Q: And do you see that individual in the courtroom?

10   A: Yes, he is that man over there (indicating).

11   Q: Your honor, may the record reflect that the witness is pointing to the defendant,

12   David Devine.

13 **The Court:**   It may so reflect.

14   Q: What happened next?

15   A: I shined my flashlight into the car and I asked him to produce his license and

16   registration.

17   Q: And how did he respond?

18   A: He stammered, looked jumpy, looked kind of wired. He did not immediately

19   produce the license so I requested that he exit the vehicle. I opened his door and

20   he proceeded to exit. I asked him again for his driver's license and he replied that

21   he had left it at home. I asked him again for his registration and he said it was in

22   the glove compartment. I told him to retrieve it. He got back into the vehicle and

23   reached over to open the glove compartment. When he opened it, a sandwich-size

24   zip-lock bag fell out of it onto the floor and came into plain view. I saw that it

25   contained a white substance. I reached in and retrieved the bag. Detective

26   Hellman removed $275 in cash from the glove compartment. I ordered Mr. Devine

27   to exit the vehicle and put his hands on the roof of the vehicle. He did so and I

28   patted him down for weapons. I visually checked the bag and believed that it

29   contained cocaine.

30   Q: What did you do at that time?

1 Q: So it wouldn't surprise you to learn that someone smoked up as much as 13 grams
2   of crack over a period of several days, would it?
3 A: I guess not.
4 Q: In fact, it would be typical for a crack user to consume this much crack in two to
5   three days, isn't that true?
6 A: If they can get their hands on it, they will smoke it.
7 Q: So it wouldn't surprise you that an affluent crack user could consume as much as
8      $1,000 worth of cocaine in two or three days?
9 A: No.
10 **Atty. Delbert:** No further questions.
11 **The Court:** All right. We'll adjourn for the day. Ladies and gentlemen of the jury, please
12   remember my admonition that you should not discuss the case with anyone and so
13   forth. You're excused for the day. Will counsel please stay for a minute?
14   [Jury leaves the courtroom. Court and counsel confer in the absence of the jury.]
15 **The Court:** Counsel, I have an engagement that's going to keep me away from court
16   tomorrow, so we'll reconvene at the usual time the day after tomorrow. Mr.
17   Paulson, when do you plan to rest?
18 **Atty. Paulson:** Well, your honor, I have some redirect for Mr. Ripka. I intend to elicit some
19   further testimony based on what he saw two days before the defendant's arrest.
20   While on stakeout in the Frog Hollow neighborhood, Mr. Ripka saw Mr. Devine pass
21   a small plastic bag, about 1" x 1" in size, containing what appeared to be cocaine
22   through an open car window to another individual. He saw that individual give Mr.
23   Devine some money. I also want to call Officer Fusco, the arresting officer in a prior
24   conviction of Mr. Devine, to testify about the circumstances that led to his prior
25   conviction for the sale of narcotics. Your honor, Mr. Devine had been out of jail for
26   only six months at the time of his arrest by Mr. Ripka. I have already given Ms.
27   Delbert Rule 404 notice of Officer Fusco's testimony and a copy of the report he
28   filed at the time of the prior arrest. I am now giving my notice under 404 of Ripka's
29   testimony.
30 **Atty. Delbert:** I object to the testimony of both officers. First of all, it's too late to give

1   notice under 404. Second, the testimony about each prior incident is out under 404.

2   And, in any event, each incident is out under 403.

3 **The Court:** Well, look. In light of what happened on cross-examination of Ripka, I'm going

4   to excuse the late 404 notice. Ms. Delbert, the recess will give you the time you

5   need. It's the end of the day. Why don't you both file briefs that address the

6   admissibility of the proffered testimony of officers Ripka and Fusco and Ms.

7   Delbert's objections to their admissibility under 404 and 403. I'll rule when we

8   reconvene.

Beckley Police Department Arrest Report

INCIDENT NO.			DATE OF STATEMENT January 30, 1996
NAME OF PERSON GIVING STATEMENT Devine David		DOB: 6-15-68	PHONE
STREET ADDRESS:: 555 Franklin St.	CITY: Beckley	STATE: Franklin	ZIP CODE: 33331		
STATEMENT TAKEN BY Det. G. Fusco, Narcotics # 7105		IN PRESENCE OF	

STATEMENT

Information supplied by reliable informant (#107) that a WM named "Dave" was selling heroin from his vehicle, blue 1992 Buick LeSabre (license plate #PEX 711), at the corner of Westin Hills Blvd. and Meadowood Dr. On January 30, 1996, at 2230 hours proceeded to Westin–Meadowood intersection in the Frog Hollow area of city with Officer T. Seyfat in an unmarked vehicle. Positioned vehicle about 50 ft. south of intersection on west side of Meadowood with a clear unobstructed view of intersection. At 2247 hours the suspect vehicle, blue '92 Buick with license plate #PEX 711, arrived and parked on south side of Westin Hills Blvd., about 15 ft. from corner. Only one person observed in vehicle, WM with dark hair and white shirt, who moved from driver's position to passenger seat. Observed two vehicles pull in front of suspect vehicle (at 2252 and 2258 hours). An individual exited each vehicle and proceeded to passenger side window. Observed WM in suspect vehicle turn on interior light, take something from glove compartment, and exchange unknown item for some amount of currency. At 2259 Officer Seyfat and undersigned officer exited police vehicle and proceeded to suspect vehicle. Seyfat approached driver side as I approached passenger side, identifying selves, ordering occupant out of vehicle. Patdown search of person revealed no weapons but a large bulk in rear pants pocket that proved to be $792 in cash, no bill larger than $20. Search of glove compartment produced 43 small glassine baggies (about 1" x 1" in size) of a white substance. Visual and texture check suggested heroin. Suspect advised of rights and taken into custody. Identification revealed name David Devine, above address.

_____

Signature

FRANKLIN GENERAL STATUTES

ARTICLE XVI. CRIMES AND PUNISHMENTS

Section 286. Unlawful manufacture, distribution, and possession, etc., of controlled substances.

(a) Except as authorized by this subheading, it is unlawful for any person to manufacture, distribute, or dispense or to possess a controlled dangerous substance in sufficient quantity to reasonably indicate under all the circumstances an intent to manufacture, distribute, or dispense a controlled dangerous substance;

(b) Any person who violates any of the provisions of subsection (a) of this section with respect to a substance classified in Schedules I or II which is a narcotic drug is guilty of a felony and is subject to imprisonment for not more than 20 years, or a fine of not more than $25,000, or both.

FRANKLIN RULES OF EVIDENCE

Rule 403. *Exclusion of Relevant Evidence on Grounds of Prejudice, Confusion, or Waste of Time*

Although relevant, evidence may be excluded if its probative value is substantially outweighed by the danger of unfair prejudice, confusion of the issues, or misleading the jury, or by considerations of undue delay, waste of time, or needless presentation of cumulative evidence.

Rule 404. *Character Evidence Not Admissible To Prove Conduct; Exceptions; Other Crimes*

(a) Character evidence generally. Evidence of a person's character or a trait of character is not admissible for the purpose of proving action in conformity therewith on a particular occasion, except:

(1) Character of accused. Evidence of a pertinent trait of character offered by an accused, or by the prosecution to rebut the same;

* * *

(b) Other crimes, wrongs, or acts. Evidence of other crimes, wrongs, or acts is not admissible to prove the character of a person in order to show action in conformity therewith. It may, however, be admissible for other purposes, such as proof of motive, opportunity, intent, preparation, plan, knowledge, identity, or absence of mistake or accident, provided that upon request by the accused, the prosecution in a criminal case shall provide reasonable notice in advance of trial, or during trial if the court excuses pretrial notice on good cause shown, of the general nature of any such evidence it intends to introduce at trial.

* * *

Rule 608. *Evidence of Character and Conduct of Witness*

(a) Opinion and reputation evidence of character. The credibility of a witness may be attacked or supported by evidence in the form of opinion or reputation, but subject to these limitations: (1) the evidence may refer only to character for truthfulness or untruthfulness, and (2) evidence of truthful character is admissible only after the character of the witness for truthfulness has been attacked by opinion or reputation evidence or otherwise.

(b) Specific instances of conduct. Specific instances of conduct. Specific instances of the conduct of a witness, for the purpose of attacking or supporting the witness's credibility, other than conviction of crime as provided in Rule 609, may not be proved by extrinsic evidence. They may, however, in the discretion of the court, if probative of truthfulness or untruthfulness, be inquired into on cross-examination of the witness (1) concerning the witness's character for truthfulness or untruthfulness, or (2) concerning the character for truthfulness or untruthfulness of another witness as to which character the witness being cross-examined has testified.

The giving of testimony, whether by an accused or by any other witness, does not operate as a waiver of the accused's or the witness's privilege against self-incrimination when examined with respect to matters which relate only to credibility.

Rule 609. *Impeachment by Evidence of Conviction of Crime*

(a) General rule. For the purpose of attacking the credibility of a witness,

(1) evidence that a witness other than an accused has been convicted of a crime shall be admitted if the crime was punishable by death or imprisonment in excess of one year under the law under which the witness was convicted, and evidence that an accused has been convicted of such a crime shall be admitted if the court determines that the probative value of admitting this evidence outweighs its prejudicial effect to the accused; and

(2) evidence that any witness has been convicted of a crime shall be admitted if it involved dishonesty or false statement, regardless of the punishment.

(b) Time limit. Evidence of a conviction under this rule is not admissible if a period of more than ten years has elapsed since the date of the conviction or of the release of the witness from the confinement imposed for that conviction, whichever is the later date, unless the court determines in the interests of justice, that the probative value of the conviction supported by specific facts and circumstances substantially outweighs its prejudicial effect.

* * *

Milford v. State
Franklin Supreme Court (1994)

The appellant, Edward Milford, was convicted of the unlawful possession of cocaine in sufficient quantity to reasonably indicate an intent to distribute. In this appeal he claims that the trial court erred in permitting the introduction of evidence revealing other criminal activity on his part.

On December 12, 1992, three officers of the Franklin State Police executed a search and seizure warrant at the residence of Edward and Lena Milford. At the time of the search, Edward Milford was not at home, although Lena was. The police recovered from a bedroom a large plastic baggie containing five smaller baggies, each of which contained cocaine.

The fact that the appellant was not caught with the contraband in his hands is not legally fatal to proof of possession. Possession and control need not be immediate and direct but may be constructive.

In terms of legal sufficiency, Edward Milford argued that he was not only not in the bedroom from which the cocaine was seized at the time of the search, he was not even in the house. Nothing suggested that the bedroom was his. Nothing made him a more likely possessor of the narcotics than any of the other five residents of the home.

Milford's connection with the house would probably have been enough to permit the State to clear the low hurdle of legal sufficiency but the margin of clearance would have been narrow. In this case, however, we are not called upon to make these closer decisions, for, despite Mr. Milford's insistence, we are not going to look at the events of December 12 in a vacuum.

If the evidence of December 12, standing alone, might have given rise to arguable ambiguities, the observations of December 10 dissolved those ambiguities. On December 10, Herman J. Grunion, a neighbor of the Milfords for two years and a frequent visitor in their home, went to their home in the company of Mike Wiehl, an undercover State Trooper. In the presence of Wiehl, Grunion purchased directly from Lena

Milford a one-eighth-ounce package of cocaine for $280. Edward Milford was present when the sale was consummated.

This narcotics sale on December 10 was a crime other than the charged possession on December 12. The question for decision is whether it was relevant and important in establishing guilt with respect to the December 12 charge of possession.

The relevance and vital importance of the "other crimes" evidence here in issue looms large. Close proximity between appellant and the cocaine was shown on December 10 even if the connection was less proximate on December 12. The presence of the cocaine was, moreover, shown to be within his knowledge on December 10.

It has long been recognized that evidence of other bad acts, although relevant and having some probative force, presents the problem that it is difficult to prevent a jury from improperly using evidence of other bad acts or giving it more weight than it deserves. The policy that other bad acts should be excluded is driven by two fears. One fear is that jurors will conclude from evidence of other bad acts that the defendant is a "bad person"

and should therefore be convicted of the current charge, and the other fear is that jurors will conclude that the defendant deserves punishment for the other bad conduct.

Evidence of other bad acts may, however, be admissible if it is relevant to the offense charged on some basis other than mere propensity to commit crime, and if it passes muster under the ever-present test of balancing relevance against unfair prejudice. The threshold inquiry a court must make before admitting similar acts evidence under Franklin Rule of Evidence § 404(b) is whether that evidence is probative of a material issue other than character. Evidence of other crimes may be admitted if it is substantially relevant to some contested issue in the case and if it is not offered to prove the defendant's guilt based on propensity to commit crime or his character as a criminal.

When evidence of other bad acts is relevant for reasons other than general criminal propensity, the trial judge must determine whether the accused's involvement in the other crimes is established by a preponderance of the evidence. If this requirement is met, the trial judge must then carefully weigh the necessity for and probative value of the evidence of other bad acts against any unfair prejudice likely to result from its admission. This approach recognizes that evidence of other bad acts usually has some relevance and that relevant evidence is usually admitted unless some good reason is shown to exclude it.

When a disputed issue involves the accused's state of mind, and especially when the only means of ascertaining that mental state is by drawing inferences from conduct, then prior instances of the conduct of the accused are relevant. Here, evidence of other offenses is admissible on the trial of the current charge to prove state of mind. To be admissible as relevant, such offenses need not be exactly concurrent. If they are committed within such time, or show such relation to the current charge, as to make connection obvious, such offenses are admissible. Where the other crime is so linked in point of time or circumstances as to show state of mind, the evidence is admissible.

This case is distinguishable from *Mellish v. State* (Franklin Supreme Court, 1992), involving the charge of possession of heroin with the intent to distribute. At issue was the admissibility of evidence that at some unspecified time in the past, the defendant and the witness had "worked together selling narcotics." This Court held the evidence inadmissible, finding no special relevance, and, indeed, questionable probative value even for criminal disposition. Proof that the accused had previously sold narcotics perhaps as long as five years before the crime charged in the indictment hardly tends to establish a disposition or propensity to commit the offense alleged, let alone an intent to do so. The remoteness in time of prior conduct has always been a consideration in determining relevancy, particularly when prior misconduct is alleged. Passage of time may actually indicate rehabilitation of the person.

In this case, the evidence, although involving other uncharged crimes, was admissible because of the strong inference that could be drawn from such evidence that Milford knowingly possessed the cocaine found on the day of the search and that he possessed it with the intent to distribute it. Evidence of the other offense possessed special relevance transcending mere criminal character. The necessity for the evidence was obvious. Proof of the other acts was clear, convincing, and uncomplicated, and the probative value of the evidence clearly outweighed its potential for unfair prejudice. Accordingly, we affirm.

*

CHAPTER 11

Taking the Bar Exam

Being in the Moment

No matter how hard you've studied and how many practice exams you've taken, once you get to the bar exam, you must let go and "be in the moment." This means that you respond to what the bar examiners ask of you and not what you want to tell the bar examiners you know. Trust me—there's no better way to ensure a poor grade than to ignore what is asked of you. By answering the question, you'll be showing what you know.

Everything you've been doing during your bar review has prepared you for this moment. And, if you've prepared properly and you're willing to surrender to the questions, you'll find the "exam zone." Like a "runner's high," it's a feeling that there is only "the now." It's where you're on auto-pilot and your training takes over. You've connected with whatever it was you were working to achieve: for the athlete, it's that connection of mind and body that allows for peak performance; for the law student, it's that command of the material that lets you see the issues in the facts and allows you to write with clarity and cogency. Your thinking and writing come together—it flows because you flow.

Implementing the Method

It's finally arrived. Your test booklet is on the desk in front of you. What follows is a step-by-step approach for taking the exam.

It's a blueprint you can follow to guide you through practice sessions and then implement on test day. Following this plan saves time and prevents anxiety: if you know exactly what you're going to do, and practice sufficiently, the process becomes second nature. On exam day, you can count on the routine to take over and prevent you from freezing up. You'll soon be in the "exam zone."

1. What should I do in the moments before the exam?

    ☐ Sit calmly and do not think about anything or anyone else while the proctors are handing out the exam materials.

    ☐ Be alert and listen carefully: you must follow all instructions.

    ☐ Do not worry about any other part of the exam. Focus solely on what is right in front of you. It requires and demands your full and undivided attention.

2. What should I do when told to begin?

    These are critical minutes for setting the pace and tenor of your exam experience. You want to start smoothly, work efficiently, and above all, remain focused and calm. Here's how to do it:

    ☐ Make sure you've followed the proctor's directions for identifying your exam papers.

    ☐ Write down what you're afraid you'll forget on scrap paper.

    If you're worried that there's something you're likely to forget during the course of the exam, write it down on scrap paper. It only takes a few minutes and buys peace of mind.

    ☐ Scan the exam

    Since you know the composition of the exam from your preparation, there's no need to scan any part of the bar exam except for the essays. Here you may want to get a sense of the general topics before you begin. More than that is not necessary.

3. How should I allocate my time?

Just as you "set your clock" during practice sessions, do so now:

☐ Using the exact time you were told to begin the exam, set your timetable as you did during practice sessions.

☐ Write down the starting and ending times for each question.

☐ Follow this clock throughout the exam to stay on track.

4. How do I keep a handle on my timing with the MBE?

As you know from practicing MBE questions, they are presented in a completely random manner so that both the subject matter and the complexity of the question varies from one question to the next. As you work through the exam, keep an eye on your clock to gauge your progress. This should keep you in line.

You have to complete between 16 and 17 questions in a 30–minute period, averaging 33–34 questions every hour to complete the 100 questions in a three hour period; set your "clock" on the half hour with appropriate milestones.

Assuming your exam begins at 9:15 and ends at 12:15:

Time	Question Number
9:45	17
10:15	33
10:45	50
11:15	67
11:45	84
12:15	100

5. What if I get stuck on an MBE question?

Here you have two options:

☐ You can circle the question in your test booklet and return after you've completed the entire exam.

☐ You can make your best choice and move on.

With only 1.8 minutes per question, there's only so much time to allow for doubt. No matter how well you've prepared, there are bound to be questions that present difficulty. Don't squander precious time that could be spent on questions you can answer.

6. What if I get stuck on an essay question?

While we've covered this topic in Chapter 8 in the Checklist, *Emergency Measures or "What to Do If,"* we'll review some relevant points again here:

☐ Have I forgotten the rule of law? What should I do if my mind goes blank when I read the question and nothing comes to mind?

    ☐ Ask: *"What is the issue?"*

    You can formulate the issue from the question you are asked to answer. Focusing on identifying the issue will allow you to regain your composure and lead you back to the process of thinking like a lawyer.

    ☐ Write the issue, whether or not you "know" the rule at this point. Formulating the issue will get you points from the grader because it shows that you can identify the legal problem from the facts.

    ☐ Next ask: *"What principle of law is implicated by this issue?"*

    Now you're thinking like a lawyer. This will either lead you to the rule from the recesses of your memory or you'll have to improvise. When you improvise, rely on your knowledge of general legal principles and standards to guide you.

☐ How do I use what I know about a topic to build on it?

If you're asked about recoverable damages, rely on what you know about "damages" in particular areas of the law and proceed from there.

    ☐ For example, if it's a contracts problem, you know every breach of contract entitles the aggrieved party to sue for damages. The general theory of damages is that the injured party should be placed in the same position as if the contract had been properly performed, at least so far as money damages can do this.

Ask,

- ☐ Is plaintiff entitled to his "expectation interest" or "the benefit of his bargain"?

- ☐ If not, can plaintiff seek reliance damages?

- ☐ Was defendant "unjustly enriched" so plaintiff recover in restitution?

- ☐ Does an action lie in specific performance? Was the contract for a sale for real property or a unique piece of personal property?

☐ On the other hand, if it's a torts problem, very different policy considerations are involved. The tort system compensates for both economic and non-economic loss since its goal is to provide redress of a civil wrong.

☐ What if I can't find the issue or principle of law?

If you really hit a roadblock, you can break down the problem into the elements common to every case and proceed from there. The following prompts allow you to gain access to the problem when your initial read is fruitless. From any one of these topics, it is but a short step to finding the principle of law implicated in the question:

☐ Identify the parties and the nature of their relationship.

Is it that of employer/employee, landlord/tenant, buyer/seller, parent/child, teacher/student, husband/wife?

☐ Identify the place(s) where the facts arose.

Did the events occur in a public area, a private home, a school, a waterway, a farm?

☐ Identify whether objects or things were involved.

Was there a transaction involving the sale of goods?
Is the ownership of land or chattel in dispute?

☐ Identify the acts or omissions which form the basis of the action.

Was there a robbery, a breach of contract, an assault, an act of discrimination?

☐ Determine whether there is a defense to the action.

Is there a basis for self-defense, justification, privilege?

☐ Characterize the relief sought.

Are the parties seeking damages?
Are they monetary or equitable damages, or both?

7. Should I "skip around" on the MBE?

Some believe that the first twenty questions and the last twenty questions are "easier" and therefore, they should answer those first and then go back to the others. Since MBE questions appear in completely random order, both in terms of subject matter and complexity, there is no benefit from jumping around but quite possibly there is a detriment: you can lose your place on the answer sheet and enter your selections incorrectly.

Also, it takes time to read a question, decide to skip it, and then return to read it again later. You simply don't have this extra time. However, if you find that you must skip some questions to return later, leave the appropriate spaces on your answer sheet so that you don't mismark subsequent answer choices.

8. Should I "skip around" when answering the essay questions?

Generally, there's no rule that says you must answer the questions in the order in which they are presented as long as you mark your answer booklets appropriately. If you find that your reading of the first question is fruitless, then you might consider moving on to another question so as not to lose time or create anxiety. Chances are that once you're operating in "exam mode," when you return to the skipped question, you'll be able to answer it.

But be very careful—there are notable exceptions such as Connecticut where applicants must answer the questions in order because questions are collected every hour.

Mastering Anxiety

1. What if I am feeling anxious?

   Pre-exam jitters are absolutely normal and very necessary. You should expect to feel anxious. It's also useful because the adrenaline ensures that you'll operate at peak performance. The problem occurs when it interferes with your performance. It should subside once you start working.

   Take a moment to think about all the work you've done to prepare. In fact, you've over-prepared. It's the best way to provide the confidence necessary to ward off the usual exam jitters.

2. Is there anything else I can do if I'm feeling anxious?

   ☐ Recall past experiences of success. You've taken tests all your life and you've done well or you wouldn't be here now sitting for the bar exam. Just think of all the college exams you've taken and the LSAT itself. These were tough exams and you managed quite nicely. There's something to be said about the value of past experience—if you've done it before, you can do it again.

   ☐ Remember it's only an exam. In the general scheme of things, it's still only an exam.

   ☐ Conjure a "negative" role-model. This worked nicely for me. I knew several people from high school and college who were living full and productive lives as lawyers. I had not considered them particularly exceptional. I thought to myself "if so-and-so could pass the bar exam, then so could I." I'm sure you know someone who can serve as your own negative role model. Just never tell them.

☐ Begin the exam and work your way through, one question after another. As you move forward, your exam preparation will take over and you'll soon be thinking of the questions and nothing else.

FINAL PLANS

A week before the exam:

☐ Have you confirmed your hotel reservations?

☐ Have you packed what you need to take with you?

　☐ For staying at a hotel?

　　☐ Your most comfortable clothing?

　　☐ An alarm clock (or will the hotel give you a wake-up call)?

　　☐ Snack foods?

　☐ For taking to the test site?

　　☐ Test Admission Ticket?

　　☐ Appropriate forms of personal identification?

　　☐ A watch?

　　☐ An adequate supply of pencils, pens, highlighters?

　　☐ "Quiet" food?

The night before the exam:

☐ Have you put your books away and plan to relax by watching television or a movie?

☐ Have you set your alarm or left a wake-up call with the hotel?

☐ Have you packed snack foods and lunch?

The days of the exam:

☐ Are you dressed in layers so you will be comfortable during the exam whether it's warm or cold in the exam room?

☐ Are you planning to get to the test site approximately 30 minutes before the starting time, yet stay away from the crowd?

☐ If you will be with friends, have you agreed not to talk about the exam, either before or after the exam?

☐ Will you listen carefully and follow all instructions from the test proctors?

☐ When a session is over, will you leave the test site promptly and go home or to your hotel?

☐ Will you try and get a good night's rest between the days of the exam, knowing that you have done all you possibly could to prepare for this exam?

*

CHAPTER 12

When It's Over

You thought this day would never come—the bar exam is over. It's almost anti-climactic. All that you've been working for since your acceptance to law school is now behind you. Suddenly, after years of studying, and the last few weeks of intense, almost around the clock studying, you're left with nothing to do. It's possible—even likely—that you're feeling strangely out of sorts.

What You Can Expect

These feelings are entirely normal. You're finally on your own—law school is behind you and the bar review course is over. Your usual sources of support, the ones you worked so carefully to cultivate from the moment you started law school are now behind you too. You can feel a sense of loneliness, even isolation.

AFTER THE BAR EXAM

1. Do you find that you are physically exhausted yet have trouble sleeping?

    If so, you are most likely overtired from the weeks of concentrated study. You are physically and emotionally exhausted. The adrenaline you've been living on for so long is gone. It takes time to readjust—time to get back to a normal routine and time to refocus your energies.

2. Do you find it difficult to stay focused on even the simplest activities?

    This is a result of the hundreds of hours you have just spent in preparation for the exam. Because of the intensity of the effort, it will take time to feel normal again!

3. Do you find yourself reliving the exam or rethinking your answers?

    This is entirely normal but a fruitless activity. You have to try your very best to put the exam out of your mind. Find something else to occupy your thoughts. Consider the suggestions that follow in the next question.

4. Have you made plans to

    ☐ get together with friends?

        If you're feeling lonely, pick up the phone and call one of your study partners or law school friends. Chances are they are feeling just as dislocated as you. Make plans to do something totally non-law related.

    ☐ see family?

        You have probably not been able to attend family functions for quite some time. Now would be a good time to visit with family and renew those connections.

    ☐ have some fun?

        Is it possible to take a short trip or get away for a weekend? A change of scenery works wonders to renew one's outlook. Sometimes, even a day away from your normal surroundings is enough to change your perspective.

5. Have you set new goals?

    You have been living with a single focus for a very long time. It's time to set some new, non-law related goals. Of course you'll be setting career goals, but right now you need to think about the other parts of your life.

6. What did you miss most during law school?

   ☐ Was it regular workouts at the gym or sports activities? If so, consider joining a gym or starting a weekly basketball or softball game.

   ☐ Was it brunch on Sundays with your family?

   ☐ Was it simply "going out" and not having to think about studying?

7. When was the last time you read something other than a law school assignment?

   Try reading something for fun. It's the fastest, easiest, and least expensive way to get reacquainted with the rest of the world and get in touch with yourself.

8. Do you wonder if life will ever return to normal?

   The weeks and months following the bar exam will be different for everyone, but chances are that you'll all experience some of the same things. Truthfully, no one really relaxes until the bar results come out and you know for sure whether this "thing" is really behind you. Until then, no matter how you look at it, you're still living in limbo. Do the best you can to stay positive, remain confident, and go about the rest of your life. It's important to remember that being a lawyer is only one small part of who you are—don't let it become everything.

*

CHAPTER 13

Advice for the Re-Taker

If at First You Didn't Succeed

Of all bar-takers, it might be said that you face the most daunting task of all: overcoming your fear of failure. My heart is with you. But I know that you can pass the bar exam because I've worked with so many re-takers to know that it's possible. It's possible because you're going to follow the plan this time.

There are any number of reasons candidates don't pass the bar exam: the reasons are almost as varied as the test takers themselves. There are always a small minority of candidates who walk into the exam unprepared, knowing that they're unprepared. But this isn't typical. The vast majority work hard in preparing for the exam but working hard is not the same as working smart.

It won't be easy to pick up your books once again, but pick them up you must if you want to be the attorney you went to law school to become. Allow yourself some time to regroup emotionally and physically before taking up the task of bar preparation once again. But once you do, don't look back! You're not the same person you were the first time around, and now you're going to do things very differently.

And you must proceed differently to achieve a different result. Some re-takers erroneously believe that if they had simply spent more time on their studies, they would have passed. However, I can practically guarantee that spending more time doing what you've done before will do nothing to change the outcome. A different result requires a different approach, not more of the same. It also requires that you be brutally honest with yourself: you have to face the truth about you did or did not do. For example, if you did not learn the black letter law—really learn it so that you could recite it automatically—then no study schedule or checklist will compensate for this deficiency, no matter how elaborate or comprehensive.

Before we get involved in an intense examination of your test-taking skills and substantive knowledge, we need to consider some of the more basic issues. The most difficult part will be getting through the first few weeks after learning the results. You won't feel like doing much of anything—least of all looking over the materials sent to you by the bar examiners. But you must. There are some time-sensitive matters that require your attention and you may not be thinking all too clearly at the moment.

Here is where I can do the thinking for you—if you let me. I've tried to make it as painless as possible. Let the Checklist do the thinking for you.

 WHERE TO START?

After allowing yourself a brief cooling off period, it's time to get moving. The steps outlined below provide a place for you to begin.

1. Look to your jurisdiction. What information does your state release to failing examinees?

   ☐ Are copies of your exam answers available?

   ☐ Are the test questions available?

   ☐ Are representative good answers or model answers available?

   ☐ Is there a fee?

☐ Is there a deadline?

☐ Is there someone who can help explain what you have received?

2. What is your state's regrading procedure?

☐ Is there an automatic regrading process or may you petition the bar examiners myself?

☐ Is there a fee?

☐ Is there a deadline?

☐ Can you have the MBE answer sheet re-scored by hand? Is this information available from your local jurisdiction or must you contact the National Conference of Bar Examiners?

Note: If your MBE score was very low and there's no way a couple of correct answer choices would make a difference between passing and failing, then you can't expect miracles. Face the facts, harden your resolve, and move on.

3. How does your performance on the essay portion of the exam compare with your performance on the MBE? Is there a significant difference?

4. Are MBE sub-scores available so you can identify particular subject weaknesses?

5. Who can you talk to about my performance? Is there someone at

☐ your bar review course?

☐ the bar examiners?

☐ your law school?

SELF-REFLECTION QUESTIONS

Before you begin a substantive review and work with MBE and essay questions, you should consider some of the other factors involved in the preparation process to see where you might have gone wrong.

The first step is answer the following questions openly and honestly.

1. Did you study for the MBE and forget about the essays because you wrongly believed that if you got a high enough MBE score the bar examiners would not read your essays?

2. Did you get so distracted by concerns about the technicalities and procedures of the bar exam (timing considerations, scoring, format, length, and pass rates) that you lost sight of the law?

3. Did you fail to reach "automaticity" by memorizing the black letter law, relying instead on only a general familiarity with concepts?

4. Were you overwhelmed by the subject matter outlines from the bar review course?

5. Did you work with released bar exam essays from your jurisdiction?

6. Even if you purchased or downloaded these essays, did you *really* work with them by

   ☐ actually writing out answers?

   ☐ writing answers under timed conditions?

   ☐ comparing what you wrote to the model/sample answer and appreciating the differences?

7. Did you practice with actual, released MBE questions?

8. Did you practice MBE questions correctly by

   ☐ answering one question at a time?

   ☐ reading the explanation even when you answered the question correctly?

   ☐ de-constructing each of the answer choices and asking,

      ☐ Do I know why each of the incorrect answer choices is incorrect?

      ☐ Can I fully articulate the reasoning to support the correct answer choice?

      ☐ Did I check my notes if I could not recall the specific language of the rule?

  □ Did I check my notes if I wasn't sure of related sub-issues, even if not necessary to answer the question?

9. If you answered a question incorrectly, did you go back over the question and try to determine where you made a wrong turn

  □ was it a problem with how I read the question?

  □ was it a problem with my knowledge of the black letter law?

10. Did you include a timed practice session to see whether you could answer between 16 and 17 questions in 30 minutes?

11. Did you include at least one practice session to simulate a six-hour test period of 200 questions?

*

CHAPTER 14

A Bar Exam Make-Over

Getting Beyond the Disappointment

It's hard to understand how hundreds of hours spent attending bar review classes, reading outlines, studying notes, and taking practice exams could possibly result in a failing score, but it can and it does. I'm not about to minimize your disappointment—it really hurts—but what matters now is what we can learn from the experience so your next attempt will be successful.

In this effort, we are going to use the results from your past bar exam to figure out what went wrong and where. What we're going to do next won't be easy but it's essential if you're going to pass the bar exam. It's what you do when you realize that you've been traveling down the wrong road: you go back to where you made the wrong turn and proceed again. It's the going back and finding out where the wrong turn was taken that's our job.

Forensic IRAC

In preparing to re-take the bar exam, you'll be writing out lots of exam answers and practicing many multiple choice questions. To be meaningful, you'll need feedback on your work. The good news is that you can learn to assess it yourself. By applying what I've termed "forensic IRAC" to your essays and multiple choice answers, you'll be able to identify the errors and correct them.

Forensic IRAC works by examining each sentence you've written in terms of its place in the IRAC structure of legal analysis. I've called the process forensic IRAC because the techniques are similar to those employed by crime scene investigators, accountants, medical examiners, and any of the forensic experts who go back over the trail of evidence to determine how that evidence led to a particular result. While such experts rely on fingerprints, ledger books, and DNA, we use IRAC.

This process allows us to step inside your head to see the way you thought about the exam problem–how you approached it, how you read the facts, and what they meant to you. What you've written leaves an identifiable trail–something like your DNA but instead of identifying your biologic self, it identifies your cognitive self. You should think of forensic IRAC as deciphering a code, where each sentence you've written is a clue to piecing together how you approached a problem. It works because when you write, you take the inherently private and internal process called "thought" and make it visible—and provide just the way into your head that we need. Here's where your "baseline" becomes critical.

Using Your Baseline

Your score on the bar exam, with its individual breakdown on the MBE and essays, represents your "baseline" performance. These numbers are a guide to your strengths and weaknesses in the MBE subjects and the essays. While you might wish you didn't have the experience it took to acquire a baseline, you're going to make the best of the situation by using it to your advantage.

The checklists that follow will guide you through the preparation process, from deciding whether to re-take a bar review course to learning to assess your own exam performance. In effect, you'll become your own personal grader but with one significant advantage: you'll be able to change the outcome!

ASSESSING YOUR SITUATION

There are two major considerations for re-takers:

1. How do you preserve the substantive knowledge base you acquired as a result of your prior bar preparation?

    The bar exam tests the black letter law to a level of specificity that doesn't stay with you for too long. You'll need to make a complete review of all subjects. What is the best way to cover all the necessary material?

    A. Should you take a review course?

        1. Can you afford to take another course?

            Bar review courses are expensive and even with the reduced fee some offer to re-takers, they can still be expensive and not necessarily the best use of your time. Unless you fall into one of the categories in question 2 below, I'd suggest you forgo a course.

        2. How long has it been since you've graduated law school?

            If it has been more than 18 months since you've graduated from law school or taken your last bar exam, then I strongly recommend a review course. You may not think it necessary but it's essential for two reasons:

            •   To make sure you are studying current law

            Bar review courses continuously update their materials so candidates have access to the current law in preparing for the exam. While your notes from one bar administration to the next will still be timely, you should not take chances with study materials older than that.

            •   To get back into the routine

                It is not easy to get back into the habit of studying and if you've been away from it for a while, it's probably best to commit to a structured program. The set schedule of classes and assignments is what you need to re-acclimate yourself to the process.

            If you fall within this category, ask:

☐ Should you repeat the course you've already taken?

Some candidates like to sit through the same course a second time because they receive a reduced rate and don't have to take any new notes. If you are an "oral" learner, then hearing the material again may be very helpful.

On the other hand, you might want to take a different course: the change in approach, focus, sequence, and study materials may be necessary to keep you engaged and lead to a different result.

☐ Should you take a different, but still traditional bar review course?

☐ Should you take one of the "abbreviated" courses offering targeted reviews of substance and skills training? There are a number of short-term bar review courses that offer intense re-taker classes. These are often ideal for those pressed for time and money who still need the direction that only a structured study environment can provide.

☐ Should you take an on-line course? Finally, there are a number of on-line programs available that allow you to work from home and still receive valuable feedback. If you are pressed for time because of work or other commitments during the bar preparation period, this is a viable option.

B. Do you have the discipline to follow a study schedule on your own?

If you're a conscientious worker and a recent re-taker, it's possible, even preferable to work on your own. There is no need to sit through lectures and gather the material again. Instead, you can use these precious hours to study the material and practice questions.

If you plan to work on your own, then follow the schedule from your prior bar review course to make sure that you cover all the topics. However, be sure to adapt the schedule so that you spend more time where you need it. This assumes you've kept your bar review materials. If not, get in touch with a law school buddy and see if you can borrow them.

2. How do you improve your performance on individual sections of the bar exam to achieve an overall passing score?

    By taking a targeted approach to the topics and areas of the bar exam that caused you difficulty, you can concentrate your efforts where they're needed most and will do the most good. How do you determine what and where your weaknesses lie?

    A. What can you learn from your MBE scores?

        If used correctly, your MBE score report can help you identify your strengths and weaknesses on the six MBE subjects. Then you can use this information to target your study efforts.

        1. What do the numbers mean?

            When you receive your MBE results, they will include a subject breakdown of your scores. Because each jurisdiction determines the weight it will accord the MBE portion of the bar exam, you'll want to look at the "raw" scores and not the scaled scores. The raw score represents the actual number of correct answers. For example, if you got a raw score of "18" in Criminal Law, this means that out of the 33 possible Criminal Law questions, you got slightly more than 50% correct. If you can add but two or three more correct answers, your raw score will increase a bit, but your scaled score will jump. Because of each jurisdiction's individual scaling system, numbers do not have the usual one-to-one relationship. This means that one right answer can be worth more than one point.

        2. How do you use the numbers to identify strengths and weaknesses?

            You can use the numbers to see if there are significant differences in your performance between individual subjects. For example, if you scored a "23" in Constitutional Law and only a "9" in Property, then you know you have a lot of work to do in Property.

        3. What does it mean if the numbers are pretty consistent between all the MBE subjects?

If the numbers are consistent, then you may have a reading comprehension problem in addition to a gap in substantive knowledge. You'll want to drill yourself on reading the questions and focusing on the bar examiners' very particular use of vocabulary. Your ability to identify signal words and legally significant phrases will help to compensate for some reading deficiencies.

4. What does it mean if the numbers vary widely from subject to subject?

    If there's a wide variation in scores between subjects, then it's not likely to be a reading comprehension problem, but a true subject-specific deficiency. In this case, you have to make some tough decisions. Some subjects are easier to master than others. Pick your subjects and focus on increasing your score in the areas where you're most likely to have success. In addition to the subjects for which you have the greatest affection (if that's true of any of the subjects at this point), I'd suggest that you hone in on those topics which feature a more direct application of rule to fact, such as Torts, Criminal Law, and Constitutional Law. Then you must buckle down and practice, practice, practice.

B. What can you learn from your essays?

    1. What do the numbers mean?

        If your jurisdiction breaks down your essay scores, then look for any significant differences between individual essays.

        ☐ Do your essays show a range of scores?

            If you find a range of scores, including some rather high scores, then your problem is most likely a function of the subject matter and not your general essay writing skills. You need to concentrate on learning the substantive law in the low-scoring areas and practice the technique for constructing solid statements of the rule. Write sample answers and lean heavily on the "building block" approach by incorporating elements, definitions, exceptions, or distinctions, into your articulation of the rule. See Chapter 8.

☐ Are your essay scores consistent?

If your scores tend to be consistent, then you need to focus on both substance and form. You should work on improving your performance on each part of an essay, beginning with articulation of the issue and following through with a complete rule section and a thorough analysis of the applicable facts. Refer to the following section on forensic IRAC.

2. How do you use the copies of the exam answers you requested from the bar examiners?

You are going to use "forensic IRAC" to identify the flaws in your work and correct them. Refer to the Checklist in this chapter, *Using Forensic IRAC to Diagnose Your Essays*.

C. What can you learn from your MPT score?

Since the bar examiners give you the "law" on the MPT, how and where did you go wrong?

1. Did you finish the MPT?

Typically, a low score on the MPT results from a lack of practice. It is not difficult "legally" but it can be a race against the clock. Adequate practice is essential to master the MPT. Your goal is to make your approach to the material so mechanical that come test day, it's purely automatic.

2. Did you use an outline to prepare your answer?

The MPT includes so much material that it's easy to get lost. It is necessary to draft an outline before you write to organize your response.

3. Did you re-state the facts and background material instead of addressing the issues?

If you have the opportunity to review your MPT response, then look to see whether you included unnecessary background facts before finally getting to the issue. This just takes up your valuable time without adding any point-worthy material. Instead, practice beginning your response with a direct reference to the issue you're asked to resolve.

4. Did you include long, quoted passages from the cases?

Once again, this is a major time-waster. While you want to cite to the Library cases to support your rule statements, rely on quoting key phrases rather than copying whole passages.

 ## USING FORENSIC IRAC TO DIAGNOSE YOUR ESSAYS

Each sentence you write in an essay should serve some identifiable function: stating the issue, articulating the relevant rule of law, or developing the analysis of the facts. As you read your essay answer, consider each IRAC element against the criteria outlined below. By showing you exactly what to look for in each step of an IRAC analysis, you'll be able to pinpoint exactly where in the process any weakness occurs. Then, by following the suggested remedies for that particular problem, you'll be able to correct it.

What follows is something like a troubleshooting section in a technical manual where system faults are identified and applicable solutions are provided. It works by examining what you've written to reveal your thought process.

1. Do you have trouble finding the "issue"?

A failure to properly identify the issue(s) in your exam question results in a "scattershot" approach in the rest of your answer—a real "hit or miss" situation when it comes to racking up exam points. Generally, you can tell that you've had difficulty in "spotting the issue" by what you've written in either the rule or the application portion of your essay, or both.

A. How you can tell when it shows up in your statement of the rule?

☐ Is your rule section so general and open-ended that it completely overlooks the precise rule implicated by the facts?

☐ Does your analysis gloss over the rule so lightly that the grader can't be sure whether you knew the relevant rule or merely happened to mention it?

☐ Have you stated the wrong rule altogether?

☐ Have you danced around the topic without really engaging it by writing lengthy, treatise-like discussions of general legal topics?

B. What is the remedy?

The following is a suggested strategy for identifying the legal issue and writing a rule section that addresses the issue:

☐ Begin your analysis by identifying the call-of-the-question.

☐ State the issue based on the interrogatory.

☐ Develop an outline of the rule according to the issue.

2. Do you have trouble writing the "rule"?

There are two separate problems which can show up in the rule portion of your exam analysis. The first is where there's a genuine ignorance of the law. You may state the wrong rule for the issue in controversy or refer to the right rule, but state it incorrectly, either in whole or in part. The second problem occurs where there's a demonstration of substantive knowledge, but it's sketchy and incomplete. Here you don't state "enough" rule to provide an adequate context for analyzing the facts.

A. How can you tell when what you've written shows you don't really know the applicable law?

Look for examples of the following in the "rule" section of your essay:

☐ Have you substituted your words for legally significant language?

☐ Have you used imprecise language and meaningless phrases?

☐ Have you relied on buzz-words?

☐ Did you misstate the law?

☐ Did you write illogical, disjointed statements of the rule?

☐ Did you neglect to use the "language of the law" so that your essay did not sound as if it were written by a lawyer?

Look for examples of the following in the "application" section of your essay:

☐ Did you merely repeat the facts without stating their legal significance?

☐ Did you write logically inconsistent statements?

☐ Did you fail to distinguish between relevant and irrelevant facts?

What is the remedy?

There are a number of reasons why you don't know something. The most obvious reason is that you simply didn't spend enough time studying and memorizing the black letter law. On the other hand, a lack of knowledge can result from an inability to integrate and learn legal principles. Sometimes, you may spend adequate time in study but the time spent is ineffective because you're not focused on the right stuff.

In addition to reviewing your notes and memorizing black letter law, you are going to integrate the following tasks into your study plan:

☐ Re-write the rules of law in your own words while conserving the legal "terms of art."

☐ Put the parts/elements of rules together in a way that forms a logical whole.

☐ Learn the language of the law by memorizing basic vocabulary.

☐ Memorize basic definitions and the elements of rules because you need to know the law to write the law.

☐ Having memorized the rules, make sure you understand how to apply them to new fact situations. Write out answers to hypotheticals and practice answering objective, multiple choice questions in that area of the law.

☐ Practice turning rules into issues and questions. Don't stop at memorizing the definition of a "merchant." Learn to ask yourself, "what's the *consequence* of finding that the party was a merchant with respect to the transaction in dispute?"

B. Is your statement of the rule incomplete or unorganized?

Look for examples of the following in the "rule" section of your essay:

☐ Have you failed to write "snippets" of law, buzz-words, and catch phrases in place of complete sentences and full explanations?

☐ Are there lists of "elements" without definitions?

☐ Have you identified the relevant exception but there's no statement of the general rule to provide context?

☐ Are there statements of law without a logical connection between them?

☐ Have you failed to write the rule in its logical order from the general to the specific?

What is the remedy?

☐ Follow the building block approach to construct a rule of law:

    ☐ *Explain* the elements of the rule.

    ☐ *Define* the legal terms.

    ☐ Identify the *general rule* that provides the context for the exception.

    ☐ Include any relevant *federal/state distinctions* or *common law/statutory law distinctions*.

    ☐ Follow a hierarchy of concepts by moving from the general to the specific and defining all legal terms of art.

Look for examples of the following in the "application" section of your essay:

☐ Is there a solid factual discussion that appears element-based but without any explanation/identification of the element?

☐ Have you analyzed the legally-relevant facts but without reference to the supporting legal framework?

What is the remedy?

☐ Build your legal context by working backwards from what you've stated in the facts to determine the scope of the rule necessary to provide a foundation for what you've discussed.

☐ With respect to a fact, ask yourself *why* you found this fact sufficiently important to be discussed. This forces you to identify the legal basis for relevancy.

3. Do you have trouble writing the "application"?

In these cases, your discussion may ramble and roam, moving without any logical transition from topic to topic. Or it may simply repeat the facts from the hypothetical. This is by far one of the easiest problems to correct—that is, once you understand what it means to "analyze the facts." That's because identifying the issue and articulating the rule is the hard part; once you've done that, it should be clear sailing. So why is it such a stumbling block for so many?

A. How can you tell if you have a problem with analysis?

☐ Is there no connection between the call-of-the-question and the application section of your answer?

When you're asked a specific question in a problem, then your analysis must be tailored to that question.

☐ Are the facts in the hypothetical repeated instead of analyzed?

One very good reason for restating facts instead of analyzing them is failure to work from the legal question. The issue provides focus and direction: it's the "problem" you solve with your "analysis." Without identifying a problem, you have nothing to answer, so you flounder and fall back on narrative.

☐ Is there a contradiction or discrepancy between what the rule requires and how the facts are analyzed?

Here the problem is that the analysis does not follow the requirements of the rule. Instead, there is a disconnect between rule and fact, indicating a genuine lack of under-standing

- ☐ Do you rely on conclusory statements?
- ☐ Do you rely on such language as "obviously," "clearly," and "evidently," thus avoiding analysis?
- ☐ Do you avoid the question to be analyzed by using "if" and "should"?

For example, do you leave the discussion at stating "*if* the breach was material" instead of evaluating whether or not it was? Or do you turn the question over to the judge—"*should* the court find that the words constituted a dying declaration"—and then not evaluate whether they were and what consequences flow from that finding?

- ☐ Is there no mention of any of the individual facts—no use of dates, times, ages, amounts, relationships, locations—nothing that ties the analysis to the specific facts of the problem?
- ☐ Is there an absence of the word "because"?

What is the remedy?

- ☐ Match up each element/sub-element in the rule to a fact.
- ☐ Make sure that every conclusion you reach is supported by an explanation of the "why" behind it (which usually means adding "because" to link rule and fact).

What not to write:

The specifications in this agreement are express conditions.

What you should write:

*The specifications in this agreement can be considered express conditions **because** the contract language uses that of express condition **when** it states the hardwood floor "shall be" of a particular type.*

What not to write:

In addition, Newman will say that the oral agreement contradicts the written agreement which is not allowed under the parol evidence rule.

What you should write:

In addition, the oral agreement contradicts the written agreement **because** *the oral conversation between Ben and Newman allowed Ben to paint the kitchen at any time while the written agreement specifies that the painting must be done after the cabinetry is completed.*

☐ Make sure you "use" every fact of consequence in your analysis.

B. How can you train yourself to engage in thoughtful analysis and not simply restate the facts of the problem?

☐ Examine the inferences/implications of each fact in light of the rule.

☐ Look for the ambiguities in the facts.

☐ Focus on explaining how these facts can be interpreted.

☐ Expect to show *how* each fact fits with the requirements of the rule and *why* it fits, **and** the opposite—why it doesn't.

☐ Consider the underlying policy of the rule and how it is implicated in the facts.

 ESSAY PRACTICE CHECKLIST

Here is a checklist to use for self-evaluation of practice essay exams:

1. Did I scan the entire exam to get a sense of scope and substance before I started to read and answer questions?

2. Did I allocate the use of my time properly?

☐ Did I apportion my time according to the point allocation of each question?

☐ Did I set up a timetable and then follow it?

☐ Did I complete the exam?

3. Did I follow all exam instructions?

☐ Did I answer the specific question that was asked of me?

☐ Did I follow all formatting and procedural requirements?

4. Did I read the question at least twice before beginning to outline?

5. Did I outline before I began to write by "charting" the rules with the relevant facts?

    Example of a rule chart for promissory estoppel:

Rule/Element	Fact
Promise	To give money to granddaughter so she would not have to work
Reasonably foreseeable reliance	If he promises to pay her what she earns at her job, she'll give it up
Actual reliance	Gave up job as sales clerk
Detriment	Now has no income

6. Did I develop the legal issues sufficiently?

    ☐ Did I identify each issue using 'whether, when"?

    The "whether, when" construction leads you to connect the legal question with the specific facts in controversy. For example, *"The issue is **whether** Ben committed a battery **when** he threw the vase at Amy and hit Jill instead."*

    ☐ For each issue and sub-issue, did I articulate the relevant rule of law?

    ☐ Did I stray from the relevant issues and discuss irrelevant ones?

7. If appropriate for the question, did I write a complete paragraph of law for each issue by working from the general to the specific?

8. Did I analyze the facts sufficiently?

    ☐ Did I use the word "because" to match the fact to the rule?

    ☐ Did I "use" each fact in the analysis?

    ☐ Did I simply recite a fact without explaining its significance?

9. Was my writing clear, organized, and "lawyerly"?

☐   Was my writing organized so the reader could follow my reasoning?

☐   Did I use topic sentences to introduce my points?

☐   Was my essay organized properly to address the question?

    ☐   By party?

    ☐   By cause of action?

☐   Did I use appropriate legal vocabulary?

10. How can I improve?

_____

_____

_____

_____

_____

_____

_____

_____

_____

_____

USING FORENSICS ON
MBE QUESTIONS

Our use of the forensic IRAC method operates somewhat differently when we apply it to objective, multiple choice questions. That's because in some way, short answer questions have already narrowed the field of possible errors. As we discussed Chapter 9, there are two basic skills at work in answering multiple choice questions: your knowledge of the law and your ability to analyze the questions, which in turn relies on your reading comprehension skills. An incorrect answer choice, therefore, is the result of an error in one of these areas.

The key to working with MBE questions is learning to identify the flaw in the reasoning behind an incorrect answer choice. This means getting inside your head and figuring out what you were thinking when you selected a multiple choice answer.

Developing Your Thought Monitor

As we discussed in Chapter 9, there are a number of reasons for incorrect answer choices. The most obvious is ignorance of the law. A superficial or general understanding of a rule is insufficient to distinguish between the answer choices. Still, a number of errors have nothing to do with "knowing the law" and everything to do with answering a question correctly.

A. To determine whether you may have problems in one of these other areas, ask:

☐ Do you comprehend what you read?

Maybe you misread the question—either the question that is asked or the facts in the problem, or both. Sometimes you mis-characterize the facts. These are essentially reading comprehension problems where you do not interpret correctly what you've read.

☐ Do you add facts to the hypothetical?

Here you read into the facts and sometimes add your own—which of course changes the problem and leads to an incorrect answer choice. Or you may see implications which have no basis in the facts but which then lead you astray in your analysis.

☐ Do you fail to identify the issue?

Maybe you ignore the specific question you are asked to address in the question stem and allow all the presented facts in the problem to lead you astray. Since you've failed to identify the "issue" in the problem, you have no means by which to identify the correct answer choice.

If you've answered "yes" to any of the above questions, then it's essential to learn to detect the errors in your thinking and reading processes. The following exercise will let you get inside your own head and detect any flaws—whether you've misread a word, made an inappropriate inference, or ignored critical language.

B. To develop self-awareness of your thought process:

1. Select an MBE question.

2. Begin by reading the interrogatory and proceed to the fact pattern.

3. As you read, pause after each sentence and write down exactly what you think. Don't stop to censor your thoughts; just write them as you have them. To borrow an old phrase, "go with the flow."

Note: By committing your thoughts to specific words, you are forced to be aware of what you are thinking. This will then allow you to backtrack to find any errors in your thought process should you select an incorrect answer choice.

4. After you complete your reading of the fact pattern, form your own answer in response to the call-of-the-question.

5. Read each of the answer choices and once again write down exactly what you think. Translate your "answer" to fit one of the available answer choices.

6. Check your answer. If you've answered incorrectly, go back over what you've written to find where in the process you made an incorrect assessment.

C. Now you need to practice.

D. Let's work with a real problem. An example from a past MBE will work nicely:

Bye Bye telegraphed Vendor on June 1, "At what price will you sell 100 of your QT–Model garbage-disposal units for delivery around June 10?" Thereafter, the following communications were exchanged:

1. Telegram from Vendor received by Bye Bye on June 2: "You're in luck. We have only 100 QT's, all on clearance at 50% off usual wholesale of $120 per unit, for delivery at our shipping platform on June 12."

2. Letter from Bye Bye received in U.S. mail by Vendor on June 5: "I accept. Would prefer to pay in full 30 days after invoice."

3. Telegram from Vendor received by Bye Bye on June 6: "You must pick up at our platform and pay C.O.D."

4. Letter from Bye Bye received in U.S. mail by Vendor on June 9: "I don't deal with people who can't accommodate our simple requests."

5. Telegram from Bye Bye received by Vendor on June 10, after Vendor had sold and delivered all 100 of the QT's to another buyer earlier that day: "Okay. I'm over a barrel and will pick up the goods on your terms June 12."

Bye Bye now sues Vendor for breach of contract. Which of the following arguments will best serve Vendor's defense?

(A) Vendor's telegram received on June 2 was merely a price quotation, not an offer.

(B) Bye Bye's letter received on June 5 was not an acceptance because it varied the terms of Vendor's initial telegram.

(C) Bye Bye's use of the mails in response to Vendor's initial telegram was an ineffective method of acceptance.

(D) Bye Bye's letter received on June 9 was an unequivocal refusal to perform that excused Vendor even if the parties had previously formed a contract.

1. Read and write your thoughts on the problem as outlined in the steps above.

2. Now read my thoughts on the problem and compare them to what you've written. Don't expect them to be the same but your thinking should parallel mine. While what we've written won't be exactly the same, it should be close—what I found important, you should have found important, what I questioned, you should have questioned, and how I responded to each of the issues raised in the facts, you should have responded. After all, the same problem should elicit a similar analysis.

3. Here's what I'm thinking as I read this problem, sentence by sentence. My thoughts are in italics.

Okay, what does the interrogatory ask me to do?

Bye Bye now sues Vendor for breach of contract. Which of the following arguments will best serve Vendor's defense?

I'm looking for a defense to a breach of contract and it seems like a sales contract, why else "vendor."

Bye Bye telegraphed Vendor on June 1, "At what price will you sell 100 of your QT–Model garbage-disposal units for delivery around June 10?" Thereafter, the following communications were exchanged:

I was right. It's a sales problem because garbage-disposal units are goods so I have to apply the UCC. There's a lot of info here. I have dates, quantities, and writings because "telegraphs" are writings. But they are not signed. I don't know if that's important yet, so I'll have to watch it. I'm going to think about each exchange separately and see what it means. I hate series of exchanges, but there's no other way to deal with them. As to this first volley, it sounds like a preliminary inquiry because it's asking "at what price" the goods would cost.

Telegram from Vendor received by Bye Bye on June 2: "You're in luck. We have only 100 QT's, all on clearance at 50% off usual wholesale of $120 per unit, for delivery at our shipping platform on June 12."

Okay. This looks like the offer. It's definite in terms of delivery terms, quantity, and price. It doesn't need a payment term because the UCC has gap fillers for this. This is something Bye Bye can accept.

Letter from Bye Bye received in U.S. mail by Vendor on June 5: "I accept. Would prefer to pay in full 30 days after invoice."

Now we have a letter instead of the usual telegraph. Doesn't seem to mean anything so don't read into it now. Date makes it seem timely. The words are those of acceptance. But then it adds a payment term. There was nothing mentioned about payment in the offer so this is an additional term. Does that impact the acceptance? No, not here. The common law requires a mirror-image. This looks like it might be a 2–207 problem where there's an additional term in the acceptance. There's still an acceptance but we may have to figure out what to do with the additional term. It doesn't seem like

Bye Bye has made its acceptance conditional on this additional term, only that it would "prefer"—which says to me, "would like to" pay in 30 days. So under 2–207, this is still an acceptance but the additional term becomes a "proposal" for addition to the contract unless one of the exceptions for merchants apply.

Telegram from Vendor received by Bye Bye on June 6: "You must pick up at our platform and pay C.O.D."

Looks like the offeror is not accepting the additional term. Certainly noted their objection quickly enough since it's the next day. Now what to do. Because the parties are merchants—the names tell me that they are, i.e., Vendor and who else buys 100 units—the additional term becomes part of the deal unless it's a material term. This would seem to qualify since there's a big difference between COD and credit for 30 days. So the payment term doesn't come in but we still have an acceptance and a deal.

Letter from Bye Bye received in U.S. mail by Vendor on June 9: "I don't deal with people who can't accommodate our simple requests."

Bye Bye's letter is a repudiation. It's a clear, unequivocal statement that Bye Bye won't perform. So Bye Bye is in breach.

Telegram from Bye Bye received by Vendor on June 10, after Vendor had sold and delivered all 100 of the QT's to another buyer earlier that day: "Okay. I'm over a barrel and will pick up the goods on your terms June 12."

Looks like Bye Bye is trying to retract its repudiation. But it's too late. Vendor was right to treat Bye Bye's June 9 letter as a repudiation and could sell the goods to another. Let's see which answer choice allows for this situation. On to the answer choices.

Choice A. Vendor's telegram received on June 2 was merely a price quotation, not an offer.

This was too definite to be merely a quote. It was sent in response to a pretty specific inquiry from Bye Bye which set quantity terms and a delivery date. Vendor's response was an offer so this "A" is incorrect.

Choice B. Bye Bye's letter received on June 5 was not an acceptance because it varied the terms of Vendor's initial telegram.

I've already accounted for this. The UCC rejects the common law "mirror image" rule requiring the acceptance to be the exact match of the offer. The UCC allows for an acceptance with different or additional terms, as long as it's clear that there was an expression of acceptance. So the June 5 letter was an acceptance even though it added the term for the 30 days of credit.

Choice C. Bye Bye's use of the mails in response to Vendor's initial telegram was an ineffective method of acceptance.

Finally something about all the back and forth between letters and telegrams. But it really doesn't matter because the mail is just as valid a form of acceptance as telegram. Vendor didn't specify how the offer had to be accepted and the UCC is lenient here too and Bye Bye could use any means reasonable under the circumstances. There's nothing to indicate in the facts about the goods or the market that would indicate time to be of the essence so a letter would be fine.

Choice D. Bye Bye's letter received on June 9 was an unequivocal refusal to perform that excused Vendor even if the parties had previously formed a contract.

Okay. This is it. It accounts for Bye Bye's repudiation and this would excuse Vendor from its obligation under the contract. If Vendor is excused, then it's not in breach. And that the best defense.

Choice D is the correct answer.

4. I realize it's not practical to write down your thoughts each time you answer a multiple choice question. But now that you know what you should be thinking as you work your way through a problem, your task is to be conscious and deliberate during each step of the process. This way you'll remember what you thought and can go back and revisit it should you arrive at an incorrect answer choice.

Be sure to make the effort to put your thoughts into some concrete form—even if it's just in your head. Words give form to thoughts. And once there's form, there's something to remember.

†